AFTERMARKETING
How to Keep Customers for Life through Relationship Marketing

AFTERMARKETING
How to Keep Customers for Life through Relationship Marketing

Terry G. Vavra, Ph.D.

Associate Professor of Marketing
Lubin School of Business
PACE UNIVERSITY
and
President
MARKETING METRICS, INC.

IRWIN
Professional Publishing
Chicago • Bogotá • Boston • Buenos Aires • Caracas
London • Madrid • Mexico City • Sydney • Toronto

Sponsoring sponsoring editor:	Cynthia A. Zigmund
Senior marketing manager	Tiffany Dykes
Project editor:	Mary Conzachi
Production supervisor:	Laurie Kersch
Assistant manager, desktop services:	Jon Christopher
Compositor:	Electronic Publishing Services, Inc.
Typeface:	10/12 Times Roman
Printer:	Buxton•Skinner Printing Company

Library of Congress Cataloging-in-Publication Data

Vavra, Terry G.
    Aftermarketing : how to keep customers for life through
relationship marketing / Terry G. Vavra.
        p.   cm.
    Includes bibliographical references and index.
    ISBN 0-7863-0405-7
    1. Customer relations.   2. Customer services.   3. Consumer
satisfaction.   4. Advertisers—Attitudes.   I. Title.
HF5415.5.V38   1995
658.8'12—dc20   92–16232

Printed in the United States of America
1 2 3 4 5 6 7 8 9 0 BS 2 1 0 9 8 7 6 5

This book is lovingly dedicated to the most important relationships in my life—my parents, Marv and Gwen, and the four members of my immediate family: Linda, Stacy, Kerry, and Tammy.

Preface to the Paperback Version

Since the first printing of *Aftermarketing* in June of 1992, I have been pleased to witness an impressive growth of interest in relationship marketing. When I conducted my final literature search in early 1992 (as the hardcover version was about to go to press), there was scarcely a handful of articles from the prior year on the topic of "relationship" or "retention marketing." Today, in the fall of 1994, a similar search will identify over 100 articles in the course of only a half year! And professional conferences have also acknowledged the growing interest in relationship marketing. The American Marketing Association's 1994 Faculty Consortium was directed at ways of teaching relationship marketing and concurrently Professors Jagdish Sheth and Atul Parvatiyar of Emory University hosted their second annual conference on relationship marketing. Other organizations, like the Institute for International Research have also hosted conferences on relationship marketing and customer retention.

I have been extremely gratified by the reception of *Aftermarketing* in its original hardcover edition. Both the business and the academic community have been very complimentary of the book. I'm indebted to several very kind reviewers and to my endorsers who first saw value in my ideas. Because of the reception of the first edition, Irwin Professional Publishing has seen fit to offer a paperback version. I thank all previous readers who have validated my belief in the importance of the topic of retention marketing.

One note of caution is required. As relationship marketing has gained a following, equal attention has been generated, it seems, by the topics of database marketing and integrated marketing communications. Readers familiar with my ideas will share my impatience in a focus on database marketing as its own field or topic. Database building and manipulation are simply new tools for mainstream marketing to practice; just as segmentation is a tool. It is unacceptable in my eyes to study "database marketing" per se. The goal of any database of customers is to identify current clients so that they may be better marketed to, and their patronage acknowledged. Both of these activities (identification and acknowledgment) are valuable only insofar as a business wishes to retain its customerbase—retention marketing is the strategy, database utilization is simply the tactic to help better retain customers!

Integrated marketing communications also is subject to some misfocus. Integrated marketing communications may be overemphasized because so much of marketing communications is directed at conquering new customers. And, in today's market, *customer conquest* is an archaic strategy. In a similar fashion, integrated marketing communication has received a lot of attention in the business press. Of course you should deliver the same basic message to your target audience regardless of whether the medium is television, direct mail or matchbook covers. But it's not a strategy it's just good, common sense! And don't let a communications expert tell you advertising helps retain customers—it's a very inefficient retention tactic!

The general business community is becoming sensitized to the terms of retention and relationship marketing. My own, second industry survey suggests a substantial increase in the *claimed* practice of relationship marketing—yet my personal experience as observer and consumer fails to substantiate this change in practice! It appears the business community may yet again have picked up a "buzzword" without fully understanding how or why to practice it.

For this edition, I and my colleagues have attempted to update as much information as possible. This has been both interesting and challenging. The arena of marketing practices is in a constant state of flux, with even the players often not knowing the status of programs in their own companies! We have, however, attempted to the best of our abilities—and the information available—to make this edition as current as possible. Mary Zerbo and Doug Pruden (of Marketing Metrics) have provided substantial assistance, they both have my profound appreciation.

I hope you, the reader, will find substantial value in this book, and will put into practice all of the retention marketing efforts you can. But be warned, you'll meet with strong resistance as you advocate reassigning marketing dollars from advertising to retention activities. You can be prepared for this challenge. Do two things. First, put together a "pro-forma" P&L statement. This P&L will help you convince your management of the potential payout from spending for retention. Second, as you institute your retention program, isolate a small, "hold-out" sample of your customers. Track their purchases as you track your total customer base, but isolate them from your retention program. They'll serve as your "control" group. After one or two years, the value of your retention program should be evident in the difference in customer value between your total customer base and these "control" customers.

You will find my use of the terms relationship marketing and retention marketing to be reasonably interchangeable. For my own money, I view retention marketing as the preeminent issue. As someone once said to me, "I don't feel a need to have a relationship with the manufacturer of my toothpaste!" Yet, the manufacturer certainly has a need to retain this customer! So let's consider various relationship tactics as yet additional ways to build stronger loyalties among our customers, consequently retaining more of them for longer periods of time.

Now, I wish you well, and hope your experiences with retention marketing are well rewarded. If you have particular success stories to tell, or encounter unique application problems, I'd be delighted to hear them.

Terry G. Vavra

Preface to the Hardcover Version

In the spring of 1989, I was fortunate enough to have been included among four American marketers assembled by Mr. Toyo Shigeta, president of Nova Promotion Group (New York), to be guests of Messrs. S. Kouchi and H. Nakatsu of the Promotion Management Division of Dentsu, Inc. We traveled to Tokyo and presented what we considered to be some of the most important developments in American marketing and sales promotion to a select group of Dentsu executives.

The topic I chose to speak on was improving relationships with *current* customers, what I labeled *aftermarketing*. (I had developed an interest and given a talk on this topic during 1988.) My presentation was well received, and I returned to the United States intent on shifting my interests to new topics. However throughout 1990 I found that, rather than having lessened my ardor for the topic, my presentation only seemed to have increased my conviction that maximizing customer retention through improved relationships is the strategy most likely to guarantee survival and success in the marketplace of the 90s. That year I began collecting materials that I believed substantiated my viewpoint. In addition, I became sensitized to marketing activities that appeared to be oriented to customer retention.

By the middle of 1990, the topic had consumed me. I was committed to gathering together ideas for relationship marketing in a single source. This book is the result. If readers accept my premise of the importance of relationship marketing, I believe that it may create a reawakening in the marketing community of unprecedented significance. If my ideas go unheeded, I fear that American marketing will have lost much of its value or contributory impact to companies and consumers.

Many readers may be aware of the burgeoning library of books and articles addressing *product quality* (led by Deming, Juran, Crosby and Garvin) and another group addressing *customer satisfaction* (for example, Peters, Albrecht, Liswood, and Zemke). I believe that these areas represent only two of several important tactics that help a marketer to maintain his or her customer base. In this book I examine a complete inventory of actions and programs that I believe will help marketers maintain their most precious asset: loyal customers.

Marketing practitioners live a double life: one as a marketing strategist concerned with sales and improving the bottom line, and another as a consumer searching for value, service, and proper treatment from other marketers. These two perspectives are sometimes shockingly out of phase. In these cases of enlightening conflict, we are likely to agree that the ultimate golden rule of marketing appears to be this: *treat your customers and clients as you would have other marketers treat you.* This is a very simple yet eloquent way of approaching the topic of improving customer relationships. This rule brings the issue down to earth in some fairly intuitive ways, yet it also challenges us to harness the full power of our intelligent marketing systems to implement *customer retention* as efficiently and as effectively as possible.

Many people have contributed to my ideas on relationship marketing. I want to individually acknowledge some of them, though no lack of appreciation is meant by failure to specifically identify others. My parents, with whom I operated a retail business (an A&W Root Beer drive-in), had a deep respect and appreciation for their customers. They impressed upon me the importance of a long-term business view with regard to building a customer following.

On the theoretical side, several academic instructors and colleagues contributed to my interest in marketing, and to my present perspective. Acknowledgement is due Hal Kassarjian, Al Silk, Joel Cohen, Robert Mitchell, and Jagdish Sheth.

Rolls-Royce Motor Cars Inc., a long-time consulting assignment, further sharpened my focus on customer care. Reg Abbiss, Howard Mosher, Bob Wharen, and Paul Beart worked with my colleagues and me at Marketing Metrics through many a long meeting to establish programs and systems that would ensure the total satisfaction of every Rolls-Royce and Bentley owner—not an easy task, considering the size of the promise made and the admittedly demanding nature of the customers. Giuseppe Greco and Hugh Steward of Ferrari North America have similarly worked with us to create a CSI program that is uniquely Ferrari! Hiro Motoshima and Craig Lynar of Seiko Instruments and Jerry Reynolds and Greg Farrell of Cellular One have also shared in our learning experiences, both as clients and as friends.

My marketing seminars at Pace University have provided me a constant platform from which to evolve more current ideas on the topic of relationship marketing. I thank Pace University and Deans Arthur Centonze and Peter Hoefer and Dr. Elayn Bernay, all of the Lubin School of Business, for supporting this project. Mr. Gerald Mentor of Richard D. Irwin encouraged me at an early stage, and Cynthia Zigmund of Irwin Professional Publishing, senior editor for this project, provided sound counsel for a first-time author.

In addition, many thanks are due to industry members who supported my writing: Don Hinman and Jock Bickert of NDL; Bill Rosenthal, WPP; Ian Thompson and Jay Denison, Thompson Habib & Denison; and Maureen Citarella, Jerry LaTour, and John Kuendig, all from Kraft General Foods. Mary Zerbo from Marketing Metrics and Nadia Maresse of Pace University scoured countless databases and journal listings to help me accumulate the vast amount of material on which this book is based. Pace University's Hayes Library, the Information Central operation of the Direct Marketing Association, and the

American Marketing Association's Marguerite Kent Library were all splendid in
responding to several requests. I am also indebted to ABI/Inform and Predicasts
for fighting through some tricky search requests.

Finally, my own personal experiences managing a marketing consulting firm,
Marketing Metrics, Inc., with my partner and wife, Linda Vavra, have further
reinforced my conviction that, if you can't satisfy your current clients, you have
no business seeking additional ones.

This explains my current preoccupation with relationship marketing. *It is my
overt mission to convince every reader of this book that relationships with existing customers are his or her first and most important obligation.* If that mission
is accomplished, I shall feel satisfied.

Throughout the book, I've attempted to offer equal examples from both product and services marketing. Although any one example may intuitively seem to
fit either product or services marketing better, it is my belief that almost all of the
aftermarketing strategies described are equally applicable to both types of marketing. I challenge the reader to test an alternative application—please don't cat-
egorize any example as relevant only to the situation as given!

This is a book of both *strategic vision* and *tactical action plans.* In it I will
establish the goal of relationship marketing and describe the aftermarketing
strategies to help marketers better relate to their customers. But I'll also propose
and discuss specific tactics to implement the strategic vision of improved customer relationships. I thus hope to appease two sets of readers, those who come
with theoretical backgrounds questioning the strategic wisdom and consequences
of my suggestions and those who come with a need to implement—who want
suggestions and action plans for retaining their customers today!

- A manufacturer of quality men's clothing launches an "educational" program directed at customers to help them better understand the quality of
  the fabric and the craftsmanship of construction in the garments they've
  purchased to maximize their satisfaction.

- A cellular telephone company dedicates itself to maintaining an active
  "dialogue" with its customers, listening to their problems and informing
  them of its service and technological commitments, making it deserving of
  their patronage and thereby reducing churn.

- A distributor of expensive European toys considers ways to expand sales
  of its line without unnecessary reliance on current retailers, who have
  proved to be lethargic, uninterested in helping the brand maintain its customer base, and otherwise apathetic about the brand's loyal customers. It
  decides to establish a customer club that allows it to talk directly to its customers, the children who own its toys.

- An automobile company dedicates itself to creating owner activities and
  events to enhance the experience of owning its cars and thereby minimize
  the possibility of a current owner buying a competitive make the next time
  he or she buys.

- A consumer packaged goods company with a low-margin product tests database marketing and direct distribution to allow its customers a greater selection of product flavors and varieties and to remove its quality products from the increasingly cluttered and costly shelf space of supermarkets.
- A hotel chain, intent upon providing its guests the absolute best treatment, "blueprints" the contacts its staff members will have with guests. As a result of the blueprint, new training programs are devised to develop better interpersonal skills among lower-level employees, who have the greatest frequency of contacts with guests.
- An insurance company creates a financial planning club to stimulate word of mouth for its current products and to generate leads for its salespeople from current policyholders.

All of these marketing needs have a common solution: an aftermarketing perspective and program. This book helps the reader understand the most important philosophical change in marketing practice since the inception of consumer-oriented marketing.

Terry G. Vavra

Contents

Chapter One

A Change of Orientation
Retention Instead of Conquest

Today's market is quite unlike any in which American marketers have previously competed. It is more aggressive and is composed of more competitors, each offering relatively equivalent (parity) products or services. Consumers, sometimes characterized as fickle, flit from one brand to the next without qualms of "betraying" a favorite brand or fear of losing value by switching between brands.

Competing in such a market by winning *new customers* (the apparent preoccupation of most contemporary marketers) can be rather easily accomplished because consumers exhibit so little loyalty. And customers won over may repurchase once or twice. What is considerably more difficult in such a dynamic market is retaining *customers currently buying* a brand or service. Given constant costs of winning new customers, the only way to make a profit in such a situation is to increase the life time spending of current customers. Customer retention is, therefore, far more important than customer attraction.

THE CHALLENGES OF THE CHANGING U.S. MARKET

Astute marketers, no doubt, silently cringe at the poignant prophecy in Bob Dylan's lyrics for "The Times They Are A-changin'":[1]

> The order is rapidly fadin'.
> And the first one now, will later be last
> For the times they are a-changin'.*

Marketers are constantly on the lookout for change; current plans are adjusted, and future plans are structured based on anticipated changes in the marketplace. Naisbitt and Aburdene have suggested that the United States is currently undergoing such massive changes that totally new approaches to conducting business may be necessary.[2] Borrowing their prescription, it may be time to "reinvent" marketing.

EXHIBIT 1–1
U.S. Population Growth

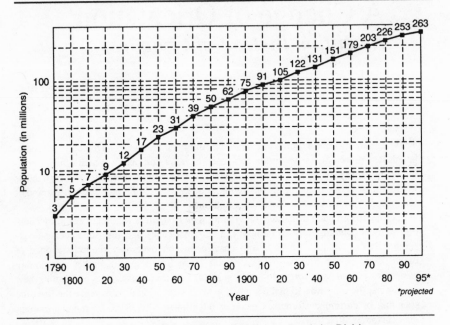

Source: *U.S. Statistical Abstract 1993* and Bureau of the Census, Population Divisions.

One aspect of marketing that surely needs to be reevaluated is the practice of inordinate attention to winning new customers. In yesterday's rapidly expanding American economy, there were always more and more new consumers whose loyalties could be conquered. But in today's market there is no longer an ever-increasing body of customers. The number of consumers is quickly reaching a plateau. The United States economy has matured.

The Economy

The U.S. population is plateauing. Whereas the population grew by nearly 56 million in the 25 years from 1965 to 1990 and is expected to gain an additional 56 million people before peaking, this gain is expected to take a period twice as long: the next 50 years![3] (See Exhibit 1–1.)

Concurrent with the slowdown in population growth, the growth of the gross national product has also slowed substantially. Compared to the 7 percent growth experienced in 1984, annual growth throughout the decade of the 1990s is expected to remain at 5 percent or less (see Exhibit 1–2).

EXHIBIT 1–2
Growth in the Gross National Product (Constant 1987 Dollars)

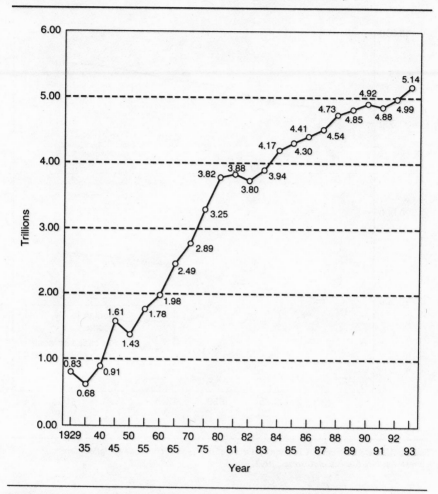

Source: *U.S. Statistical Abstract 1993*, Bureau of Economic Analysis, National Income and Product Accounts of the U.S. 1929-1959, and Survey of Current Business, May 1993.

The marketplace is already beginning to adjust to these new trends. Marketers are tightening their belts, assessing very carefully the contribution of each brand and product in their portfolios. For example, it is rumored that venerable Procter & Gamble is considering pruning some of its "dinosaur" brands. However, despite findings from a Bates USA survey indicating reluctance on the part of both retailers and consumers to stock or try new products, the long-expected decrease in new product activity has yet to manifest itself.[4]

EXHIBIT 1–3
Median Family and Personal Disposable Income

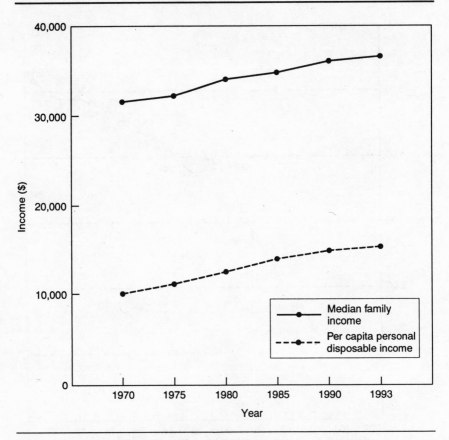

Source: U.S. Department of Commerce, Bureau of the Census, *Current Population Reports*,
pp 60–184; *U.S. Statistical Abstract*, 1993.

The consumer is feeling the pinch directly. As shown in Exhibit 1–3, disposable personal income and median family income are both leveling. This has
reportedly caused some consumers to break loyalties to national brands.[5]

The Competition

Products and services in nearly every segment of the economy are reaching market parity. Prior to the 1980s, product categories could be dominated by a giant
such as Procter & Gamble, Exxon, or American Airlines. This is no longer the
case, owing to the hard work of the former "also-rans." Virtually every category

EXHIBIT 1–4
Industry Structure Influences Industry Focus

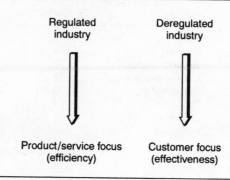

Regulated industry → Product/service focus (efficiency)

Deregulated industry → Customer focus (effectiveness)

shows this: for example, Head & Shoulders, the leading shampoo, has only a 9 percent share of the market—no more than 9 percent! Texaco, the second-best-selling gasoline, has 7 percent of the U.S. gasoline market, and Exxon, the leader, has only 8 percent.[6]

As industries have been deregulated, the structure and competitive mannerisms of the industries have reacted dramatically. The basic change has been in the marketer's orientation toward customers. In a regulated industry, it is assumed that demand (a base of loyal customers) will always exist. So the marketer focuses on the product or service produced. Efficiency of production and marketing activities is generally the key concern. When deregulation opens an industry to competition, marketers learn that they must actively court their customers to stay in business. In deregulated situations, marketers come to recognize that efficiency is far less important than doing the right things, that is, being *effective*. Exhibit 1–4 demonstrates this principle.

The deregulation of industries causes havoc because it forces companies to adopt a consumer perspective in place of their distribution mentality; they are forced to engage in marketing! And this requires information about consumers.

Information is no longer a scarce commodity among competitors in the 90s. Extensive research capabilities are now within the reach of almost all competitors. No single firm is likely to be able to capitalize on a unique view of the market, as has happened in the past.

The marketplace has also grown more complex. Channels of distribution have multiplied, as have channel intermediaries. The net result has been to move marketers further away from their end users (a trend labeled *intermediation* by economist Paul Hawken).[7] As the distance from marketer to ultimate customer has increased, marketers' control over the conditions of the sale and over the offering of after-sale service has diminished. In a 1986 survey of 214 large manufacturers

EXHIBIT 1–5
Industries That Care for Their Customers

Industry	Percentage*
Drug	75
Food processing	74
Telecommunications	72
Electric utilities	72
Automobile	70
Cosmetic	64
Chemical	46
Petroleum	46

*The table shows the percentage of consumers who rated particular industries as "very" or "moderately" caring about their customers.

Source: *Roper Reports,* February 1988, Roper Organization.

(which unfortunately has not been updated), the Conference Board found that over half were using distribution channels rather than their own sales force to reach their customers.[8]

The resulting separation allows marketers to diminish their perceived sense of obligation toward customers, as well as to psychologically excuse themselves from responsibility for the way in which their customers are treated. Marketers assume that profit will motivate intermediaries to look after their customers. But marketers fail to recognize that most intermediaries carry products from many different marketers. The intermediaries' economic livelihood is rarely dependent upon just one brand or product. Consequently, they often fall short of adequately representing any one marketer's products or services in the manner that the marketer would have desired.

The customer relations focus of offshore marketers, primarily the Japanese, has significantly altered the U.S. marketplace. The care for customers evidenced by some Japanese companies has reminded U.S. consumers of days when U.S. companies expressed similar concern and care for them as customers. This is a rediscovery for some consumers and is still, unfortunately, a relatively rare feeling for the majority of American consumers. Exemplifying this attitude are findings from a one-of-a-kind 1988 *Roper Report* survey, in which less than half of all Americans polled believed that the oil industry was even "moderately caring" about its customers. And, only two-thirds of Americans rated the cosmetics industry as "moderately caring" (see Exhibit 1–5).

In another survey in the same year, expectations for future improvement among industries were not optimistic. The Opinion Research Corporation asked a national sample whether American industries were improving (in caring for their

EXHIBIT 1–6
How Americans Rate Industry Improvement

	Getting Better	Getting Worse
Supermarkets	40%	16%
Telephone companies	30	29
Clothing stores	29	20
Appliance stores	24	9
Automobile dealerships	20	24
Airlines	16	19
Insurance companies	14	38

Source: *ORC Issue Watch*, December 6, 1988. Opinion Research Corporation.

customers), a majority expressed the belief that American industry is not likely to become more caring about customers, and 20 percent believed that concern for the customer in the future would deteriorate still further (see Exhibit 1–6).

The Consumer

As the nature of competition has changed, so too, has the consumer, as shown in Exhibit 1–7. The typical consumer of the 90s is no longer young, making first choices of products and services. More people are working beyond what was previously the normal retirement age, and more people are going into business for themselves after retirement. Retirees have more disposable income than ever before. The graying of the marketplace means that older consumers are making more purchasing decisions, based on their previous experiences with products and services. The majority of households today function as dual-income households, which means shared purchase responsibilities by several members of the household: female head of house, male head of house, and teenagers as well. All of these changes have effectively weakened the brand loyalty that many marketers depend so much on.

As consumers have become increasingly skeptical about marketers' interest in satisfying their individual needs, class-action suits against American corporations have increased exponentially.[9] The Yankelovich Clancy Shulman Monitor documents this rising skepticism among consumers. Consumers are more interested in warranties assuring them that manufacturers will be held responsible for defects in products.[10] Scandals on Wall Street, in the banking industry, and in Washington have made consumers wary of sleaze. They want high quality products and expect straight talk from manufacturers. The consumerism movement, another result of this growing distrust among consumers toward business, is what Peter Drucker has labeled "the shame of marketing." Drucker's thesis is that if

EXHIBIT 1–7
Composition of Households: (a) in 1980; (b) in 2000

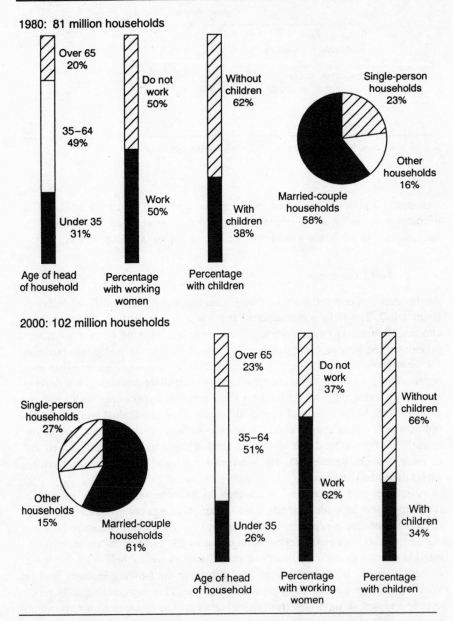

1980: 81 million households

Over 65
20%

35–64
49%

Under 35
31%

Age of head
of household

Do not
work
50%

Work
50%

Percentage
with working
women

Without
children
62%

With
children
38%

Percentage
with children

Single-person
households
23%

Other
households
16%

Married-couple
households
58%

2000: 102 million households

Single-person
households
27%

Other
households
15%

Married-couple
households
61%

Over 65
23%

35–64
51%

Under 35
26%

Age of head
of household

Do not
work
37%

Work
62%

Percentage
with working
women

Without
children
66%

With
children
34%

Percentage
with children

Source: U.S. Department of Commerce, Bureau of the Census, *Current Population Reports*, p 25,
No. 1018.

marketing had been doing what it was supposed to do—listening to and serving consumers—a consumerism movement would never have been necessary!

Brand loyalty among consumers has virtually disappeared, as they perceive all brands to be about the same. A survey by BBDO Worldwide of consumers in 28 countries found that two-thirds believed that no differences exist in the quality of brands in 13 different product categories![11]

THE PURPOSE OF A BUSINESS OR ORGANIZATION

Ask most businesspeople what the goal of their business is, and the reply will probably be, "To make a profit." Organization leaders will say that they want "financial survival." And most of our business students emerge from B-schools with an inordinate fixation on the profit motive. But should profit be the primary goal of a business?

Professor Ted Levitt, in *The Marketing Imagination,* argues a different viewpoint. To say that making a profit is a motive of business is as shallow a statement as to say that the goal of living is eating. Eating sustains life in order for people to accomplish other goals. So too, Levitt argues, should profit be considered a requisite of business, allowing the enterprise to accomplish other goals. To do otherwise, Levitt says, is to be guilty of short-sightedness, moral shallowness, and strategic misdirection.[12]

Kenosuke Matsushita, founder of the Japanese electronics giant bearing his name, appears to agree with Levitt.

> The purpose of an enterprise is to contribute to society; profits come only in proportion to the contribution. Profit is a result, not a goal of business.[13]

Levitt goes on to observe that this difference in perspective is as fundamental as the now widely acknowledged difference between sales and marketing.

Peter Drucker voices an opinion similar to Levitt's definition of the purpose of businesses and organizations as *attracting and holding customers,* which

> forces [us] to face the necessity of figuring out what people really want and value and then catering to those wants and values. It provides specific guidance and has moral merit.[14]

MARKETING'S CURRENT ORIENTATION

Current textbooks on marketing and the American Marketing Association define marketing as

> a social and a managerial process by which individuals and groups obtain what they need and want through creating, offering, and exchanging products, goods, and services of value with others.[15]

Six key elements have been associated with such a definition:

- Selecting a target market or markets.
- Identifying the wants, needs, and demands of the selected market group.
- Matching present or new products, goods, and services to these wants, needs, and demands.
- Delivering satisfaction.
- Establishing and managing an "exchange process" to logistically price, promote, and deliver the products, goods, or services.
- Anticipating change that will occur in the target market and in the environment.

These elements describe an outlook that can be called *conquest marketing*. The goal is volume—to unabashedly "conquer" as many customers as possible. In this scenario, the main thrust of the organization's marketing effort is devoted to *creating more and more new customers*. Marketers' priorities evolving from this perspective have been the following:

1. To identify a target market.
2. To determine the target market's needs.
3. To match a product or service that they currently do or potentially can produce to the market's needs.
4. To attract the maximum number of target market consumers to try the product or service.

This sequence has been repeated again and again in an attempt *to gain the maximum number of new customers*.

The fixation on new customers has no doubt been fueled by the marketer's desire to increase revenues and profits. It is human nature to look beyond one's present business (and one's customers) in the quest for expanded profits. American marketers in particular, with their unbridled expectations of ever-expanding markets, have traditionally looked beyond their current franchise to those not yet buying their products and services. The search for new customers sends marketers out on quixotic missions, while they take their current base of customers for granted.

The sins of this mindset are subtle. Marketers, focusing on winning new customers, concentrate effort and capital on these elusive potential customers. Research may even be conducted with a mind to possibly modifying the company's product (or service) to be even more appealing to a greater number of people.

But, as an organization focuses on conquering new customers, present customers are often overlooked. Their continued patronage or participation is assumed. Their value to the enterprise is forgotten; their contribution to profit is taken for granted. Their satisfaction is presumed. The organization fails to

---

AFTERMARKETING NEEDED
Disregarding Current Customers

In 1989 "Audi-phobia" was at its height. The prestigious German automaker's U.S. sales had plummeted from 80,000 a year to a disastrous 15,000 (partly caused by a story on *60 Minutes* about Audi's purported "unintended acceleration" problems). In 1989 I traded in my 1984 Audi for a new Audi. If not a brave move, it was certainly a move counter to the trends of the marketplace.

At this time every "returning" Audi owner and every owner simply staying loyal to the marque ought to have been worth his or her weight in gold to the German manufacturer. And so I found it exceptionally odd that I never received a communication from Audi thanking me for my purchase or attempting to reinforce my rather bold reaffirmation to the marque. As precious as each of the 15,000 purchasers of 1990 Audis ought to have been to this car company struggling to stay alive in the American automotive market, the company was still apparently blasé about communicating with its current and new owners.

While Audi was apparently disregarding loyal current owners, it allocated ample funds into attempting to attract new customers! It produced a very expensive $40 videotape presentation kit introducing its new V8 model. It sent a reported 250,000 of these to *non-Audi owners* in an attempt to entice new customers into its franchise.

Audi's actions appear to be the ultimate example of a fixation on conquest with absolutely no concern about the value of aftermarketing.

---

maintain them. And when current customers take their business elsewhere, their defection is often dismissed by the rationale that you can't please everybody.

THE COSTS OF CONQUEST MARKETING

Attracting new customers is becoming an increasingly costly effort as mass media costs for advertising continue to escalate.

Over the 30-year period from 1960 to 1990, advertising expenditures in the United States have quintupled, as Exhibit 1–8 demonstrates. Over approximately the same period, the costs of television advertising have similarly increased from $19,700 for a 30-second spot in 1965 to $92,700 in 1993.[16] *Advertising Age* reports that in 1993 the top 100 advertisers spent a combined $37.9 billion in advertising![17] The leading spender, Philip Morris (including the spending of its Kraft General Foods unit) spent $2.4 billion by itself. The average expenditure for these top 100 advertisers was $379 million.

From 1984 to 1991, the number of television advertising vehicles has also increased by about 25 percent to an annual volume of 333,164 commercials per

EXHIBIT 1–8
U.S. Advertising Expenditures

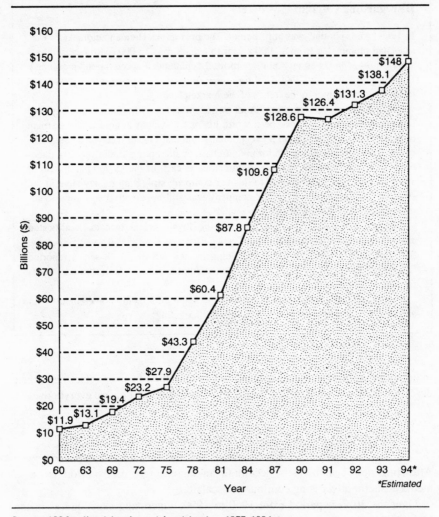

Source: 100 Leading Advertisers, *Advertising Age*, 1977–1994.

year.[18] This is in part due to the amoeba-like multiplication of advertising slots caused by the downsizing of commercials from 60-second spots to 30s, and then from 30s to the all too prevalent 15-second commercial of the 1990s.

Next, consider all of the new advertising media that are developing:

Cable television.

Proprietary cable television programs.

Syndicated television programs.

Specialized magazines.

Events: entertainment, sports, cultural.

In-store media.

Videocassette sponsorships.

"Wallboards" in professional offices and schools.

Specialized television networks in schools, airports, restaurants and supermarkets, and so on.

Targeted direct mail.

Outward and inward telemarketing.

To exist in such a complex media environment and to maintain one's "share of
voice" commensurate with one's intended market share is to require a level of
spending far exceeding that which most American companies can today afford.
And even if such advertising is affordable, it may be of questionable value in
attracting new customers.

As a side note, any advertising agency executive will affirm that advertising
serves multiple purposes:

- Creating awareness among nonaware potential customers.
- Stimulating trial among current nonusers.
- Reinforcing current users to enhance brand loyalty.

These multiple results of advertising are neither being denied nor overlooked.
But successful competition today requires a reallocation of marketing effort
between tools and tactics that champion conquest and those that foster retention.

THE VALUE OF CURRENT CUSTOMERS

Their industry is labeled the "hospitality" industry, and, indeed, two hoteliers
have led the concern for customers. Conrad Hilton was one of the first American
marketers to preach concern for customers. His book, *Be My Guest*, acknowledged his drive to care for those who visited his hotels. Two generations of the
Marriott family have endorsed similar care for customers. Both the current chairman, Bill Marriott, and his father, Willard, have reaffirmed the Marriott credo,
"We are all at Marriott to make our guests' visits as comfortable as possible."

Both Hilton and the Marriotts were addressing simpler times and left uncon-
sidered (or at least unspoken) the difficulty of a marketer seeing to it that his philosophy toward customers was actually carried out. Both Marriott and Hilton had
the added advantage of having their customers on their premises, where they
were more in control of the customer's experiences. When marketers don't have

the opportunity to directly interact with customers, it becomes far more difficult to effect quality marketing programs.

Recent studies conducted and sponsored by various groups and organizations objectify more dramatically the business value of retaining current customers:

65 percent of the average company's business comes from its present, satisfied customers.[19]

It costs five times as much to acquire a new customer as it costs to service an existing customer.[20]

A business which each day for one year loses one customer who customarily spends $50/week will suffer a sales decline of $1,000,000 the next year.[21]

91 percent of unhappy customers will never again buy from a company dissatisfying them, and will communicate their dissatisfaction to at least nine other people.[22]

Beyond the loss of their own business, studies show the tremendous destructive potential of dissatisfied customers. It has been determined that more than 90 percent of dissatisfied customers won't exert effort to contact a company to complain; they simply take their business to a competitor. But they do voice their dissatisfaction to other potential customers. So losing one dissatisfied customer may be more injurious than it appears; one defecting customer may speak to as many as nine other current or potential customers, multiplying his dissatisfaction ninefold!

In Levitt's goals for the organization, equal importance is placed on *maintaining* current customers and on *creating* new customers. Maintaining customers is a very different mindset, which requires a different set of marketing activities.

AN INTRODUCTION TO AFTERMARKETING

In *Serving Them Right,* Laura Liswood's excellent book on customer service, she traces the somewhat "abnormal" evolution of marketing:

In the past, acquisition and retention marketing went hand in hand. Selling and service were part of the same ongoing company-customer relationship... However, as we matured into a more mobile, industrialized, technocratic society, a distinction arose between selling and everything that came after the sale... We relegated the second half of the sale to "customer complaint departments," "service departments," and "warranty departments."

This mentality has been reflected for years in the formal structures, hierarchies, and budgeting philosophies of companies. Acquisition marketing and promotion continue to dominate, while customer-service activities are typically underbudgeted, understaffed, viewed strictly as cost centers and assigned to the periphery of a company's competitive strategy.[23]

There is some evidence that the marketing community is beginning to recognize the importance of relationship marketing. For example, in the seventh edition of Kotler's *Marketing Management* text, he embellishes the exchange process component of marketing by discussing the importance of customer relationships in marketing.

> Transaction marketing is part of a larger idea, that of *relationship marketing.* Smart marketers try to build up long-term, trusting, "win-win" relationships with customers, distributors, dealers, and suppliers.[24]

Other marketers are catching on, too. At the 1992 Fall Conference of the Direct Marketing Association, 28 package-goods companies announced their exploration of building customer databases. Their motivation is to build relationships with their high-value customers. John Kuendig, of Kraft General Foods, questioned, "When you see the importance of your heavy-users [in IRI scan data], how are you going to communicate with [relate to] these people through mass media?"[25]

Characteristic of the needed change in marketing perspective is the newly introduced signature line of the brokerage house Paine Webber:

> We invest in relationships!

Although bankers have discussed relationship banking for many years, their definition is much narrower than that required in today's marketing. Relationship banking seems to apply to humanizing the otherwise impersonal industry of financial services. It also incorporates the recognized ability to sell current customers more services! Maintaining customers requires the establishment of a relationship with them. But this relationship unites two relatively different points of view.

Ted Levitt proposes that marketers deal with these differences through *relationship management.* In *The Marketing Imagination,* he characterizes the marketing relationship not as a "momentary flirtation," but rather as a "marriage" of a customer to an organization. And, as is the case in marriage, each partner has rather distinct expectations, and rather particular needs.

From the customer's perspective, a purchase is most likely viewed as *initiating* a relationship. The customer feels considerable desire or need for a continued interaction with the selling organization. But this view of an ongoing relationship probably runs directly against the mindset of the selling organization, which may consider the sale of its products or services as *culminating* its effort and relationship with the customer.

Continued after-sale interaction is a very important part of aftermarketing. And it is as necessary as the sale itself if an organization wishes to count on continued business opportunities with the same customer in the future (see Exhibit 1–9).

Marketing must change its mentality from completing a sale to beginning a relationship; from closing a deal to building loyalty. Yet in the daily planning of marketing effort, more attention is generally directed at conquest—winning new customers to one's brand, product, or service. It is much rarer to find a company

EXHIBIT 1–9
Expectations at the Time of Sale

From the Seller's Perspective	From the Buyer's Perspective
Culmination of a long sales negotiation	Initiation of a new relationship
Time to cash-in on labors	Concern about the support the new vendor will provide
Closure opens the way to cultivating new potential clients	Concern about the amount of attention and help that will be received after purchase decision
Shift account from sales team to production team	Desire to continue to interact with sales team

also devoting attention to maximizing the satisfaction of current customers. In such a company, the customer would not only be right, but his or her opinions would be actively sought out. This is the spirit of aftermarketing activities.

Ask any marketing executive about her budget for relationship marketing. Generally it is not even acknowledged as a role of marketing. Where the aftermarketing spirit does live, it is effected in the operating policies of a number of different departments or activities: customer services, consumer affairs, return policies, and sporadic customer bulletins or communications.

Dick Berry, a marketing academician, has recently suggested modifying marketing's revered 4 P's. Berry says that today's marketplace requires that new elements be added to the marketing mix to help the marketer stay competitive.[26] Adapting Berry's ideas to an aftermarketing perspective, the new marketing mix might be as follows:

- *Product:* product quality management, reliability, and features.
- *Price:* price charged, pricing terms, and pricing offers.
- *Place:* accessibility to the marketer's goods or facilities.
- *Promotion (market communication):* pre-sale advertising, publicity, and sales promotions.
- *Customer communication:* post-sale communication programs (proprietary magazines, events, etc.), 800 telephone center, complaint and compliment handling.
- *Customer satisfaction:* monitoring customer expectations and satisfaction with the existing product or service and the delivery system, striving to improved satisfaction.
- *Servicing:* servicing quality management pre-sale service and post-sale service, and customer convenience activities.

This marketing mix fully acknowledges the value of customer retention activities. Retaining customers requires marketers to exhibit care and concern for them

EXHIBIT 1–10
The Role of Aftermarketing

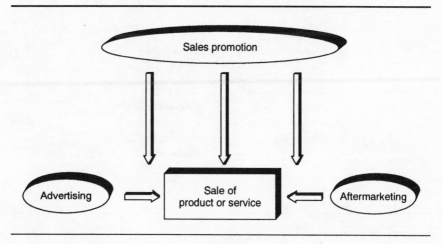

after they've made a purchase. This care and concern is part of aftermarketing because it applies marketing principles to customers *after* they have purchased a company's goods or services.

Aftermarketing includes the following elements:

- Activities and efforts to keep customers satisfied, even after purchase.

- Doing everything possible to increase the likelihood that current customers will buy a company's product or brand for their next and future purchase occasions.

- Increasing the likelihood current customers will buy *another of the company's products* (a complementary product or line) rather than a competitor's when they need such additional products.

- Repeatedly measuring the extent to which customers are satisfied by current products or services; letting them know they are cared for and utilizing the collected information in strategic planning.

Each element of the marketing effort hits customers at different points in the consideration–purchase–use sequence. Advertising's primary effort is to inform and remind—activities that normally precede a sale or purchase decision. Sales promotions occur immediately before, during, or after the sale; promotions tend to stimulate purchase and influence the brand or product purchased or repurchased. Aftermarketing encompasses an entire range of activities that a marketer can engage in after a customer has committed to the marketer's brand, product, or service (see Exhibit 1–10). Aftermarketing's goal is to maximize satisfaction.

Aftermarketing expands the activities included in the marketer's promotion activities (or the "marketing communications mix"):

Traditional Communications Mix	Aftermarketing Communications Mix
Advertising	Advertising
Sales promotion	Sales promotion
Public relations	Customer relations
Personal selling	Public relations
Packaging	Personal selling
	Packaging

AFTERMARKETING WORKING
The Value of Relationship Marketing

The first objective of customer-focused marketing is to *obtain* the full lifetime value from every customer—and then some. The second objective of customer-focused marketing is to *increase* the lifetime value of every customer and keep increasing it year after year. The third objective of customer-focused marketing is to use excess profits from the success of the first two objectives to pay for obtaining new customers at an ever lower cost of acquisition. The goal is long-term, profitable survival.

You cannot reach that goal if you are driven only by short-term profits. You cannot reach that goal if you are driven only by quality. You cannot reach that goal if you are driven only by productivity. You cannot reach that goal if you are driven only by technology. *The only path to long-term, profitable survival is customer-focused marketing.* All business begins and ends with the customer. In the beginning, there was the customer. In the end, there will be the customer. The company with the most customers wins.

Reflect for a moment on all of the companies you have patronized. Is there a department store or a grocery store that you use exclusively? How many florists have you tried? Is there one restaurant that you go to that is so perfect that you go nowhere else? When have you last encountered excellence? Or is your personal experience a gray panoply of trade mediocrity?

This creeping malaise is spreading into every aspect of American commerce. The inevitable result is economic deterioration. Forget the deterioration that can be measured; the lethal damage is the unseen, undeveloped potential of what could be but never will be. Global greatness is dying on the cross of mediocrity. As a nation, we are abdicating our leadership and our potential for greatness. As a nation, we have lost our customers to international competition; we have lost our capacity to survive because we have accepted mediocrity as a norm.

Had we attended to business and focused on the lifetime value of a nation of automobile customers, we might still have an automobile industry. Had we focused on the lifetime value of electronics customers, we might still have a television industry. Had we focused on the lifetime value of microchips, we might still have a microchip industry. And if we don't focus on the lifetime value of education, transportation, communications, and information technology customers, we might not have those industries soon. In the end, the country that has the most customers wins.

If economic deterioration is the inevitable result of failing to attend to customers, then economic survival must necessarily begin with a renewed focus on those customers. Consider the most common trade experience—buying food. You buy one-hundred fifty dollars of food products every week—seven-thousand eight-hundred dollars' worth a year. If you are satisfied with the supermarket, you will spend seventy-eight thousand dollars over a lifetime of ten years. If something happens that causes a customer trust to be broken, you could walk away from that store with over seventy thousand dollars of lifetime value and deposit it in the cash register of a rival store. It would appear that you should have some leverage with that supermarket. In fact, you don't because that supermarket doesn't know you from John Doe. Only the cash registers talk to you, not the managers.

Now consider how many things can go wrong in a supermarket–customer relationship. Milk can be spoiled, bread can be stale, meat can be tough; the potentials are endless. Has anything been done to identify you as a customer of that store? No. You will have the spoiled milk replaced, the stale bread exchanged, and maybe the tough meat refunded (probably not), but there is no genuine caring for having broken a trust with you, the valued customer of that store. Why? Because, as consumers, we don't demand it! Ninety percent of the time we don't even complain! That is how used to mediocrity we have become. The result? Seventy-eight thousand dollars of potential lifetime value transfers to another perhaps equally uncaring supermarket and both of the markets get a diluted share of the potential; neither gets the full lifetime value or the potential of increasing it. Consequently, the grocery chains have to compete with coupons, double coupons, and triple coupons. In other words, give up margin to maintain economic volume. That doesn't make sense.

Source: D. R. Libey, "New Customers as Lifetime Profit Generators: A Customer-Focused Marketing Strategy," Third Annual Conference on Database Marketing, The National Center for Database Marketing, Inc.

In this new communications mix, four elements need to be explained and the distinction between customer relations and public relations needs to be made:

• *Advertising and sales promotions* are primarily considered "outreach": conquest techniques ideally suited for winning over new customers to a brand, service, or company. The image enhancement capabilities of advertising—even among current customers—is not overlooked.

• *Customer relations* is defined as encompassing all aftermarketing activities, that is, all activities with current customers for purposes of enhancing satisfaction with a company and its products or services.

• *Public relations* is defined as all activities and communications with current noncustomers for purposes of enhancing the image and maximizing the operational latitudes of a company and its products or services.

Aftermarketing is manifested in many different marketing activities, all of which have current customers as their focus:

• Identifying the customer base.
• Acknowledging individual customers.
• Understanding their needs and expectations.
• Measuring satisfaction delivered to them.
• Providing ample channels of communication.
• Actively showing appreciation for their business.

Customer satisfaction programs are the first component of an aftermarketing program to be verbally endorsed by the contemporary marketing community. But good aftermarketing requires more than lip service:

Although two recent studies conducted among high-level business executives found 100 percent stating that long-term customer satisfaction was, indeed, their first priority; *none* had a formal program to measure customer satisfaction currently active![27]

Aftermarketing is a long-term strategy; its immediate goal is not to simply trigger another purchase, but rather to reassure the customer that he or she has purchased the right product.

No better example of marketers' discovery of the importance of aftermarketing can be found than in three industries that are currently focusing the majority of their efforts on customer retention:

The cable television industry, where churn (disconnects) exceeds 50 percent of the subscriber base per year.[28]

The cellular telephone industry, which is beginning to experience the cost of disconnects (running at 30–45% per year).[29]

The pager industry, where churn is reportedly 40 to 70 percent annually.[30]

THE PSYCHOLOGY OF AFTERMARKETING

Interestingly, numerous studies on the effectiveness of advertising have repeatedly discovered that one of the most attentive audiences for a product's advertising is recent buyers of the product. This surprising finding has been explained by the belief that recent buyers turn to advertising (print, radio, television) in an effort to reinforce the wisdom of the purchase they have just made (whether it is the brand or model they selected, or the fact of making the purchase at all). Obviously, the larger, more significant, and more costly the purchase, the stronger will be the motivation to find confirming information. But even with small purchases there is still, no doubt, some desire on the part of the customer to know that he purchased wisely.

This information-seeking activity is a process of reducing or trying to avoid *cognitive dissonance*—the mental recognition that one has purchased something that may not have been the smartest, most rational alternative. The customer's need for after-purchase reassurance is a strong one, and one not overlooked by some smart salespeople. There is real value in speaking to a customer after she has purchased your product or service to reassure her that she has purchased wisely and that she is getting her money's worth.

Aftermarketing performs just such a role. It focuses the customer's attention on appropriate (reinforcing) elements of the product or service. In so doing, it can help reassure an anxious buyer who is rethinking his product or brand selection. It can also help a buyer "fore-arm" himself for the onslaught of questions and barbs from friends and relatives when they learn of the buyer's purchase. In such cases, aftermarketing, by providing additional information or "evidence," can fortify a buyer against these questions, which are sure to come.

The information offered to new buyers should be very strategic. It should point out specific superiorities of the chosen product, service, or brand over competitors, facilitating *comparative* satisfaction. It should also address the buyer's performance expectations from the product or service purchased, helping to keep the buyer's expectation levels in a realistic range and helping to control *absolute* satisfaction.

There is another psychological principle that confirms the value of post-purchase reinforcement through aftermarketing. Learning theory describes the increased likelihood of repeating responses (purchases) that are viewed as rewarded. The problem in marketing is that with many products and services consumers do not overtly experience any direct or immediate reward. Marketers are often quite smug about their product's or service's performance, assuming that their customers will self-experience the benefits of having purchased their products or services. It is far better for marketers to be less smug and to actively direct their customers toward discovering reward in the selected products or services through aftermarketing activities.

From this perspective aftermarketing activities become critical components of any satisfaction or service project because, through their supply of post-purchase information and reassurance, they help influence how customers perceive the quality of the product or service purchased.

AFTERMARKETING NEEDED
Responding to Customers

To test just how customer oriented today's automobile manufacturers really are, an enterprising reporter at *Advertising Age* wrote to 25 companies complaining about problems with a one-year-old vehicle. The letter read as follows:

Dear (name of appropriate CEO):

I'm a big believer in advertising. I was a big believer in your company's advertising when I bought my car late last year.

When I drove the car off the lot, I noticed some immediate problems. The salesman said, as he was pushing me out the door, "Don't worry. Just bring it back and they'll fix it."

I live 35 minutes from the dealer, and it took three visits just to get the factory foul-ups fixed.

Now, a mysterious "clunking" sound is coming from the right front wheel. The selling dealer hasn't been able to correct it; the dealer in my neighborhood keeps pushing me back to the original dealer, saying it's not his problem.

My salesman has left the dealership, my warranty expires in two weeks, and I have a car I don't even know is safe to drive.

Should I have believed your ads claiming quality, service, and reliability? I'm beginning to think not.

Can you suggest how I can get my car out of this rut?

Over the next 30 days, a varied amount and quality of responses arrived:

Day 7	Saab-Scania national customer service department leaves a phone message.
Day 8	Rolls-Royce Motors' Midwest zone service manager leaves a phone message.
Day 11	Volkswagen leaves an 800 phone number; Rolls-Royce leaves two phone messages.
Day 12	BMW's central regional office and Yugo America leave messages.
Day 13	BMW's national consumer services office sends a Western Union Mailgram; a letter arrives from Peugeot Motors; Isuzu leaves a phone message.
Day 14	"Send us your phone number" requests Volvo in a Mailgram, "or call," Volvo adds. Buick sends a letter, and Honda, Nissan, and Chevrolet all leave phone messages.
Day 15	Letters arrive from Rolls-Royce, Cadillac, and Volkswagen.
Day 18	Letters arrive from Audi and Pontiac, and Isuzu leaves a phone message.
Day 19	Ford's Dealer Affairs Office writes to say they "sincerely regret" the problems; Mitsubishi's letter is the first to claim that the Chairman actually read the complaint letter; Honda and Isuzu leave phone messages.
Day 22	Letters from Isuzu and Oldsmobile arrive.

Day 27   Honda writes a letter.

Day 28   Mercedes-Benz phones.

Day 29   Mercedes-Benz sends a Mailgram.

The most condemning aspect of this experiment: Seven of the 25 automakers *fail to respond in any form!* In general, the reporter concludes, imports were speedier to respond than were the domestics. Although a telephone number was not included in the letter, Saab looked it up. Rolls-Royce is declared the winner for persistence—a telephone call on the eighth day, two messages on the 11th day, and a letter on the 15th day.

How would you rate the general level of responsiveness to a current customer expressed by these 25 major companies? Except for Rolls-Royce, Saab, and BMW it is not exemplary. And what about the seven companies that failed to acknowledge the letter at all? Bad customer service? Most assuredly. Bad (or nonexistent) aftermarketing? Absolutely.

Source: T. Kauchak, "A Little Service, Please!" p. S-8. Reprinted with permission from *Advertising Age,* January 21, 1991, Copyright Crain Communications, Inc. All rights reserved.

THE PERSPECTIVE OF THIS BOOK

The value of retaining current customers is equal for all marketers, whether they market goods or services to consumer, business, or industrial markets. While this evolution in marketplace orientation has occurred over the last five years, there has not been an action plan for the marketing manager who wishes to personally adopt such a perspective.

This book not only explores the philosophy and value of relationship marketing, but also identifies seven specific aftermarketing activities directed at current customers. It will describe their value and show how they can be implemented. The seven activities are as follows:

- Establishing and maintaining a customer information file.
- "Blueprinting" customer contact points.
- Analyzing informal customer feedback.
- Conducting customer satisfaction surveys.
- Managing communication programs.
- Hosting special events or programs for customers.
- Auditing and reclaiming "lost customers."

As each activity is examined, its overall value to maximizing the satisfaction of current customers will be assessed. It will be shown that successful aftermarketing also has direct impact on customers by showing them that the marketer:

- Appreciates their business.
- Is interested in maximizing their satisfaction.
- Cares about their problems.
- Is interested in their suggestions and input.
- Wants their repeat business.

This book provides the rationale, identifies specific opportunities, and suggests specific programs to establish aftermarketing at your organization.

KEY POINTS OF THE CHAPTER

Definition of aftermarketing.   Aftermarketing is the process of providing continuing satisfaction and reinforcement to individuals or organizations that are past or current customers. Customers must be identified, acknowledged, communicated with, audited for satisfaction, and responded to. The goal of aftermarketing is to build lasting relationships with all customers.

Definition of marketing.   Marketing is the process of conceiving, producing, pricing, promoting, and distributing ideas, goods, and services that satisfy the needs of individuals or organizations. It incorporates all of the myriad exchange processes needed to distribute the products and services. It also requires foresight to anticipate the changing environment and to modify the market offering to more effectively compete in the changed market.

Presumption of satisfaction.   All too frequently, marketers assume that current customers are satisfied with the marketer's products or services. They fail to take the time or show the concern to actually ask, "How are we doing?" Presuming that one's customers are satisfied, that they have discovered the quality and value of the marketers' products is short-sighted, it is not marketing myopia, but rather "customer myopia."

Appendix One
A SURVEY OF U.S. BUSINESSES TO ASSESS ATTITUDES ABOUT RETENTION VERSUS CONQUEST MARKETING—WAVE II

In the spring of 1991, an initial, benchmarking survey was fielded among the nation's top 100 advertisers (according to *Advertising Age*). In June of 1994 the survey was replicated among a national sample of two thousand businesses. The sample was stratified by size of business: small firms (those with fewer than 50 employees); medium firms (51-500 employees) and large firms (500+ employees). The 1991 wave received a 28% response rate, the 1994 wave an 8% response.

RETENTION VERSUS CONQUEST

Survey results show a perceptible shift—away from focusing on winning new customers and increasing market share—toward retaining and providing support for current customers. Respondents, on average, reported spending 53% of their marketing budgets on customer retention, against 47% for winning new ones (though large companies on a 1991 to 1994 basis show the lowest shift of spending). Previous results showed a preponderance of spending (54%) on customer conquest.

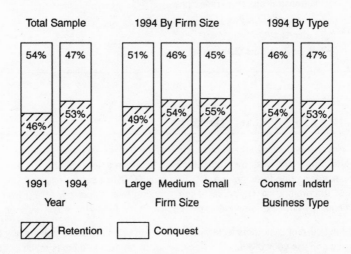

(The substantial allocation reported for retention was higher than expected. In actuality spending on retention may be somewhat lower, since respondents' later descriptions of "retention activities" frequently included advertising—which is not considered an after-marketing tool.)

RETENTION ACTIVITIES

The foremost activities reported as "important in retaining customers" changed substantially from reported usage in 1991. A number of specific activities were mentioned more frequently than in the past, including customer support and newsletters. Down from 1991 were customer satisfaction programs, public relations activities and internal training.

TABLE 1
Activities Important to Retain Customers

'94 Rank	Activity	1991	1994
1	Customer Support and Service	35%	50%
2	Newsletter and Direct Marketing	–	24
3	Sales Activities	–	19
4	Advertising	53	19
5	Quality Products and Services	50	18
6	Promotions and Offers	65	18
7	Customer Special Events	–	18
8	Personal Attention and Follow-Up	–	14
9	New or Improved Products and Services	18	14
10	Costs/Pricing/Value-Added	–	14
11	Demonstrations and Trade Shows	–	10
12	Communication Programs	–	9
13	Plant Visits/On-Site Visits	–	9
14	Public Relations/Community Involvement	29	8

BELIEFS VS. ACTIONS

To see if reported budgetary allocations were lagging beliefs, the respondents were asked overall, how important customer retention was compared to conquest. This question divided respondents into three groups. The first group (50% of survey respondents) placed the greatest importance on retention. (Their spending was allocated, 60% to retention, 39% to conquest.) They explained their perspective in the following ways:

"Retaining current customers is definitely more important, because you already know they need and use your product! Selling additional product to them is much easier than convincing a new customer that he needs your product."

"If you don't take care of your existing customers, someone else will!"

"It is very costly to regain a "lost" customer. Most of our efforts are spent keeping our existing customers very satisfied."

Only 30% of the respondents placed greatest importance on conquest. (Their reported spending was 41% for retention, 59% for conquest). Their reasoning was:

"Our strategy has been to maintain a level of brand awareness through magazine advertising, supplemented by local ROP for conquest. It's been successful for 80 years...however, we're currently considering some retention strategies for future roll-out"

"Winning new customers provides the fuel for maintaining market share, replacing customers who find other brands and growing the company"

"Both are important, however, with new products, new customers are needed. Also, as inflation rises, profit margins fall, we need more market share to stay in business."

EXAMPLES OF RETENTION ACTIONS

Asked what specific retention programs they had in place, many respondents described comprehensive customer-loyalty programs:

"Constant direct-mail programs, active customer relations department and lots of customer service."

"Customer needs-focussed sales, customer-contact training, factory-driven 'after-sale' phone follow-up to monitor sales process, quarterly direct mail digests with servicing coupons, a new program contacting 4-year old owners surveying them on repurchase intentions and presenting the current product line to those favorably predisposed, internal development of a customer database (2 years to implementation)."

Finally, a list of Aftermarketing activities was provided and respondents were asked to indicate which of the activities their company conducted on behalf of their customers.

TABLE 2
Use of Aftermarketing Activities

Activity	1991	1994	Change
Maintain a database of current customers	72%	96%	24%
Analyze and respond to complaint mail	95	79	−14
Offer an 800 telephone number for customers	70	68	2
Conduct a customer communication program	70	64	− 2
Sponsor special events/activities for customers	77	53	−24
Conduct regular customer satisfaction surveys	82	46	−36
Offer customers a frequency incentive program	53	28	−25
Publish a proprietary magazine for customers	40	20	−20
Conduct exit interviews among departing customers	43	16	−27

Somewhat at odds with the earlier, attitudinal data (which indicated increases in commitment and spending to retention over 1991 levels), the reported practice or use of specific retention marketing tactics was somewhat lower in 1994 compared with levels in 1991. While the use of customer databases was up 24 percentage points, other tactics (including analyzing complaint mail, sponsoring customer special events and conducting customer satisfaction surveys) were all down over 1991 reported activity levels.

FUTURE TRENDS

When asked to anticipate trends in American marketing related to spending on customer conquest versus retention, the vast majority (66%) indicated they thought efforts towards retention marketing would increase, only 4% thought retention marketing would command less spending in the future!

RETENTION LEADERS

Of companies identified as doing an excellent job in customer retention, Ford, McDonald's, and AT&T led the 1994 list. Mentioned at lower levels, or missing altogether were 1991 leaders, Nordstrom, LL Bean, Land's End, Honda and American Express. Marketers excelling in retention were commended for:

"Product excellence, customized customer treatment."

"Good service, responsive programs, unconditional guarantees, practice total quality management, believe 'the customer is always right'"

"Survey customers, then target programs and offerings to their needs; best customer data existing; able to target own programs and customer promotions to most valuable customer segments."

NOTES

1. Bob Dylan, "The Times They Are A-changin'."
2. The United States is undergoing changes: J. Naisbitt and P. Aburdene, *Reinventing the Corporation* (New York City: Warner Books, 1985), pp. 2-7.
3. The U.S. population is plateauing: U.S. Department of Commerce, *Projections of the Population of the U.S. by Age, Sex and Race: 1988 to 2080*, p. 3.
4. To stock or try new products: Stuart Elliot. "How New Brands Become Too Much of a New Thing," *The New York Times,* June 2, 1992, Sect. D, Page 19.
5. Some consumers have broken loyalties to national brands: "What Happened to Advertising?," *Business Week,* September 23, 1991, p. 68.
6. Virtually every category shows this phenomenon: C. Knowlton, "Consumers: A Tougher Sell," *Fortune,* September 26, 1988, p. 70.

7. A trend labeled "intermediation" by economist Paul Hawken in "The New Di-Economy:" *Marketing Communications,* March 1987, p. 43-48.
8. Survey of 214 large manufacturers: Conference Board, "Rethinking the Company's Selling and Distribution Channels," Report No. 885, 1986.
9. Consumers are becoming increasingly skeptical: P. W. Huber, *Liability: The Legal Revolution and Its Consequences* (New York: Basic Books, Inc., 1988), p. 69.
10. Consumers are interested in warranties: D. Pearl, "More Firms Pledge Guaranteed Service," *The Wall Street Journal,* July 17, 1991, p. B-1: C. Knowlten, "Consumers: A Tougher Sell," *Fortune,* September 26, 1988, p. 70; and S. Stern, "Guarantees at Fever Pitch," *Advertising Age,* October 26, 1987, p. 3.
11. Survey by BBDO Worldwide: R. Rothenberg, "Preserving Value of Brands," *The New York Times,* October 27, 1988. p. D22.
12. To do otherwise, Levitt says, is to be guilty of short-sightedness: T. Levitt, *The Marketing Imagination* (New York: The Free Press, 1983), p. 6.
13. The purpose of an enterprise: Harvard Business School Case No. 9-481-146, Boston, HBS Case Services, 1981.
14. Levitt, p. 7.
15. A social and managerial process: P. Kotler, *Marketing Management; Analysis, Planning, Implementation and Control* (Englewood Cliffs, NJ: Prentice Hall, 1991), p. 4.
16. Over the 26-year period from 1965 to 1991: Personal communication, Television Bureau of Advertising.
17. $37.9 billion in advertising: "100 Leading National Advertisers," *Advertising Age,* September 28, 1994, p. 2.
18. From 1984 to 1991, the number of television advertising vehicles: Personal communication, Television Bureau of Advertising.
19. American Management Association, New York, NY.
20. Forum Consulting, Boston, MA.; Customer Service Institute, Silver Spring, MD.
21. Customer Service Institute, Silver Spring, MD.
22. Technical Assistance Research Programs, Washington, D.C.
23. In the past, acquisition and retention marketing went hand in hand: L. Liswood, *Serving Them Right* (New York: Harper Business, 1990), pp. 14-15.
24. Transaction marketing is part of a larger idea: Kotler, p. 8.
25. Communicate with the people through mass media?: Gary Levin. "Package-Goods Giants Embrace Databases," *Advertising Age,* November 2, 1992, pp. 1, 37.
26. D. Berry, "Marketing Mix for the 90s Adds an S and 2 Cs to 4 Ps," *Marketing News,* December 24, 1990, p. 10.
27. J. W. Duncan, "U.S. Businesses Focus on Customers," *D&B Reports,* September/October 1988, pp. 8 and 51.
28. "How Five Companies Targeted Their Best Prospects," *Marketing News,* February 18, 1991, p. 22.
29. The Cellular Telephone Industry: Personal Communication, Herschel Shostack Assoc., Silver Spring, MD.
30. The pager industry: ProNet Annual Report, 1989.

Chapter Two

What You Need to Know
Collecting the Right Information

Just as the market of the 1980s became characterized by phenomenal amounts of information at the aggregate (macro market) level, the market of the 1990s and beyond is becoming characterized by information at the individual consumer (micromarket or "one-on-one") level. This progression will occur largely as the result of the evolution of the personal computer. Airlines and hotels already have begun to establish travel profiles of their frequent customers; department stores are beginning to understand the vast amounts of information they have always had access to, concerning the purchases and purchase patterns of their charge customers; and even supermarkets are collecting information on frequent customers—when they shop and what they buy.

The goal of relationship marketing is customer retention. Relationships are built on familiarity and knowledge. The marketer of the future will reestablish "personal" relationships with customers through detailed, interactive databases. The challenge is to quickly establish the required databases, and then to act on them to restore personal relationships in marketing.

THE CHANGING FACE OF THE MARKETPLACE

Prior to the 1960s, retailing and even manufacturing to some extent were practiced on an *individual basis*. Marketers took pride in establishing special and lasting relationships with their customers. Such relationships, they found, kept customers returning. In the 60s, 70s, and 80s these individual relationships appear to have been sacrificed in favor of economies of mass reach and distribution. And who, in the light of the tremendous growth of the American marketing system during this time, could have successfully argued against the emphasis of increasing distribution networks and efficiencies? In its quest for greater reach and distribution, the market grew far more complicated in these three decades; reaching a point that a return to the relationship basis of the previous periods surely would have seemed impossible.

The market wasn't the only thing changing. Consumers were also changing. They began to expect and demand greater variety in the products and services they were buying. With marketing's focus on the needs of the marketplace, the types and kinds of products and services were expanded to better meet these more specialized needs. Marketers responded with caffeine-free sodas, all-natural, non-allergenic cosmetics, monogrammed clothing, custom-blended gasolines, and nonsmoker hotel rooms.

Even the most traditional products in the marketplace responded. Only one type of Tide detergent was sold from 1947 to 1984, in 1985 Procter & Gamble introduced four additional types; Crest toothpaste is available in over *100 different combinations* of packaging, flavor, and size; Campbell's, with its stalwart red-and-white-label condensed soups, introduced four totally new brands of canned soups in the late 1980s; even the venerable Oreo cookie was joined by three new varieties. Today, in John Naisbitt's words,

> The time when consumers could be satisfied with black telephones, white refrigerators, and green checks is gone. A product for everyone is a product for no one in America today.[1]

In summary, by the 1980s the structure of the market had become more complex, the consumer market had fractionated, and product offerings had proliferated. Marketers, now entrapped by the complexity they had created, attempted to cope with it by collecting and studying volumes of information about the typical consumer segments of the market. Regularly fielded A&U (attitude and usage) research studies sought to help the marketer stay "in touch" with his "typical" customer. Relationships with average consumers were substituted for personal relationships with individual consumers.

However, as the marketplace was growing more complicated (and mass media advertising costs were skyrocketing), computer technology was experiencing significant improvements in both storage capacity and in storage costs. The typical costs for maintaining a customer record in a computer file fell from $10 in 1977 to less than a penny by 1990!

These improvements in the computer industry provided exactly what the marketer needs to keep track of her customers. Current and future computer developments, when directed at maintaining customer databases, will do for marketing what the steam engine did for manufacturing. Mainframe computers are no longer required for establishing or maintaining a customer file. Today's microcomputer technology places database capability on the desks of every marketer. Indeed, some of the smallest marketers have been the first to harness this power. (Take for example the local video store's computerized inventory control and billing system.) Not only can a customer information file fit on a PC, but virtually every additional data requirement is also available in PC format, including the entire U.S. census!

EXHIBIT 2–1
Relationships to Customers: (a) Hierarchical Structure

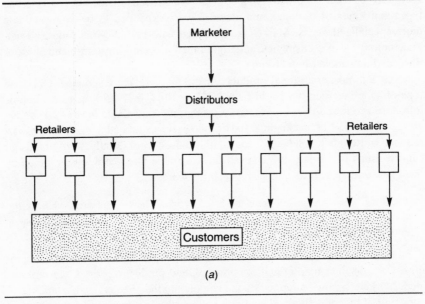

(a)

Today's marketer implementing his marketing strategies with a well-designed CIF (*customer or central information file*) is in a position to continue from where the storekeeper of the 1930s left off. Personal relationships with customers are not only once again possible, but they have become the face of marketing in the 1990s.

This increased personalization of marketing is being described in a variety of terms:

Database marketing.

Individualized marketing.

Micromarketing.

Relevance marketing.

One-on-one marketing.

Bonding.

Frequency marketing.

Relationship marketing.

Segment-of-One™ marketing.

Integrated marketing.

Interactive marketing.

EXHIBIT 2–1
Relationships to Customers: (b) Coordinated Effort

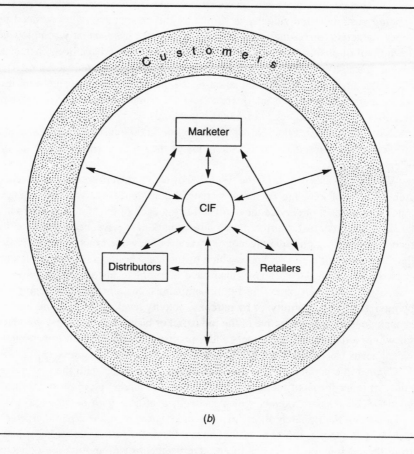

(b)

Dialogue marketing.

Curriculum marketing.

Regardless of the terminology, the emphasis is the same—the recognition of the importance of treating each customer individually, and conducting business in a totally customized fashion, no matter how large the enterprise.

The goal of returning to personal relationships in marketing also has implications for the structure of the company. No longer must retailers or manufacturers be considered the primary force in a hierarchical structure, as in Exhibit 2–1(a) Rather, the customer information file and the customers it represents will unify the effort, coordinating the entire marketing process and all of the participating business entities, as demonstrated by Exhibit 2–1(b).

WHY MARKETERS NEED TO KNOW THEIR CUSTOMERS

Treating customers individually is similar to the perspective long practiced by direct marketers (direct-mail specialists), a group that has generally been looked down upon by mainstream marketing professionals.[2] They have been characterized as "bean counters," focusing microscopically on nontheoretical issues. Traditionally, direct marketers have market-tested their every strategy and offer. It is not uncommon for a direct marketer to test 16 or more versions of an offer or execution in "matched" cells of 5,000 households or more. That means testing involving 80,000 target households! Each cell of 5,000 households is presented a different offer in terms of price, conditions of the offer, or the execution of the offer.

With actual sales data from the test cells, direct marketers are then in the enviable position of knowing (within a statistical confidence interval), *exactly* how much of a product or service they will sell using each of the 16 tested offers in a larger market context. Furthermore, direct marketers have been sticklers for recording results. Consequently, not only do they know the exact number of sales they've made, but they also know which of the households in their data file purchased and which did not. They also have a complete history of the previous responses of each customer. For future campaigns, customers can be segmented by interests, by profitability, or by purchase activity level. This attention to detail is analogous to the perspective of the industrial or business-to-business marketer, for whom a database of customers and a precise knowledge of customers' individual needs has always been the normative way to conduct business.

Contrast the certainty of the direct marketer's operation with the vast uncertainty of other forms of marketing, particularly the marketing of most consumer goods. Such mass marketers will also begin a project with some exploratory research. But the research differs in style and content from the direct marketer's. Generally, a sample of 300 to 1,200 households of the target market is extracted from the population. Reactions to an advertisement or promotion are collected from this sample. The mass marketer then generalizes results from the small sample to the larger population.

Then the marketer runs the advertisement or promotion in the market and waits to measure gross sales over an extended period of time. Unfortunately, there is no way for the marketer to definitively attribute marketplace sales to the advertisement or promotion. Further frustrating understanding, the marketer has no precise information about the types of customers motivated to purchase in comparison to those who were not.

The "accounting" of the marketing perspectives is radically different. The *mainstream marketer* hopes that her mass media advertising creates awareness and interest, among both retailers and consumers, that ultimately are translated into marketplace availability and sales. There is, however, no direct way of

AFTERMARKETING WORKING
How Marketers Are Building Customer Information Files

Philip Morris's recent Penske RM1 Corvette Sweepstakes is an excellent example of how aggressively some marketers are establishing databases of their customers and category customers in general.

It has been suggested that this is more than just an occasional project for Philip Morris. Some believe that the tobacco giant is creatively seeking solutions for a "doomsday marketing scenario," in which over-the-counter sale of cigarettes in many retail establishments may be prohibited by law. In such a case, direct-mail sales would be the only viable distribution channel. Rather than wait until such a scenario is imminent, some believe Philip Morris (and its chief competitor, RJ Reynolds) are seizing every customer identification opportunity and are constructing the most accurate and complete customer lists possible. These lists would serve as a platform for the direct distribution of tobacco products in the future.

Regardless of Philip Morris's intentions in running the Corvette sweepstakes, the entry form is more a questionnaire than a traditional entry form. Among the items of information requested are the following:

A signature guaranteeing that the respondent is 21 years of age, a licensed driver, and a cigarette smoker.

Regular brand of cigarettes.

Type of cigarette considered regular brand.

Length of time smoked regular brand.

Quantity in which regular brand is purchased.

Gender.

Birthdate.

Telephone number.

relating any sale to a specific advertisement or even to the advertising in general. The mainstream marketer (especially in the introduction of a new product) does not have a clear idea of the success or profitability of the product because she is spending to create awareness and interest—both unacceptable items on the company's P&L.

In contrast, the *direct marketer* spends for a specific customer. The success or profitability of the effort is immediately readable by the sale or rejection of the offer as presented. Each offer is therefore clearly analyzed.

The *database marketer's* accounting is different yet again. The database marketer spends to acquire a long-term relationship with a customer. The bet is that the customer will transact a string of purchases with the marketer. Because every purchase the customer makes is recorded, and because the length of the customer's relationship with the marketer is also measured, the database marketer will be able to determine the customer's long-term value to her.

It may be said that the database marketer's approach is different and better in terms of of the following:

- *Addressability*—being able to identify every customer and reach each one on an individual basis.

- *Measurability*—knowing whether or not each customer purchased, exactly what he or she purchased, and how, where, and when he or she purchased (and his or her purchase history).

- *Flexibility*—having the opportunity to appeal to different customers in different ways at different times.

- *Accountability*—having precise figures on the gross profitability of any marketing event and qualitative data showing the type of customers who participated in each particular event.

These criteria have been missing from traditional marketing. Unsure of the identity of their actual customer, mainstream marketers have relied on global information about the behavior of the aggregate market or "average" consumers.

This perspective must change. As Stan Rapp, a direct marketer and frequent author, said in a recent AMA speech,

> *Dialogue* and *information* will be the new order. This represents the beginning of a great turnaround in marketing. The computer changed production. The computer changed how we work in the office. Now, the computer's going to change marketing. The ability to have a database of end users' names, addresses, and information, is the great turnaround in marketing. It means you have to start thinking differently if you want to keep up with a competitor who is already thinking that way. We are looking at the birth of a new marketing, an individualized marketing.[3]

Current marketing practitioners must quickly acquire the technical skills and capabilities to create corporate and organizational marketing programs aimed at the individual customer. Failure to do so will result in the loss of the organization's confidence in the marketing function and the ultimate reassignment of control.

But members of the mainstream marketing community are only slowly recognizing the value of addressing individual customers and are taking cautious steps in that direction. It is not that current marketing practices should be set aside in favor of *database marketing,* but rather that the techniques used in database marketing must be generalized and incorporated into mainstream marketing practice and thought.

The massive change in perspective required will not be easy for all marketers to accept. Many are clinging to activities and tactics in which they were trained. For example, few advertising agencies have bothered to study or adopt database skills. Despite a recent flurry of ad agency "repositionings," bringing the concept of integrated marketing out of textbooks and supposedly into practice, few agencies are equipped to practice integrated marketing. Most advertising agencies continue to focus on creating and placing mass media advertising (aimed at customer conquest)—avoiding issues as seemingly mundane as building lists of customer names and as foreign as recommending a special event instead of another 30-second TV commercial.[4]

Yet as agencies' conventional attitudes prevail, the real need for databases is all too apparent in the businesses of many clients who never previously considered a database. A 1991 study by the American Association of Advertising Agencies showed that 67 percent of large advertisers already integrate their marketing efforts. However, their lack of belief in agencies' ability to service such integrated needs is testified to by their expressed preference of "playing one [type of marketing agency] 'off against another' rather than allocating an entire marketing budget to one agency."[5]

Only the fittest marketers will survive during the 90s, the "decade of the database." And the strength of the CIF will begin to be felt in most American companies throughout the remainder of the 1990s. The battle lines are drawn. Across the marketplace competitors are quickly amassing as much information about their customers as they can, hoping to seal customer relationships before anyone else in their category does.

The strategy, therefore, must be to expand the understanding and use of the more helpful tools of direct marketing within mainstream marketing. One of the most important tools is the establishment and maintenance of the customer information file. Simply using database tools should not be seen as a move to database marketing, but rather must be properly viewed as aftermarketing, implemented by database and other selective technologies.

WHOSE BUSINESS IS RIGHT FOR CUSTOMER INFORMATION FILES?

Customer information files are a natural component of most financial services. Consumers cannot refuse to answer a bank's questions when they apply for a loan. Number of children? The question is readily answered. Ages of children? Also answered. Any older dependents? Again, no problem. In this short series of questions the consumer has provided the financial services marketer with a wealth of information with which to properly target him for future campaigns. And as the bank studies the applicant's investment activity, it can begin to make some educated guesses about his ultimate value as a depositor and borrower.

Information routinely collected on its established application forms should assist the financial services marketer to accomplish many of the aftermarketing activities already described. But there are opportunities to collect even more information. Marketers in industries using applications and questionnaires

AFTERMARKETING NEEDED
Ignored Owner Registration Cards

Think about, for example, the customers of a particular electronic appliance manufacturer. The manufacturer's factory packed an owner registration card in each
appliance it shipped. Many purchasers of the appliances dutifully completed the
forms and returned them to the company's headquarters.

The company's executives, however, did not have a clear idea of the value of the
cards constantly arriving in their post office box. They did not have the staff to
process the cards and were unwilling to hire an outside agency. Consequently, they
unceremoniously dumped the returned cards into crates, which were then placed in
a corner of one of their warehouses.

An inspection of samples of the tens of thousands of cards so stored brought to
light, in addition to the returned cards, the following items:

- Checks and cash with requests for supplies and accessories.
- Letters containing questions or comments about the company's products.
- Letters of satisfaction and praise for the manufacturer.

The enormous amount of potential goodwill represented by these returned
owner registration cards was never realized. If the cards had been properly
processed, each customer would have been sent an acknowledgment. Those
requesting supplies or special assistance could have been handled in a courteous
and satisfying manner. Most importantly, a tremendously valuable database of the
company's customers could have been established.

Consider the feelings of those appliance owners who sent money for supplies
and never heard from the manufacturer! It is unlikely that they will ever buy
another of the manufacturer's products.

should capitalize on these accepted procedures and amass all of the information
they legitimately require.

Many other service marketers are in the similarly enviable position of being
able to collect information from their customers as a normal part of doing business. And, interestingly, this valuable information doesn't always have to be volunteered through applications or questionnaires completed by the customer.
ChemLawn, a lawn maintenance company, reportedly plans to develop several
additional door-to-door services from its customer information file of customers
whose lawns it services. Consider similar opportunities for the pizza delivery
services of Pizza Hut, Domino's and Little Caesar's; they know who their customers are, where they live, what their phone numbers are, and what, when, and
how often they eat home-delivered fast food.

Durables Marketers

Durables marketers (especially those whose products are represented and sold by middlemen) are not yet convinced that databases are a useful tool. Many claim that customer relationships are the responsibility of their channel representatives. The problem is that the typical dealer or agent handles a wide range of products or services from several marketers and thinks nothing at all about trading "his" customers from one brand to another.

Consumer Packaged Goods Marketers

At the opposite end of the spectrum, many manufacturers of consumer packaged goods prejudge customer databases as too costly and offering too little return on investment. Except for the tobacco industry, which, as has already been mentioned, is motivated to construct databases to ensure a long-term distribution channel, most packaged goods manufacturers have been slow to experiment with databases. The primary reason for this appears to be their overwhelming focus on *short-term results.* Ten million dollars spent in advertising or promotion will almost surely spike sales in the short term, relaxing pressure from upper management and satisfying stockholders. But database construction and maintenance are, by definition, a *long-term venture.* Results of an equal investment in database construction may take several years to be realized, exceeding corporate executives' average position tenure, or one or more corporate "lifetimes."

Another factor inhibiting the ready adoption of databases by packaged goods marketers is the corporate organization-by-brands characteristic of most packaged goods marketers. This organization fosters a parochial, brand-centered view; it does not encourage a multibrand, corporate orientation. In contrast, databases offer the potential of integrated marketing activities.

Payback is yet another reason for the slow adoption of databases by packaged goods marketers. Whereas an automobile manufacturer can somewhat more easily justify maintaining files on a customer who will ultimately spend $15,000 to $50,000, the manufacturer of a $2.95 razor finds database expenditures greeted with less plausibility within his company. Many times, costs will simply exceed gross profits. A Colgate-Palmolive executive tells of a database program in a South American country, which, by all standards, was a phenomenal success in triggering repeat purchases. The only trouble: The program cost $3.50 per household per year, but gross profit per household was only $4.00![6]

Consequently, many packaged goods marketers have been slow on the uptake. Some marketing experts believe that this avoidance will ultimately be buried by the rush of technological advancements, making databases much less costly. And there are a number of other reasons to believe that databases are in the future of virtually all packaged goods marketers:

- Couponing efficiency has seriously eroded in the last few years, causing many packaged goods marketers to rethink the wisdom of participating in the circulation of 300 billion coupons per year (more than 3,000 coupons per household per year).
- Continuity programs are increasingly finding favor over coupon programs. Continuity programs can quite innocently create databases almost incidental to the marketer's main intent.
- Supermarket point-of-sale data technologies are creating their own databases almost independent of specific intent.
- As retailers increasingly utilize their databases to run their businesses more profitably, marketers will be forced to design their own to maintain their competitive posture versus the retailers.

THE BENEFITS OF A CUSTOMER INFORMATION FILE

The customer information file helps to implement aftermarketing in several ways (See also Exhibit 2–2):

- Marketing efforts become both more efficient and more effective because the marketer is able to identify her most important customers and then can present to them the right offer, product, or service at the right time.
- Computer technology is harnessed to manage the vast amounts of data the marketer requires to interact with her customers in a truly personalized manner.
- A true "dialogue" can be maintained with consumers by tracking interactions over time, identifying changes in purchasing, and allowing the marketer to anticipate future changes.
- New product development is facilitated by knowing who has purchased a product, how satisfied he or she is, and whether any changes would enhance the performance of the product.

These benefits, however, carry a concurrent liability of database-supported aftermarketing. Utilizing a customer information file requires the marketer to totally rethink the way she conducts business. Marketing plans must be completely redesigned to properly exploit the CIF.

The CIF is capable of bonding customers to marketers as never before. This bonding fosters aftermarketing through customer retention in two special ways: through *appreciation* and through *relevance* (see Exhibit 2–3).

Appreciation means actively acknowledging the value of a customer by recognizing his existence and by establishing a knowledge of his particular needs and desires. Appreciation is dramatically evidenced when customers' opinions are constantly invited and when customers are even asked to review product development plans or prototypes. For example, Apple computer previewed the Mac

EXHIBIT 2–2
Benefits of Knowing Your Customer

"Ted, look. Someone else who knows their customers the same way Carol Wright does."

Source: Used by permission of Donnelley Marketing.

computer with a panel of 100 influential Americans, asking for their reactions and suggestions before introducing the product to the general market.

Relevance will result if appreciation is practiced. Customers will experience the marketer's concern for them by seeing how well the marketer's products and services fit their specific needs. The marketer's total marketing activities will be more related to the customer's needs than they would if they were developed in a "consumer-less" vacuum.

EXHIBIT 2–3
Benefits of Aftermarketing

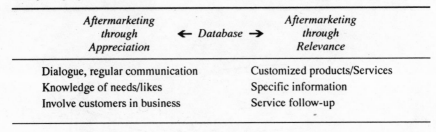

Aftermarketing through Appreciation	← Database →	Aftermarketing through Relevance
Dialogue, regular communication		Customized products/Services
Knowledge of needs/likes		Specific information
Involve customers in business		Service follow-up

The result is true to Peter Drucker's 1973 description of customer-oriented marketing:

> The aim of marketing is to know and understand the customer so well that the product or service fits him exactly and sells itself.[7]

Specific Benefits

The customer information file lets the marketer assess the value of individual customers in ways never before possible in mainstream marketing. Three of the most important measures are as follows:

- Determining the lifetime value of a customer.
- Identifying the costs of acquiring a new customer.
- Facilitating customer "scoring" and "affinity modeling."

Lifetime customer value.   One of the most useful constructs of a customer information file is the ability to calculate the *lifetime value* of a customer. This measurement tells the marketer what each customer is worth. Procedures for calculating lifetime value range from pragmatic to sophisticated modeling procedures.

Pragmatic methods of calculating lifetime customer value can be based on the total customer base, or can more precisely be calculated within customer cohorts that are determined by some event: date of first purchase, type of offer originally redeemed, and so forth. The first step is to define which customers are to be considered *active* customers. Customers have a distinct life with an organization, from their first purchase to their last. The problem is that, although a first purchase is easily identified, a customer's last purchase is not as evident. But a customer will at some time stop purchasing a company's products or services. Whatever the reason—receiving poor service, purchasing a defective product, moving out of the trading area, and so on—there comes a time when every customer stops buying from a firm.

The definition of who an active customer is should depend on the purchase cycle of the category or industry. A customer missing three purchase cycles should probably be considered lost. It is human nature to try to deny the loss of a customer, but it serves no purpose to delude oneself by optimistically extending the definition of an active customer beyond a certain number of missed purchase cycles. The definition of an active customer is then used to identify all the customers who meet this criterion.

An aggregate estimate of lifetime customer value can be made by determining their total lifetime purchases and dividing by the total number of active customers:

$$\text{Lifetime value} = \frac{\text{Total purchases of all active customers}}{\text{Total number of active customers}}$$

Average lifetime value is then defined as the average dollar amount of purchases made by the typical customer during his or her lifetime as a customer.

A more precise estimate of lifetime customer value would utilize cohort analysis. A weighted average of the lifetime of the typical customer would be calculated. This would be multiplied by the known average monthly or yearly purchase amount within the cohort (L_1 = number of customers lasting 1 period, L_2 = number of customers lasting 2 periods, and so forth).

$$\text{Lifetime} = \frac{(L_1 \times 1) + (L_2 \times 2) + \cdots + (L_n \times n)}{L_1 + L_2 + \cdots + L_n}$$

Then,

$$\text{Lifetime value} = \text{Lifetime (in periods)} \times \text{Average period expenditure}$$

Obviously, the magnitude of the lifetime value is completely dependent upon the time definition given to an active customer. Extend the definition, and lifetime value will necessarily increase. Contract the definition, and lifetime value also decreases.

Some argue that, for the concept of lifetime value to be of any real use, it must be an actual, not a mathematically projected, number. But regardless of how it is derived, the concept has pragmatic value. Its message is that *the longer a customer stays with a firm, the greater the customer's value.* If a customer stays longer, lifetime value increases. If that same customer leaves sooner, lifetime value decreases. As simple as this maxim is, some marketers operate as if they are totally unaware of its existence. Once lifetime sales are calculated, it is easy to determine the net profit associated with each active customer. Using a marketer's average percentage for net profit before taxes, the average lifetime value can be easily transformed into the average lifetime net profit before taxes.

Costs of acquiring a customer.   Calculating lifetime value encourages the calculation of an additional per-customer figure, the *average cost of acquiring a customer.*

Costs for acquiring new customers may be less certain in mainstream marketing than in direct marketing, but estimates can be made based on typical conquest rates. In any campaign or promotion in which results can be traced, this figure will be much more easily obtained. It should be immediately apparent that the cost of acquisition should be less than the lifetime net profit before taxes in order to survive and profit.

Customer scoring models.   Another concept supported by the customer information file is *scoring*. This means rating, or scoring, each customer's likelihood of purchasing on the basis of a typical offer. Direct marketers use scoring models to more efficiently allocate their marketing efforts by the following methods:

- They present new products, services, or offers *only* to those customers who evidence the greatest likelihood of buying.
- They treat prospects *differently* according to their scored likelihood of purchasing.

Affinity modeling.   Another process supported by the fully functioning customer information file is *affinity modeling*. Affinity modeling is making guesses about how likely customers are to purchase *other products or services* (hence the term *affinity*). Affinity scores can be very useful in ranking customers by their likelihood of responding to cross selling.

HOW TO CONSTRUCT A CUSTOMER INFORMATION FILE

There are four maxims for building an effective customer database:

1. Anticipate the major information needs.
2. Plan the components of the database carefully, but allow for future changes.
3. Don't delay building the database while trying to specify the ultimate structure: construct and use a smaller, less grandiose database sooner rather than later to assess its value to the business.
4. Involve as many departments and individuals in the construction as possible.

The key to the design of a successful database is viewing the customer file as both *available* and *dynamic.*

Making the file *available* to all relevant departments means that the file will get more use, and that it will also be improved by the input from many different sources. As the data added to the CIF becomes more diverse, the CIF serves the indirect purpose of helping to integrate the many activities and departments of the organization. For example, the following activities could be captured within or linked to the CIF:

Field sales reports.

Customer financial reports.

Product development opportunities.

Customer service requests and reports.

Processing of customers' orders.

Literature fulfillment.

Lead qualification.

Research data and information.

Lead generation.

Use of and redemption from sales promotions.

The successful file must capture virtually all interactions between customers and the organization.

The file should also be *dynamic* (expandable). The ability to grow should itself be highly flexible and should not be restrictive. Ask these questions before starting to construct a customer information file:

- What *department or organization* will build the CIF?
- *Who* will be included in the CIF?
- *What information* will be collected in the CIF?
- How will the CIF be *organized?*
- How will the CIF be *used?*

What Department or Organization Will Build the CIF?

Considering who will build the customer information file includes the question of its propriety. Generally, if a CIF is constructed internally, it will be a proprietary database. Several combinations of origination and access can be imagined (see Exhibit 2–4). In the case of a proprietary database built by an external service bureau, the database could ultimately be brought in-house for daily upkeep and maintenance.

Deciding whether to construct the database internally or externally is a difficult decision. Few managers wish to advocate spending money on "the outside" for resources available internally. However, many experts warn of the likely problems of relying on a corporate Management Information System (MIS) department to construct and maintain the customer information file.

EXHIBIT 2–4
Options for Database Construction and Maintenance

	Access		
Where Built	*Proprietary*	*Shared*	*Syndicated*
Internally	✓	?	
Externally	✓	✓	✓

- Generally, an MIS department will not be equipped with either the right machinery or talents to construct the database. It will be unfamiliar with software to perform geocoding and statistical modeling or to supply on-line, direct access to the database.

- Placing the database in-house may create a "tug-of-war" over storage space, and talk of downscaling the database to fit in current surplus space.

- In-house production priorities will generally work against the customer information file. MIS's primary function is usually overseeing and producing the payroll, inventory control, and accounts receivable, and overseeing manufacturing. A marketing project is likely to receive a lower priority than any of these existing assignments.

- The MIS "culture" is at variance with the dynamic nature of a customer information file, which will require testing, constant updating, and on-line access. The MIS orientation is programming and installing systems and then allowing them to run, unchanged, for several years.

- On-line operations require a special know-how and a real-time system. MIS departments frequently bring their systems down for repairs and other reasons. The need to access a CIF on a reasonably continual basis will not easily coexist with the arbitrary shutdowns of many MIS operations.[8]

The decision comes down to control. Marketing rarely, if ever, manages the MIS function. Therefore, the marketing department will have little clout within the MIS department. The speed with which changes are made will depend on whether programmers are available. On the other hand, an external database supplier will have the appropriate expertise and should meet requests in a timely fashion to keep the business.

The issue of access is equally complicated. Constructing a proprietary database can be a very expensive project. Costs can easily reach $2 per name or household. For this reason, many marketers choose the services of a "syndicated" database supplier such as National Demographics & Lifestyles. NDL will manage the collection of a marketer's customer information or will transfer existing records into its formatted files for a reasonably small fee. However, in exchange for its services, it requires the marketer allow her customers' information to become part of NDL's own Lifestyle Selector™ database.

NDL uses the information in its Lifestyle Selector database to produce syndi-cated reports showing the zip code locations of high likelihood prospects for generic products and services. (NDL does not disclose brand purchases of its clients' products.) Although this process may ease the financial burden of estab-lishing the customer information file, it does place the file somewhat at arm's length. Requests for custom reports and analyses must be made to NDL and will likely incur charges. On the other hand, the expertise of an "off-site" database operation will benefit the marketer in the professional way in which the list is organized and maintained.

Shared databases are also becoming popular. Sharing means that two or more noncompetitive marketers whose products are likely purchased by the same con-sumers will join together to co-fund the formation of a database that each can use. Sharing is an attractive alternative, but it may be difficult to find the right partners for such a collaboration. One marketer must make the extra effort to organize the venture. Usually an external vendor would construct and maintain a shared database.

Who Will Be Included in the CIF?

Although there are many specific groups to consider, there are generally four constituencies that ought to be included in the customer information file:

- *Current customers,* marked by frequency of purchase, average order vol-ume, lifetime value, and recency of last purchase.
- *Prospective customers;* knowing who current customers are gives a mar-keter a better description of target customers. With information on current customers a marketer can assemble lists of similar individuals.
- *Lapsed customers* or lost customers; although they are beyond the imme-diate goal of retention, they still ought to be retained and communicated with.
- *Information on stores, dealers, or merchandise* that is derived from cus-tomers' purchases. Indirectly, information such as the preference for dif-ferent departments, stores, branches, or dealerships, or the attractiveness of merchandise lines offered can be deduced from the purchase records of customers identified in the file.

Other groups may be included for specific applications. Flexibility and imagi-nation should prevail in the selection of each component group.

What Information Will Be Collected in the CIF?

The information to be included in the customer information file will necessarily be customized to the marketer's specific needs, yet there are some reasonably universal components. Traditionally, the three most important components of a customer database have been the following:

- Recency: When was the customer's last purchase made?
- Frequency: How often does the customer purchase?
- Monetary value: How much money has the customer spent over a specified period of time?

These components have generally been collectively referred to as RFM in direct marketing.

As the costs for computer database storage have dramatically fallen, marketers have become more ambitious about the range of information they would like included in a CIF. Here's one marketer's "wish list":

A customer identification number or code.

Customer's name and address (both the billing and the shipping address).

Name of key decision makers (I).

Titles and positions of key decision makers (I).

Size and composition of household (H).

Customer's telephone number.

Date of customer's first purchase.

Dates of all subsequent purchases.

Date of last purchase.

Frequency of purchases.

When product or service is likely to next be required.

Items or services purchased by item or service ID number, category, and department.

Distribution channel from which each purchase was made (for example, retailer, catalog, and so on).

Items returned and services discontinued.

Purchase amounts.

Average purchase volume.

How purchase was made (telephone, mail, in person, and so forth).

Method of payment.

Bad debt history, if any.

Dates of all promotions, offers sent to the customer, and responses to these promotions and offers.

Source code indicating the medium or vehicle from which the customer originally responded (such as referral, telephone solicitation, print ad response, direct mail solicitation, coupon redeemer, and so on).

Personal information generated through interaction with the company (applications, for instance).

Media habits (TV, radio, magazines).

Activities enjoyed.

Personal information obtained from external databases (through database enhancement).

Product or service usage information inferred from the product or service purchase transactions.

Product or service usage information obtained by merging disparate internal databases.

Product or service usage information obtained from responses to product or service usage questionnaires.

Perceptions of the organization or company obtained from responses to product or service usage questionnaires.

Perceptions of competitors obtained from responses to product or service usage questionnaires.

How they can be better served (desired product or service improvements)[9].

    I—databases of *industrial* customers.

    H—databases of *private (household)* customers.

How Will the CIF Be Organized?

The physical type of storage used has profound ramifications on how flexible and easily updated the file will be. But it also affects how easily the file's structure is understood and how quickly the file can be built. There are two types of structure for the customer information file:

- *Flat* (or sequential). In a flat file the customer records are all the same length, being composed of the same number and type of fields (whether each field is relevant to each customer or not). All records reside in one database.

- *Relational.* In relational files an indefinite number of physically separate database files can be linked together. When new information is to be incorporated into the customer information file, the file containing the new information is simply related (indexed) to the main database.

The computer hardware itself is the second concern. Although it has been generally assumed that a large-scale customer information file means storage and access through a mainframe, the powerful personal computers containing a 486 chip (or a more advanced chip) have made the PC a feasible alternative for all but the very largest of applications.

Controlling software is another concern. "Off-the-shelf" programs are able to handle standard applications. But for highly customized applications, a more sophisticated software package or custom programming will be required (see Exhibit 2–5).

EXHIBIT 2–5
Relationship between CIF Size, Complexity and Construction[10]

	Database size	
Database complexity	**Small**	**Large**
Simple	Who: Marketing department or vendor Hardware: PC Software: Standard	Who: MIS or vendor Hardware: Mainframe Software: Standard
Complex	Who: MIS or vendor Hardware: PC/ mainframe Software: Custom	Who: Vendor Hardware: Mainframe Software: Custom

How Will the Customer Information File Be Used?

The primary aftermarketing use of the CIF (as distinct from a pure direct marketing perspective) is to ensure that customers are

- Known (and therefore addressable).
- Acknowledged and appreciated.
- Satisfied (they feel that their expectations were met by the product or service as delivered).

The CIF can be used for a variety of practical activities:

- Segmenting the customer base according to purchase frequency and volume and use occasions (surmised from lifestyles).
- Tailoring marketing programs to fit the individual needs of customer segments to make the marketing mix more relevant.
- Generating a profile of customer types to guide current marketing procedures and to stimulate the development of complementary new products.

AFTERMARKETING NEEDED
When Accountants Are Placed in Charge of the Customer
Information File

For 10 years I have had a Sunoco Credit Card. During that time I averaged 1½ tankfuls of gas each week. I bought all of my gas from Sunoco, and I bought all of it from the same Sunoco gas station.

Occasionally, if my account became overdue, I would receive reminder (dun) letters. When the account was more than 45 days overdue, I would even receive a telephone call. Sunoco was watching my account! They became extremely unhappy when I let the account become overdue. Their systems were very sensitive to changes, or the problem of no change (reduction) in my balance.

Six months ago, I became quite upset with my Sunoco dealer. The problem, I suspected, was something that Sunoco should have known about, so rather than switch to another Sunoco station, I changed brands of gas. I paid off my account and stopped buying Sunoco gas.

In the subsequent six months I haven't received one communication from Sunoco asking why I have stopped using my Sunoco account. Am I deceased? Have I stopped driving? Have I changed brands of gasoline? Sunoco appears completely satisfied my account is paid up, and they could not care less. (During the same time period, they initiated a very expensive television advertising campaign to win *new customers!*)

While they had me, they had a guaranteed annuity of $1,500 a year. But when they lost me, no one cared enough to even write a letter or send a lost customer questionnaire. I can only conclude that accountants are in control of the Sunoco customer information file because anyone with a marketing perspective would have realized that it was equally important to talk to me when I wasn't using my Sunoco credit card as when I was late in paying!

My local Sunoco gas station also lost an important opportunity to find out why I wasn't buying gas there any longer. Because I was a charge customer, they could have captured my name and tracked my visits. But they didn't, and they therefore also failed to notice my absence and lost an opportunity to bring me back.

- Further enhancing the customer file with surveys and lifestyle databases to increase the degree of intimacy with which the customers are "known".
- Supporting customer service operations better by making information in the CIF available to customer service representatives as they interact with customers.
- Identifying additional, high-likelihood purchasers based on their profile similarity with current customers.

THE COSTS OF ESTABLISHING A CUSTOMER INFORMATION FILE

Establishing a customer database incurs costs of money and time. The potential cost can be negotiated with relative ease. Companies seem less reasonable when it comes to time. No one wants to advocate constructing an inferior database, so everyone may set their sights at a database of "unreachable" quality.

Industry experts agree that it's better to start experiencing the value of an imperfect database than to aspire to a perfect but unattainable one. If construction of the database will take longer than 12 to 18 months, the planned database is unrealistically complex. The project should be abandoned. Here's why:

- Computer hardware and software evolve so quickly that to take longer than 12 months is to build the database on obsolete equipment and programs.
- Organizations resist change; the longer it takes to get a CIF into active use, the more likely it will be canceled without ever being used.
- A CIF needs an upper management "champion"—but even a committed mentor needs to see and to show progress.
- While waiting for construction, the company is incurring opportunity costs.
- By waiting longer than a year, competition has the chance to surpass the company.
- Customer information files are a process, not a goal. The sooner the file is established, the sooner the learning experience can begin.*

Because of the generally fluid structure and composition of most customer information files, the database will never contain everything that every user wants.

Consequently, it will always be outdated or inadequate. As with learning to use any new tool, usage will prompt ideas for more applications. Additional applications will suggest the need for additional data.

There are three distinct costs involved in setting up a CIF: *data* (basic information and enhancement), *processing,* and *output.*

Data Costs

Costs of data concern the acquisition of the information and its enhancement. If the names are generated by the marketer, then there are no list purchase fees. However, the costs of fielding a well-designed "registration program" will not be inexpensive. The most significant component will be postage. It is always worth

---

*Adapted from B. Spaisman, "Building a Marketing Database," Third Annual Conference on Database Marketing, The National Center for Database Marketing, December 1990.

using first-class mail service. And don't ever expect customers to spend their own stamp to mail a questionnaire back! Always supply a postage-paid business reply envelope. Costs of postage alone using first-class service both ways (plus a business reply service fee) at current postal rates will amount to $0.74 per returned questionnaire.

If names for the customer information file are purchased from an outside list broker, the fees will range from $40 per thousand for one-time use to approximately $120 for unlimited, one-year use.

Fees for the use of enhancement files will vary by the amount of information needed and the list owner. Charges tend to run from $4 to $15 per thousand per data item for one year's use; a flat additional fee of $30 to $40 per thousand will provide access to all of the list's information fields.

Processing Costs

Processing charges, the second major cost, depend in part on how much must be done to the customer information file as it is established and periodically updated. Generally a new file is "cleaned" to correct for the following items:

Titling (ensures that prefixes—Ms. or Mr.—are appropriate).

Address accuracy NCOA processing and standardization (NCOA is a USPS-sanctioned system offered by approved vendors to check addresses against change of address forms filed with the U.S. Postal Service).

ZIP code corrections, possibly adding carrier route codes.

Processing costs are further composed of the sum of two components: computer time and data storage. Data storage may not be charged for unless the database is maintained on-line. Usually computer time is a function of the size (number of records) of the database. Annual charges will depend on the cost of transactions required and the number of records processed. The frequency of updating can influence processing charges substantially. Different information components of the CIF can be updated in different periods. For example, new customers might be added weekly, purchases added on a monthly basis, and addresses updated biannually.

Output (Reporting) Costs

Output is the third charge. Service bureaus will customarily have rate schedules for each type of "report" (output option) required. Each charge will be record based, except in the case of smaller jobs, which will incur some form of minimum setup fee.

If the customer information file is to be maintained internally, the costs will be quite different. For internal maintenance, the major expenses will be the capital acquisition of the PC hardware and software and the labor costs of a

dedicated or part-time operator. There will be no incremental charges by the type
of operation performed.

Typical costs for establishing a customer information file run from $200,000
to $10,000,000. A good rule of thumb is to plan on $2 to $3 per household or
customer. (R.J. Reynolds has reportedly invested over $100,000,000 in its work
to establish a database of all Americans who smoke cigarettes.)

ENHANCING THE CUSTOMER INFORMATION FILE

Once a customer information file is established, its value can be enhanced by
adding information to it. It has been suggested that information contained in a
database falls into one of four categories:

- *Declared information:* facts that the database members have voluntarily
  supplied about themselves.
- *Implied information:* assumptions that the marketer makes about database
  members based on generally accepted correlations (for instance, high-
  income customers living in the suburbs will probably own 2 or more automobiles).
- *Overlaid information:* using a key variable, drawing information into the
  database from an external source, often the U.S. Census (the postal ZIP
  code allows overlaying census data into a CIF).
- *Appended information:* matching two or more different CIFs can provide
  additional information to be added to customers' records.

There are two major sources for appendable information to add to a company's own customer information file:

1. *External databases.* There are several national suppliers offering major
   database files that can be combined with internal customer files to further
   enhance them. Major types of lists include the following:

   - Mass compiled
   - Finances based
   - Questionnaire generated
   - Combinations of the above (known in the industry as multisourced
     enhancement files)

   These databases include information on consumption behavior, financial
   interests and status, automobile ownership, and so forth.

2. *Proprietary databases.* These lists belong to another marketer, but one
   operating in a noncompetitive category. There are many well-known companies with their own lists, which may be available:

- DAK Industries
- Bloomingdale's By Mail
- Hertz Rent-A-Car Gold Club

Once an information file of current customers has been established, the marketer can increase the possible marketing opportunities supported by the database with information from external sources.

External Databases

In general, information drawn from the external databases to enhance the CIF can be described as one of the following basic types:

• *Demographic data.* Demographics, the bare bones of consumer descriptors, are provided most accurately by the U.S. Census, which collects 73 different variables.

• *Geodemographic data.* Geodemographic data is usually based on the notion that birds of a feather flock together. They are all based on geography implemented either by ZIP code, ZIP plus 4, or census tract data. They provide thumbnail sketches of the psychographics of people residing in various clusters of ZIP codes or census tracts. Generally, marketers find that certain clusters contain a disproportionately high concentration of their customers in a small set of such ZIP clusters. Knowing the psyche of these clusters helps the marketer better understand and therefore better communicate with her customers. Vendors supplying such databases include the following:

CACI, Inc.—ACORN.™

Claritas—PRIZM.™

Donnelley Marketing—Cluster Plus.™

Equifax—MicroVision.™

• *Psychographic data.* So-called life-style segmentation of customers has been carried out on an ad hoc basis over the past 20 to 30 years. Only with the advent of VALS™, however, was psychographic segmentation formalized with a theoretical underpinning. Psychographics are based on the implicit reasoning that similarities in attitudes, interests, and opinions can better anticipate purchase and behavioral actions of consumers than demographics alone. VALS 2™ is the latest formulation from SRI, Inc. to offer a truly "tested" schema for psychographic segmentation.

• *Behavioral data.* Data recording actual behavioral transactions are beginning to be sought as the most relevant for the marketer. The UPC scanner and mass surveys of consumers will make this kind of information more readily available in the near future.

The second consideration is the source of this external information. One way of classifying sources is to use the method by which the data has been accumulated by the third-party vendor. The following descriptions identify the most important sources of external data:[11]

- *Mass-compiled databases,* essentially owned by three companies:
  - R.L. Polk & Company.
  - Donnelley Marketing.
  - MetroMail (a division of R.R. Donnelley & Sons).

- *Financial databases,* the result of the two consumer credit-clearing companies:
  - TRW.
  - Equifax.

- *Questionnaire-generated databases,* a relatively new endeavor:
  - BehaviorBank (Computerized Marketing Technology).
  - Lifestyle Selector (National Demographics & Lifestyles).
  - Shareforce (Donnelley Marketing).

(See Appendix 2 for a detailed description of each of these sources.)

Information from these sources is either rented from the vendor or obtained through program participation and "overlayed," combined with the marketer's customer information file based on a particular "key" such as ZIP code or some other element in common between the external resource and the internal database. ZIP codes are the handiest and the most frequently used key.

The cost of such external information can vary immensely, from annual licensing fees of thousands of dollars to single-use fees assessed by the individual characteristic required. Exhibit 2–6 provides examples of some possible costs for specific demographic characteristics. Of course, a vast number of other characteristics can also be added to a customer file, all from external sources.

Proprietary Databases

There are, today, a great many marketers with well-maintained customer information files who will rent their lists to other noncompeting marketers. These are sometimes the very best sources for enhancement. Because another marketer is placing its survival on the performance of the list, it is more likely that the data will be accurate.

The challenge is to creatively identify a beneficial list. One of the best clues for the kind of list to look for is contained in the reported behaviors of the current customers in the marketer's own customer information file.

EXHIBIT 2–6
Costs for Demographic Characteristics[12]

Characteristic	Cost per 1,000
Number of children	$ 7.00
Number of adults	5.00
Estimated household income	10.00
Occupation	10.00
Working women	5.00
Auto make and year	12.00
Home value	35.00
Date home purchased	25.00
PRIZM cluster	10.00
Phone number	20.00
Exact birthdate	20.00

Other Sources for Database Enhancement

There are a number of other recently developed technologies that can be used hand-in-hand with marketers' customer information files to achieve aftermarketing. Two of the more important are UPC scanning and desktop demographic or mapping systems.

UPC scanning. For retailing and for some service operations, UPC scanning is probably the most significant development aiding database maintenance. Designed originally as a labor-saving device for grocery checkout lines, the Universal Product Code scanner has become the marketer's frontline ally. It is now possible for a retailer to accumulate vast amounts of purchase data with absolutely no direct contact with customers. The data is unobtrusively collected as the customer's purchases are tallied. No customer is inconvenienced by being asked to report her purchases, and no behavior is biased by the collection of data.

The real surprise is how quickly local retailers have discovered the value of information provided by scanners and how aggressively they've leveraged this value against marketers and manufacturers. Several grocery chains—such as Ralphs in Los Angeles, Ukrops in Richmond, Virginia, and Wegman's in Rochester, New York—have positioned their stores as consumer laboratories, able to study the power of retailing tactics such as price reductions, point-of-purchase displays, promotions, and couponing. In addition, they sell the data they collect to manufacturers.

This information means three things:

- They are the first to know consumers' reactions to a manufacturer's products or marketing tactics.

- They maximize their stores' retail space and inventory by stocking according to their observations of sales.
- They increase their income by the revenues produced through the sale of the data.

Desktop demographic or mapping systems.   Recently, each of the four major geodemographic vendors have introduced desktop PC-based systems allowing marketers to perform highly sophisticated analyses using national or regional databases. These systems are meant to replace some of the analyses and services previously offered by these vendors on a service bureau basis. They give the marketer direct access as well as the ability to perform an infinite number of iterations or "what-if" scenarios without worrying about service bureau costs involved. The systems currently offered include the following:

- Claritas—COMPASS™
- CACI, Inc—Insite USA™
- Equifax—Infomark™
- Donnelley Marketing—Conquest/Direct™

Claritas's COMPASS system, for example, is an integrated package containing both decision models and databases. The system includes PRIZM (Claritas's geodemographic database); P$YCLE, a segmentation system designed for financial services marketers; and access to the syndicated databases from SMRB, MRI, and R.L. Polk. The system is marketed as a repository for the marketer's customer information file as well as an analytical tool kit. Its access to the other supplemental databases promises easy enhancement of one's own database. With a marketer's database installed in the system, it is said to be capable of conducting a wide range of analyses and applications, including customer profiling, market potential estimates, site selection, trade area evaluation, and mapping.

KEY POINTS OF THE CHAPTER

Customer information file (CIF).   The CIF is a database that enables aftermarketing activities to occur. It contains the identities and addresses of all present customers, and perhaps past customers and potential ones as well. This database provides four improvements over current marketing practice: *addressability* (knowing one's customers); *measurability* (capturing transaction information); *flexibility* (enabling an individualized approach to each customer); and *accountability* (knowing the gross profitability of each marketing endeavor). Traditionally, CIFs have been noted for providing RFM (recency of each account, frequency of purchasing, and monetary spending).

Database marketing. Database marketing, whether labeled relationship marketing, sole or single-source marketing, integrated marketing, marketing information systems, one-to-one marketing, micro-marketing, the new direct marketing, or database marketing, involves at least the following element: managing a computerized relational database system in real time, that contains comprehensive, up-to-date, relevant data on customers, inquiries, prospects, and suspects. This will help identify the most responsive customers for the purpose of developing a high-quality, long-lasting relationship of repeat business. This relationship is aided by development of predictive models that enable one to send desired messages at the right time in the right form to the right people—all with the result of pleasing customers, increasing response rates per marketing dollar, lowering costs per order, building business, and increasing profits. (Skip Andrew, The National Center for Database Marketing.)

Integrated marketing. This is a concept of marketing communications planning that recognizes the added value of a comprehensive plan that evaluates the strategic roles of a variety of communications disciplines—for example, general advertising, direct response, sales promotion, and public relations—and that combines these disciplines to provide clarity, consistency, and maximum communication. (American Association of Advertising Agencies, 1991.)

Lifetime customer value. Finding the value requires using a calculation to determine the total spending accounted for by a typical customer throughout the customer's dealings with an organization. To determine lifetime value, the average customer lifetime is defined, and then purchases of all customers fitting that definition are averaged.

Appendix Two
SUPPLIERS OF EXTERNAL DATABASES AND MASS-COMPILED DATABASES

R.L. POLK & CO.

Polk's principal mass-compiled database, X-1, was created in 1973. By 1990 it contained data on more than 87 million U.S. households (well over 96 percent of all U.S. households). The X-1 is produced by cross-referencing data from 22 different data sources and updating the file six times a year. The most important source files are the following:

103 million current auto registrations.

17 million truck registrations.

23 million households contacted by Polk's door-to-door interviewers.

66 million residential telephone listings.

22 million new car buyers.

53 million records of births, high school and college enrollments, and graduations.

64 million known direct mail respondents.

52 million home owners.

140 million credit card users.

27 million consumer questionnaires.

13 million members of the NDL database.

DONNELLEY MARKETING

Donnelley's master file, the Donnelley Quality Index[2] Peoplebank, is a super database of 124 million consumers at their home addresses. The database has been culled from 4,700 telephone directories, automobile registrations, drivers license data, voter registrations, birth records, survey respondents and coupon redeemers from Donnelley's Carol Wright™ distribution program, direct mail donors, and mail order buyers. The database can be accessed at any level of geography from the smallest (block group) to the largest (nationally).[13] The database includes the following information:

Age.

First name and middle initial.

Gender of up to five family members.

Household income.

Credit card holders.

Creditworthiness (1 to 9 trade lines).

Presence of children.

Purchasing power.

Dwelling unit size.

Length of residence.

Mail responsiveness.

Make, model, and year of auto.

Telephone number.

Up to 500 other census characteristics.

DQI[2] offers five subsets:

The Automobile File—64 million automobile owners.

The Seniors List—31.5 million consumers 50 years or older at home.

New Movers List—approximately 600,000 households each month.

The Creditworthy Enhancement—38 million creditworthy consumers.

The Affluence Model—20 levels of net worth from under $10 K to over $10 MM.

METROMAIL

This division of R.R. Donnelley maintains a national consumer database of 83 million households and 185 million individual names and addresses. The database includes information from new home owners, new movers, families with births, and households with high school or college students. The database is updated 65 times a year.[14]

The national consumer database can be tied directly into R.R. Donnelley's Selectronic printing and binding technology, offering the possibility of totally customized mailings to members of the database.

FINANCIAL DATABASES

TRW

TRW, a longtime credit-checking service, has recently entered the consumer information services field by upgrading the contents of its database. It offers the PerformanceData system, a database of 143 million individuals with credit and demographic information.[15] TRW draws its information from three sources:

Public records.

Financial institutions.

Retailer accounts.

The database contains over 300 demographic characteristics and 400 financial variables.

Equifax

This company, one of the largest credit bureaus, offers the Equifax Consumer Marketing Database which contains financial and retailer credit information, U.S. Census variables, public records, and cluster membership information from MicroVision, an Equifax geodemographic model. The database includes information on over 135 million consumers.[16]

QUESTIONNAIRE GENERATED DATA

Computers for Marketing Technology

This company offers BehaviorBank™, a questionnaire-generated and maintained database of 25 million consumers. CMT is very active in mailings to its database members, offering sample packs and updating questionnaires.

National Demographics & Lifestyles

NDL pioneered the field of questionnaire-generated databases with the 1978 introduction of The Lifestyle Selector®. By 1994 The Lifestyle Selector contained over 33 million names with demographics and lifestyle information. The list is established and maintained by questionnaires included with consumer products from about 100 major manufacturers. Most of the products are consumer durables such as cameras, electronic equipment, appliances, and sporting goods. NDL receives over 15 million new questionnaires a year. Information on returned questionnaires is used to expand and refresh The Lifestyle Selector as well as to build a database of proprietary information for each participating manufacturer.[17]

The Lifestyle Selector® data elements consist of 12 key demographics:

Gender.
Location.
Home ownership.
Exact age.
Household income.
Marital status.
Number, gender and ages of children at home.
Occupation.
Credit card usage.
Religion/Ethnicity.

The elements also include descriptions of individual participation in more than 60 lifestyle activities and interest areas such as tennis, foreign travel, and gourmet cooking.

Donnelley Marketing

Donnelley Marketing's Shareforce™ database is a 17 million strong file of individuals by demographic, geographic, and lifestyle characteristics. The file is maintained through responses to a questionnaire inserted in Donnelley's Carol Wright co-op direct mail program. The questionnaire includes occupation, presence of children, hobbies and interests, and some financial information. Shareforce clients, primarily in the packaged goods industry, also submit some questions that remain proprietary to them.

MULTI-SOURCED DATA: INFOBASE SERVICES

InfoBase Premier is InfoBase Services' consumer enhancement file. Because of its size—200 million American consumers with 170 different data elements—this file is able to offer an enhancement match rate of 60 to 80 percent. (The common match rate in enhancing an internal database is usually only about 45 to 60 percent.)

NOTES

1. The time when consumers could be satisfied: J. Naisbitt, *Megatrends: Ten Directions Transforming Our Lives* (New York: Warner Books, 1985).
2. Generally looked down upon: G. Day, Guest spot, *Adweek*, April 8, 1991, p. 26; and R. Kilgannon, Guest spot, *Adweek*, April 22, 1991, p. 22.
3. Dialogue and information will be the new order: S. Rapp, "The Great Turnaround: How Marketing Will Change in the 90s," presented at the American Marketing Association's Annual Sales Promotion Conference, New York, NY, May 23, 1990.
4. Few are the agencies who can really demonstrate: "Integration and Reality: Ross Roy Group," *Promo*, March 1991, pp. 6-7, 16, 24..
5. A 1991 AAAA study showed: R. C. MacClaren, "Four-A's Told Clients Want Control," *Promo*, June 1991, pp. 1, 64.
6. A Colgate-Palmolive executive tells of a databased program: B. Spelling, Panel participant in "Is Database Marketing Really Working for Package Goods?" at Direct Marketing Day, New York, May 22-23, 1991.
7. The aim of marketing: P. Drucker, *Management: Tasks, Responsibilities, Practices* (New York: Harper & Row, 1973), pp. 64-65.
8. Many experts warn of the likely problems: Adapted from B. Spaisman, "Building a Marketing Database," Third Annual Conference, The National Center for Database Marketing.
9. R. M. MacDonald, "CIC-A Money Machine," Third Annual Conference on Database Marketing, National Center for Database Marketing, December 1990.
10. D. Raab, "Estimating and Controlling the Cost of Your Database," Third Annual Conference on Database Marketing, National Center for Database Marketing, December 1990.
11. The following descriptions identify the most important suppliers: J. Bickert, *Adventures in Relevance Marketing* (Denver, National Demographics & Lifestyle Inc., 1990), pp. 13-26.
12. Cost per characteristic sample from: D. Raab, "Estimating and Controlling the Cost of Your Database."
13. Donnelley's master file, the Donnelley Quality Index: Corporate literature from Donnelley Marketing, Stamford, CT.
14. This division of R.R. Donnelley: Corporate literature from R.R. Donnelley, Chicago, IL.
15. TRW, a long-time credit checking source: Corporate literature from TRW Marketing Services, Richardson, TX.
16. Equifax, one of the largest credit bureaus: Corporate literature from Equifax Inc., Atlanta, GA.
17. NDL offers the Lifestyle Selector: Corporate literature from National Demographics & Lifestyles, Denver, CO.

Chapter Three

The Value of a Customer Information File

The customer information file, or CIF, as financial service marketers abbreviate it, is second nature to the delivery of most financial services. Yet, despite its familiarity, few financial service marketers have truly exploited the marketing potential of the CIF for their businesses. On the other hand, very few consumer packaged goods marketers have even considered instituting a customer information file.

In the information-intensive marketplace of the 90s, marketers' success is not only dependent on the extent to which they collect information about their current customers but also on how well they use the information they collect. Marketers who sell big-ticket items and who routinely collect information on their customers will adapt to the new information-intensive marketing relatively easily. Marketers who sell low-ticket items, such as consumer packaged goods, will find adaptation more challenging. But the efforts of both marketers in forming CIFs will be rewarded by increased loyalties from their customers.

The promise of the customer information file is immense. Competitors can outspend, underprice, and overdistribute a company, but if that company has achieved a strong database-implemented relationship with its current customers, it is unlikely to be immediately vulnerable. As Marshall Field said,

Goodwill is the one asset the competition cannot undermine or destroy.[1]

JUST WHOSE CUSTOMERS ARE THEY?

The emphasis in the 60s, 70s, and 80s for increased distribution resulted in the growth of countless intermediaries—middlemen. Examining the resulting structure, Hawkens describes the marketplace as suffering from "intermediation," or the proliferation of intermediaries.[2] Management theory suggests that the more organizational levels through which a request must travel, the less likely it will be followed. And the more levels that exist, the more socially distanced people in the levels become from the management. Marketing channels follow similar rules. Many marketers, recognizing their separation by many levels from their ultimate customers, have begun to shorten their distribution channels in an attempt to recapture control over the marketing to and the servicing and support of their ultimate customers.

Typically, extensively developed channels have been encouraged by larger marketers, whose breadth of product offerings and scope of operations have made use of independent distributors and retailers attractive. However, not all large companies have adopted this perspective. IBM has traditionally favored direct marketing over channel representatives, and when it has experimented with intermediaries, IBM has generally been disappointed.

As the numbers of intermediaries proliferate, separating the marketer from his customer, there is far less customer identification with the marketer who originated the goods or services. In shorter channels the marketer and an intermediary may be in relatively close contact, and in such a case the intermediary may, to some extent, identify with the marketer. The intermediary may adopt some of the marketer's values and may internalize the marketer's desire to have his product adequately and properly displayed, actively sold, and well serviced.

However, as marketers depend upon vast numbers of unknown intermediaries to represent their products and businesses, it is likely that the intermediaries will do so with very little commitment to or affiliation with the marketer. Intermediaries, thinking only about their own business and disregarding loyalties to the marketer, do little to reinforce customers' perceptions of a marketer or the quality of its products. It is human nature for intermediaries to look out for themselves— and so they perceive their role as *selling themselves* rather than as *representing a marketer's products and services*. Where would they be without the marketer's wares? No place, of course. But generally, this logic fails to motivate them to invest themselves in properly representing the marketer's products, services, and after-sale attention.

The severity of the situation is obviously intensified within the intermediaries' internal organizations among personnel who interact with customers. With only the faintest loyalty expressed toward the marketer by the intermediary's management, the marketer's products and services are even less cared for at the sales or representative level.

Marketers who rely on intermediaries place themselves at risk. They do not have the opportunity to meet with or to sell to their customers directly, so they rely on the intermediary. And the intermediary is likely to represent no one but himself. Consequently, the marketer's product is thrust into the marketplace without the care and supervision the marketer would desire.

There is an easy answer to this dilemma: the establishment of a customer information file.

OPPORTUNITIES TO ESTABLISH A CIF

Most marketers have numerous ready-made opportunities for collecting information on their customers without instituting special studies and without buying costly databases. Any interaction with customers can be an opportunity to collect information. The typical marketing organization has countless existing opportunities to ask customers questions.

Service Marketers

Service marketers, for whom an application or an enrollment form is already a natural part of doing business, have a natural vehicle with which to collect customer information. All that has to be done is to extend the form by adding questions to collect the most critical marketing information. Because customers need the marketer's service and are "trained" to respond to questions in application or enrollment forms, they will likely complete most questions without a problem.

- *Application forms.* Although all of the desired information is likely to be included in an application form, sometimes this form is not routed through the marketing department. Once the form has served its use as a financial instrument, it should be sent to the marketing department, where its marketing information value can be fully exploited.
- *Club memberships, preferred customer programs, 800 number calls,* and *letters* also apply here.
- *Customer satisfaction surveys.* During assessment of the quality of service being rendered, there is a natural opportunity to also get to know the customer better. Make use of such surveys to collect customer information as well.

Sometimes marketers are reluctant to impose on their customers by asking marketing-type questions in forms or applications. Such concerns can be accommodated by prefacing the CIF information section with a heading such as "For our information, not mandatory." Generally, marketers will be surprised at the number of customers who take the time to volunteer information about themselves. This is the result of two phenomena. First, customers are usually flattered that a marketer cares about them, and they may realize the more the marketer knows about them the better able the marketer will be to satisfy their needs. Second, there is the basic human pleasure that most people take in talking about themselves.

Durables Marketers

As a product area, durable goods—appliances, sporting equipment, cars, and so forth—have the advantage of being a highly involving purchase, owing to their nature and their relatively high price. These qualities make the typical durables

AFTERMARKETING NEEDED
Held "Hostage" by One's Intermediaries

A manufacturer of high-quality, prestigious men's clothing would like to turn the tide of eroding sales. Specifically, it would like to capture more of the business of its retail representatives. These upper-end men's stores and men's departments in the finer "carriage trade" regional department stores rely on the manufacturer's brand to assure their clientele that they carry the best in men's clothing. They also gladly use any promotional piece paid for and mailed by the manufacturer to build traffic in their stores or departments.

However, when the manufacturer's customers shop their stores or departments, the retailers think of the customer as theirs, and trade the customer away from the manufacturer's brand to their own brand without feeling any guilt at all.

It is also the case that only a few retailers carry the extensive inventory the manufacturer would like in terms of range of fabric or patterns; consequently, the customer will usually not see the full season's line of clothing. In addition, the store may be out of his size in any particular item. Special-order garments from the manufacturer are available, but, likely as not, the retailer would prefer to avoid such time-consuming orders and sell another manufacturer's garments out of his inventory.

The manufacturer is reluctant to initiate any direct interaction with its customers. It fears that such interaction will be viewed as "competitive" by the stores. Even though it retains files with each customer's measurements, it only knows the customer through his order with the retailer—there is no direct channel of communication open to the manufacturer.

It would be to the manufacturer's distinct advantage to quickly assemble an internal CIF so that it could begin a one-on-one dialogue with its customers. Such a dialogue could be conducted without disrupting customers' relationships with current retailers. Indeed, those retailers who are currently servicing the marketer's customers well could be featured in subsequent mailings. Special promotions could be offered in the name of the established retailer. The promotions would reinforce the retailer's importance but also, if made applicable to specific merchandise, could encourage the retailer to extend his representation of the manufacturer's line. Only when the retailer fails to properly represent the marketer through poor customer service or a decreased inventory might the marketer decide to mention a direct-sales source to his customers, and then only for merchandise the retailer is not willing to carry.

Too many marketers appear to be caught in the same circumstance, appreciative of retailers' representation when it is forthcoming, but also wary that retailers can just as easily trade a customer to another manufacturer's goods any time the occasion suits them.

purchaser much more likely to want to identify himself or herself to the manufacturer. Almost always such products are shipped or delivered with a warranty registration card or an owner survey. Most consumers appear to understand that it is in their own interests to provide the manufacturer with information about themselves and the uses to which they intend to put the new appliance. Also, some purchasers may be expecting or hoping for additional information from the marketer on the use or proper care of the appliance or equipment purchased.

Response rates for such cards are usually very good, especially when the manufacturer promises something in return for the completed card. An incentive is most effective when it is associated with the product itself. Generally, the more relevant the promised incentive is to the use or enjoyment of the product, the more effective the incentive will be. A natural incentive to offer customers for returning the registration information is a more complete care or use manual or something else that has to do with the better maintenance or utilization of the product. For example, Seiko Instruments sends a monitor cleaning cloth to each owner registering his purchase of a Seiko Instruments computer monitor.

The warranty or owner registration card offers a natural opportunity to collect basic descriptive information on a marketer's customers. The more important the purchase, the more likely the customer will be to register himself or herself, especially to provide the marketer with contact information if a product recall is ever necessary.

- *Warranty or owner registration cards.* These cards are often shipped with products specifically to help form a customer database. Whether or not this is the case, the information included on them ought to be made available to marketing.
- *Application forms.* All of the desired information is likely to be included in an application form, but this form is not always routed through the marketing department. Once the form has served its use as a financial instrument, it should be sent to the marketing department, where its marketing information value can be fully exploited.
- *Club memberships, 800 number calls, and letters.* There are numerous other customer contact points at which information may be collected.

The amount of customer information that can be collected on a warranty card (and still retain the impression of a warranty process) is somewhat limited. It is generally wise to exercise some restraint. The most important goal should be to begin an information dialogue. The goal should be to initiate an exchange of information between the customer and marketer that can continue in the future. The customer's name and address are critical. The most important marketing questions concern the customer's brand-choice process:

- Primary reason the brand was chosen (may be volunteered or checked from a supplied list).
- The competitive set (other brands considered).
- Price paid.
- Intended use(s) and user(s).

AFTERMARKETING WORKING
Databases for Consumer Durable Goods

Effective database marketing for consumer durable products is built upon seven principles:

1. Marketing efforts will be more effective if they are customer driven rather than product driven.
2. Information about a company's current and past customers is valuable for planning future product development and marketing efforts. Knowing who has been a customer helps predict who may become a customer.
3. A significant portion of a company's future business should come from consumers who have already purchased its products. The 80/20 rule applies. That is, 80 percent of a company's business probably comes from 20 percent of its customers. Often that 80 percent comes from repeat purchases by the 20 percent. The lifetime value of a customer can be effectively defined, measured, and tracked through database marketing techniques. Database marketing helps to develop an ongoing relationship with customers by tracking their behavior and establishing a means to communicate with them.
4. Brand loyalty becomes increasingly important as the perceived differences between competitive products decrease. As a new product comes out in the marketplace, many rush to copy it. Marketers who establish differentiated leadership positions in their product categories by demonstrating and communicating quality and service will be able to keep and strengthen their market position. Database marketing helps to determine the specific strengths and importance of pricing, features, product quality, and service to consumers.
5. Building brand and company loyalty depends upon these three factors:

   - Customer satisfaction with the product.
   - The customer's perceived reliability of the service. ("If it breaks, can I get it fixed?")
   - Effective, two-way communication between the company and its customers through systems created by marketers.

6. Effective communication based on customer knowledge. Knowing who the customers are, what they like to do, and why they bought the product means that marketers have better opportunities to communicate in the consumer's own language and thereby establish better rapport.
7. Consumers are defined better by what they do—their activities, interests, and lifestyles—rather than by their demographics—age, income, and place of residence. Their values rather than their characteristics tend to be more predictive of how they choose to spend their time and money.

   - Conversation flows when people talk about what they like to do. Customer communication should be thought of as a conversation, albeit an extended one. Too often, marketers begin the communication process in terms of demographics or the location of their market segments.

> Although such information is important, it is not sufficient to complete
> the communication process. Demographics and geography may help
> define who to talk to, but not necessarily what to say or how to say it.
> * By knowing what customers like to do, marketers have the context and
>   framework for communication and can talk to their customers in relevant
>   terms.
> * Demographics classify and help define a likelihood of buying. But other
>   data may be needed to clarify the actual buying behavior. Lifestyles
>   can show whether prospective customers spend money in ways that relate
>   to the use of the product. Previous product purchasing behavior can
>   show who has been a customer and what his or her relationship to the
>   company is.
>
> Source: D.P. Hinman, "Using Database Marketing Techniques for Consumer Durable Goods,"
> *National Demographics and Lifestyles,* November 7, 1990.

Marketers should be parsimonious at this critical stage. It is unwise to ask
every question desired because there will be future opportunities to add information so long as the customer returns the registration form with his or her name
and address. If the marketer succumbs to the desire to ask everything, return
rates will suffer and the process will defeat itself.

Consumer Packaged Goods

Consumer packaged goods is the product area requiring the most ingenuity to
economically recover customer identity information to either establish or expand
a customer information file. But even here there are numerous opportunities for
the astute (and experimental) marketer. Consider the following:

Coupon redeemers. It makes good sense to request a name and
address on every coupon distributed. Customers who fill in the information will
assist in the creation of a database. As a side benefit, requiring the customer's
name and address may also deter some misredemptions. Coupon clearinghouses
should be requested to render the coupons for complete validation. This means
that the coupon clearing center will return all redeemed coupons to the marketer.
There will, of course, be a service charge. Once the redeemed coupons are in-
house, they may be entered into the CIF at the marketer's discretion.

A cash-back (rebate-type) coupon is an excellent tactic with which to build a
database. Because redeemers must supply their name and address to receive their
rebate, the quantity of usable information will be much higher than with ordinary
cents-off coupons.

Offer redeemers: The affinity group. Customers who have com-
plied with an offer for merchandise, especially affinity merchandise, appear to be

expressing a desire to affiliate with the marketer. These customers are, no doubt, *advocates* on the loyalty ladder (see page 84). These customers are virtually volunteering to become "walking billboards" for a marketer's brand. It makes good sense to pay particular attention to who they are and to enter them into the customer information file.

Contest entry forms.   Virtually all contest entry forms request name and address. The problem is that most marketers don't recover the forms from their fulfillment house, and, even if they do, they fail to enter the names into their customer information file.

Voluntary, customer-initiated contacts.   Although these "outreaches" by customers will be discussed in more detail in Chapter 5, they represent a very important source of identity information about customers.

Calls to 800 telephone centers.   Many marketers today identify an 800 telephone number that customers can call to initiate a dialogue. Even if an 800 number exists for quality control and safety, it can be used to collect hundreds of customer names, weekly or even daily. These names are a windfall for the marketing department and ought to be made available to marketing whether the department operates the telephone center or not.

Letters.   The typical American firm gets hundreds, even thousands, of letters on a weekly basis. Some may be from school children wondering where the company's product originates or how something is made. A small number of letters will be from customers with a complaint who feel the need to "document" their grievance. Virtually all letter-writing customers, probably even those with complaints, ought to be entered into the marketer's database.

Bounce-back cards.   Again, though not normally considered an information vehicle, such cards contain a great deal of marketing information (beyond redemption rates).

Club memberships.   One of the primary reasons for sponsoring a "club" is to accumulate a database of customers. Colgate-Palmolive has established different clubs in various countries with considerable success. There is a down-side risk. Forming a club implies a long-term commitment. Unlike a one-time offer, which the marketer can walk away from as soon as it has been fulfilled, a club requires continued support. Forming a club with inadequate funding or a short-term commitment may be worse than not forming it at all. After all, the customers who join will likely have expectations about membership benefits and activities.

EXHIBIT 3–1
Involvement in Customer Databases

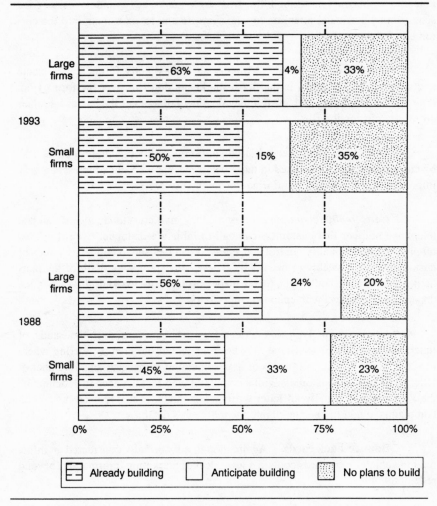

Source: Donnelley Marketing, *Eleventh and Fourteenth Surveys of Promotional Practices.*

In-pack or on-pack questionnaires. Marketers have often been gratified by the response to a questionnaire delivered in or with the product itself. The benefit is the immediacy of the information and the obvious relevance of the information request to the customer. Don't overlook this opportunity—it's efficient and free!

In the case of many of these contacts, the effort and interest of the customer in contacting the marketer ought to be acknowledged with a return call, letter, or postcard. Although a personalized letter is ideal, customers will recognize the expense involved and may be just as happy with a less personal postcard acknowledgment. The important consideration is that the customer's contact was acknowledged, not necessarily *how* it was acknowledged.

Retailers

Among retailers, department stores have had transaction-oriented databases within their reach for the last 20 years. Any department store with its own credit card program has collected information as good as that of today's expensive supermarket scanner systems for four or more decades. And it was existing and free! The trouble is that very few department stores recognized the relationship marketing value of the information they had. It was relegated to the accounting department instead and never exploited for its marketing potential.

Some retailers are beginning to use customer information files. The Sears Merchandise Group tracks in-store purchases of members of its 30-million-household database through purchases on a Sears or Discover credit card. The system can provide names and addresses of customers of any Sears vertical business, of all departments within those businesses, and of all product lines within those departments. The database functions both as a decision support tool (spotting changes in shopping habits and patterns at an early stage) and as a targeting tool (helping to identify groups of similar shoppers for future promotions or merchandise).

To get around the use of other credit cards, Neiman-Marcus has instituted the In Circle Club. Members receive special identification cards introducing them to salespeople, thus facilitating information capture of their purchases—whatever credit card they choose to use.

At the opposite end of the retail spectrum, the 7-Eleven chain of convenience stores has reported its intention to form a frequent shopper club. Because convenience stores are not scanner-equipped like supermarkets, 7-Eleven's program will use identification cards inserted into in-store kiosks. The kiosk will issue promotional coupons and will track the member's purchases during each visit.

WHO'S USING CUSTOMER INFORMATION FILES?

More and more marketers today are discovering the potential of databases to help them build a stronger bond with their customers. According to Donnelley Marketing's 1993 Survey of Promotional Practices (see Exhibit 3–1), approximately one-half of the firms surveyed (63% of the larger firms) indicated that they were currently building a customer database! Database building was slightly skewed to larger companies with sales in excess of $1 billion. An additional 10%

of responding firms indicated that they planned to build a database within the coming year while 34% said they had no current intentions to establish a database of customers.

Donnelley notes in its discussion of the results that there is still a wide latitude of activities that surround use of a customer database, so immediate generalizations are probably difficult. Also, it was observed that corporate divisions expressed overall a greater involvement in customer databases than did entire companies. Consequently, Donnelley suggests that the findings may imply that databases are more applicable to certain products or categories of products than to a corporation's overall business.[3]

Small companies (those with sales less than $1 billion) appear to have cooled somewhat in the commitment to database construction. Reasons for this are unclear.

Company involvement with database construction and database marketing increases every day. Exhibit 3–2 presents a nonexhaustive but reasonably representative list of American companies known to be experimenting with databases. Where possible, the size of the resulting database is estimated.

Some companies are establishing themselves as early pioneers in this exciting new field. In this respect, the CIF construction efforts of five national marketers—Kraft General Foods (a division of Philip Morris), Philip Morris, Sherwin-Williams, Nintendo, and Royal Viking Cruise Lines—should briefly be reviewed.

General Foods

Kraft General Foods, one of the earliest packaged goods marketers to experiment with customer databases, began its efforts in 1985, as the result of a forecast of the mass media scenario of the 1990s. Along with the growth of non-network forms of television (cable, independent channels, public television, and so forth) eating away at the three networks' share of the viewing audience, KGF foresaw enough additional mass audience erosion (through "commercial zapping," VCR use, and so on) to estimate that the average prime time commercial television audience of the 1990s would include less than 50 percent of all U.S. households! With the ever-escalating costs of television advertising, KGF began to consider other options for reaching current and potential customers. Direct marketing enabled by a customer information file was one of the options selected for investigation.

Master architect of KGF's effort was director of direct marketing John Kuendig. Kuendig led a project to collect all the corporation's loose ends of household and product use data from previous promotions and test programs and to assemble it into an organized master database.

The 35-million-name database that resulted from the collection was pared down to a more functional on-line database profiling approximately 25 million households. The database was then enhanced through questionnaires and responses to subsequent mailings.

EXHIBIT 3–2
Partial List of Companies Using or Creating Customer Information Files

Marketer	Program Specifics	Estimated Size
Airlines	Virtually every airline has a frequent flyer database, usually targeting business travelers. For example:	
	American Airlines Advantage Program	25 million
	United Airlines Mileage Plus	15 million
	USAir Frequent Flyer	7 million
	Delta Airlines Frequent Flyer Program (new program Sky Miles 1995)	16 million
	Continental Airlines One Pass	7 million
American Express	Ultra Card Member Program gives the top 5% of its customers restaurant and travel offers.	na
Avon	Announced plans to complement its direct representative marketing effort with a customer database.	na
Ben & Jerry's	Ben & Jerry's uses its database when it wants to come out with a new product—test new products—and when working on a community project like the Children's Defense Fund.	na
Blockbuster	Information gathered daily is fed from every store into the company's Ft. Lauderdale mainframe computer which then tabulates members' preferences. Blockbuster is testing a system which will then recommend additional movies for renting based on customers' past rental records.	40 million
Bloomingdales	Uses its customer database to select targeted recipients for each of its 300 annual catalog and promotional mailings.	na
Burger King	Started its Kids' Club in 1990	7 million
DowBrands	DowBrands gathers names and addresses through 800 numbers on all brand packages, mail-in offers, data collection coupons in free-standing inserts and direct response print advertising. The size of the database is not available, but Jane Jud of DowBrands reports the database has doubled in size the past two years and is expected to grow by 30% next year.	na
Farm Journal	Performed pioneer work in customizing print magazines to conform to the special interests of each of its readers as recorded in a CIF.	825,000
Fashion Bug Stores	Fashion Bug launched a one-year test of its new database marketing system. In that period the database registered 956,000 customers making 10.5 million transactions. Fashion Bug offered its best customers an opportunity to join the Fashion Bug Gold Club. These customers pay an annual fee of $10 to $15 to join the club, which offers discounts, free gifts, and membership-only mailings.	956,000

Exhibit 3–2 (continued)

Marketer	Program Specifics	Estimated Size
Frito-Lay, Inc. Smartfood	Mailed a whimsical package to a group of "innovators" and early adopters to construct a database of popcorn eaters.	na
Fox Television Network	Fox Kids Club	3.85 million
Gambling Industry	Several of the companies competing in this aggressive industry are involved in constructing very sophisticated databases of their present and potential customers (for example, Hilton Super Slots and Sands Easy Money).	na
Claridge Hotel & Casino Corp.	Comp-Card Gold Program offers discounts and tips on upcoming events to its frequent gambler card holders.	350,000
General Mills	Cap'n Crunch used an 800 number to build a database in conjunction with its Buried Treasure Sweepstakes.	24 million
General Motors	General Motors joined Master Card to offer the GM Card. GM now has a database of 12 million cardholders who they survey to learn what they are driving, when they next plan to buy a car and what vehicles they like. If the cardholder expresses interest in a particular model, information on the model is mailed out.	12 million
Hallmark	The Very Best and Keeping In Touch—two database marketing programs involving regular mailings to key customers who account for about 25% of Hallmark's sales.	3.5 million
Hallmark	The Hallmark Gold Crown Card program—Hallmark's first frequent buyer program. Customers receive 10 points for every dollar spent on Hallmark products and 25 points for each card purchased. For 4,000 points, they receive a $40 gift certificate.	2 million
Helzberg Diamonds	Helzberg captures data for 100% of its sales because it offers a product guarantee requiring collection of the buyer's name and address. The database is used for cross-selling and to determine what visuals belong in retail display.	2 million
Hotel chains	Almost all hotel chains today have a frequent guest database.	
	Hilton Honors	1.5-2 mil.
	Hyatt's Gold Passport	2 million
	Marriott Club Marquis (with one of the oldest programs)	320,000
	Marriott Miles Program	785,000
	Honored Guest Award Program	5 million
	Ramada Inns RBC—Ramada Business Card	260,000
	Ritz-Carlton—Information file of repeat guests, containing guests' needs and preferences, on-line systemwide	400,000

Exhibit 3–2 (continued)

Marketer	Program Specifics	Estimated Size
Keebler	Maintains a kids' database and Keebler Elf Fun Club	na
Kimberly-Clark	Has established a database and a Huggies Collection Catalog for new parents that is centered around its Huggies disposable diapers, baby wipes and training pants.	na
Kraft General Foods	Kraft has a database of users of its products collected when consumers send in coupons or respond to a KGF promotion. KGF constantly refines its database by sending surveys to the names on the database. Kraft users receive recipes, coupons, tips on nutrition, etc. based on interests they expressed in these surveys.	30 million
Lego Systems Inc.	Lego Builder's Club with a newsletter "Bricks Kicks."	na
Mary Kay Cosmetics Inc.	Has a 9.5 million name customer information file, used to keep track of the individual preferences of each of its customers.	9.5 million
Mattel	Created a Barbie Pink Stamps Club for frequent purchasers of Barbie dolls.	300,000
	Hot Wheels Speed Points Club.	na
	Grandparents Club.	na
McCormick	Created a Society to End Dull Meals.	200,000
Miller Beer	Enrolled beer drinkers in its Lite Beer Athletic Club for $2 to $3 annual dues.	75,000
Neiman-Marcus	In Circle Club for customers spending over $3,000 per year. In Circle benefits include a special charge card, invitations to parties and events, free gift wrapping, and free credit card protection.	na
Philip Morris	The Marlboro Store is its oldest database effort. Beyond its existence as a profit center, this program has had considerable image value for the brand as well.	26 million
Polaroid	Polaroid used its 150,000 business and technical database to set up a loyalty test program. A silver, gold or platinum program offered members various benefits, coupons and a frequent buyer catalog.	150,000 business customers
Porsche	Refined a list of 300,000 car drivers from the over 80 million registered U.S. drivers. Each member of the database was offered a test drive of a Porsche.	300,000
Radio Shack	Radio Shack has used its customer database to determine who should get its product flyers. Making the cut are those who purchase end products such as a radio, receiver or telephone.	9 million
Royal Viking Lines	Established its Royal Viking Line Skald club of frequent passengers.	100,000

Exhibit 3–2 (continued)

Marketer	Program Specifics	Estimated Size
Safeway Stores	Shoppers join Safeway Savings Club by filling out an application. They receive a membership card which, when scanned, qualifies them for a variety of exclusive discounts. Each member receives a newsletter.	na
Saks Fifth Avenue	Saks Fifth Avenue analyzed its card customer database to find shoppers with the best growth potential. These customers are enrolled in "Saks First" and receive a series of special "First Services" perks such as priority alterations, coat check and check cashing privileges. They also receive an exclusive charge card making them identifiable to salespeople in the stores.	na
House of Seagram's	Started a database effort in 1986. Uses its 10 million-name database for loyalty-building programs for existing products. Seagrams uses surveys to identify likely buyers of new products, as well as drinkers of rival brands it can send offers to.	10 million
Sears	Approximately 6 million of Sears' best customers were selected for a Sears Best Customer program. The aim of the program is customer retention. Members receive mailing from local store managers that include personal thanks, advance notice of sales and a special store phone number for their personal use.	6 million
Sears	Sears has assembled a database housing two years of purchase entry for 71 million households. In addition to using it for more direct marketing efforts, Sears will use the database to evaluate each retail store's sales potential.	71 million households
Shiseido (Japan)	This international marketer has a highly successful database of 9.6 million Japanese customers for its business in Japan. These Shiseido Club members may apply for a Shiseido Visa card, and they receive a monthly magazine.	9.6 million
StarKist	StarKist has maintained Morris the cat and its 9-Lives cat food database for several years, supplementing it with responders to the various offers made through out the year. The Morris calendar is reportedly one of the favorite programs.	na
Steinway Pianos	Almost all of this marketer's marketing effort is invested in its database and direct marketing.	na
Ukrops Supermarkets	Frequent Shopper Program	na
Vons Companies	Vons has four loyalty clubs (one for each of its operations), each with its own membership card. The chain also has developed a multifunctional electronic marketing program called Target Vons, aimed at collecting consumer	3 million

Exhibit 3–2 (concluded)

Marketer	Program Specifics	Estimated Size
Vons Companies (continued)	purchase data, tailoring offers to customer needs, generating coupons, better using manufacturer trade allowances, and more cost-effectively promoting products.	
Waldenbooks	Preferred Reader Program offers discounts and rebates. Waldenbooks reports 28% of *all* transactions are from Preferred Reader members, representing 40% of all sales.	3.5 million
Warner-Lambert	Created a highly successful pollen information center for the express purpose of establishing a database of allergy sufferers.	16,000
Wegman's Supermarkets	Preferred Shoppers Club	na
The Wella Corporation	Created a database introduction for samples of its So Fine shampoo and conditioner.	na

Software for manipulating the database cost about $500,000, but maintenance of the database was in effect already being done because Kraft General Foods was already entering all premium requests and sweepstakes entries.

Now, when new household data is entered, demographic and lifestyle information is automatically overlaid from external lists. Customer responses provide additional behavioral information for the database, enhancing it to the status of an on-going dialogue with customers. "I can continue the dialogue," says Kuendig, "by asking for additional information at any time."

Kraft General Foods has opportunistically experimented with database marketing on brands whose internal management teams were supportive of investing in new marketing programs—Kool-Aid, Crystal Light, Maxwell House, and Post cereals.

One of the more impressive tests was for Kool-Aid beverage mixes, a brand with a 60-year history, which had fallen out of favor with its primary target consumer, children 6 to 12. To revitalize the brand, KGF began building a special database of 4 million households that were current users of Kool-Aid; users of other beverages (especially more expensive canned and bottled beverages), including a competitor's drink mix; and users of presweetened cereals.

Then Kraft General Foods introduced the "Wacky Warehouse," a kids' version of the Marlboro Store. Direct mail was used to introduce the program to households in the database, and television ads and in-store materials were used for supplemental consumers. The program offered a magazine, educational articles, posters, and branded premiums including T-shirts, mugs, and coupons for other Kraft General Foods products.

The Wacky Warehouse cost $1 million and produced a 41 percent rise in sales for sugar-sweetened Kool-Aid, a 33 percent rise for Koolers, and a 23 percent increase for sugar-free Kool-Aid. Coupon redemption during the promotion increased 88 percent![4]

Kraft General Foods has created special database programs for other brands, including Crystal Light beverage mixes and Maxwell House coffee.

The database project for Crystal Light, one of KGF's earlier programs, started in 1987 with a Crystal Light Lightstyle Club. The program, according to Kuendig, was one experiment to determine the possibility of direct marketing supporting a brand image strategy. Database information told KGF that users of Crystal Light had high levels of interest in health and fitness. Several celebrities have been associated with the Lightstyle Club including Linda Evans, Priscilla Presley, and Christine Ellis.

The club featured exercise merchandise obtainable by saving proofs of purchase and a quarterly newsletter devoted to diet, fitness, beauty information, and recipes.

Philip Morris

Philip Morris, a titan of the age of mass marketing, is visibly moving in a new direction—toward finding out who their prospects and customers are and dealing directly with them as individuals. One of Philip Morris' first database efforts was the Marlboro Store, entering its twenty-third year of operation in 1995.

More recently, Philip Morris collected information on approximately 2 million smokers through its "Challenge" campaign for Merit cigarettes, which began with a double-page ad in national magazines. The advertiser was not identified, but the consumer was challenged to try a new brand of cigarette. To get free packs of cigarettes, the smoker had to fill out a lengthy questionnaire on the bound-in reply card.

The follow-up campaign focused on creating awareness of the new brand and highlighted the 500,000 (sampled) smokers of competing brands who reported that they liked Merit better. The database had been effectively used to identify the most likely purchasers of the new brand and then to build their awareness and loyalty to the brand.

In another database marketing effort, Philip Morris took the highly successful Marlboro Man and offered a Marlboro Menthol calendar. To get it, customers had to provide their name, address, and detailed information about their smoking habits.

Sherwin-Williams

Beginning in 1989, Sherwin-Williams made a commitment to shift some of its marketing effort away from traditional marketing tactics to database-driven marketing. Terry Gould, director of marketing communications for the paint and painting supplies company, describes the origin of the database as a result of the realization of how poor the quality of its information was identifying and describing its customers. "We found we had a hodgepodge of customer information and 'misinformation.'" Most of the available data came from business cards collected at trade shows, mail responses to trade ads and customer information forwarded by 2,000 store managers and 900 field sales reps. Gould undertook a massive effort to purify the existing data, and imposed restrictions to guarantee only accurate information would be entered in the future.

Sherwin-Williams' database now identifies three-quarters of a million customers' names, with an impressive 95% mail deliverability rate. Every record contains the customer's account number; SIC code; and the status of the account (active, inactive or prospect). Related databases contain: demographics (number of employees, plant size, purchasing potential, decision-maker's name, etc.), sales history (average monthly transaction, total purchases by month and year, specific items purchased), customer's total annual purchases, and "customer share" (what percent of the customer's total purchases Sherwin-Williams commands). Another database tracks marketing efforts directed to each customer, including when each contact was made and its productivity.

While several programs are driven off the database, one of the more interesting is the relationship-building magazine called *Professional Painting Contractor*. Currently, 160,000 loyal contractors receive this "proprietary" magazine. Response to receiving the magazine has been enthusiastic; readership studies show that 75% of recipients report reading all of the last three issues, with 80% or more calling the magazine their "primary source of trade-related information."

The most successful program associated with the database is called Prosell. This program is directed at reactivating past customers and opening new accounts as well, based on a profile developed within three professional contractor SIC codes. Prospects receive personalized letters tailored to their assumed interests, which invite a visit to a participating Sherwin-Williams store. Three contacts are mailed during the peak April–June season. Each contractor is given traceable "bonus bucks" which reactivate about 10% of past customers and about 5% of new.

The database is also used for developing new accounts. Specific business segments are targeted for development. Each target customer is assigned to a specific Sherwin-Williams store or sales location. If a target customer makes a purchase, the database initiates an ID file and tracks the new customer for "special handling." Gould reports more than 3,000 profitable new accounts have been developed in this way.[5]

Nintendo

From the first day of Nintendo's reentry into the U.S. video game business in 1986, chairman Minoru Arakawa placed a premium on interacting with customers.

Each of the 1.1 million home systems sold in 1986 carried a sweepstakes entry card requesting the owner's name and address. About 7 to 10 percent of the cards were returned, enabling Nintendo to begin to construct a reasonably sized customer information file.[6]

In succeeding years Nintendo began offering a new incentive to capture purchasers' names and addresses in place of the sweepstakes. The incentive was a membership in the Nintendo Fun Club, which included a membership card and a bimonthly magazine, *Nintendo Power*. The magazine began as a newsletter. But, as circulation reached 2 million, Arakawa and his director of marketing took a bold step to control costs. They began to sell subscriptions to an enhanced version of the newsletter (a 110-page magazine patterned after a successful magazine in Japan). Much to the delight of Nintendo, a substantial proportion of its free circulation converted to subscribers of the $15 a year magazine. By 1990 *Nintendo Power* had developed a circulation approaching 2 million, and the company had captured 6 million names for its database.

Information for the database comes from a player poll included in each issue of the magazine. Readers return a card that asks questions concerning the player's highest score, five favorite video games, suggestions for games to be reviewed in future issues of the magazine, purchase questions including games that the player bought in the current month, what was liked about them, and what games the player expects to buy in the coming months. Results from this poll have allowed Nintendo to successfully anticipate game sales and to manage retail inventories accordingly.

Nintendo appears faultless in its attention to customer interaction. Consider these details:

- As many as 47,000 letters have been received in one month, and each has been personally answered!
- A game counselor telephone service (120 counselors work the telephones) has logged as many as 120,000 calls in one week.
- A 900 number telephone product information center is contacted by 10,000 kids each month.
- More than 35 percent of the monthly magazine questionnaires are returned.[7]

Says Bill White, Nintendo's director of advertising, "You can't put a value on what relationship marketing has done for Nintendo. The ability to communicate with 1.5 million of our most dedicated customers is comparable to what might cost three, four, or more times as much through conventional advertising channels."

The company calls its effort to establish and maintain an ongoing relationship with its customers its "secret marketing weapon." Perhaps the best explanation of the real value of the "weapon" is a comment of Nintendo's director of marketing, Peter Main: "I think we look at things the reverse of most companies. Real-life

---

**AFTERMARKETING WORKING
A New Twist for Sales**

Launching a new product is an anxious experience for any manufacturer. How best to promote the product? Who will buy it, and why? What product features will most influence the decision to buy? Will sales have "legs," or will the product bomb like a bad movie?

The Skil Corp. faced those questions when it introduced its SkilTwist cordless power screwdriver. Skil conducts a very extensive owner registration program, including a detailed questionnaire, (Skil card) with each product it sells. These cards are closely analyzed in the introduction of new products. Returned registration cards for the SkilTwist screwdriver provided some very helpful positioning information. On the basis of initially returned cards, Skil product development people conducted follow-up interviews with purchasers.

Ron Techter, manager of worldwide product development for Skil, explains what happened next:

The research proved quickly that the screwdriver was not a fad, which had been one of our fears, but a viable power tool. That research enabled us to launch a multimillion-dollar ad campaign.

The Skil product registration cards and the follow-up interviews also yielded this surprising fact: Although the do-it-yourself aspect was a chief advantage, a predominance of purchasers were over 50 years of age, many of whom suffered reduced mobility from arthritis. "We hadn't realized the arthritis implications," says Techter. In response, Skil began advertising in publications geared to older Americans.

Adds Techter, "The Skil cards and our follow-up uncovered something we hadn't thought of." And now Skil is doing more than thinking about this unanticipated market segment. The firm is out serving it.

Source: *Focus,* National Demographics & Lifestyles, Spring 1988.

---

consumer demand, not retailer perceptions, drives a company. We are listening more intently than anyone I have ever been employed by to what the consumer is saying."

Royal Viking Lines

Royal Viking has built a 100,000-member worldwide database of previous cruise passengers. After passengers sail on their first cruise, they are invited to join the Royal Viking Line Skald Club at no cost. (*Skald* is Scandinavian for storyteller.)[8]

Royal Viking works hard to build a lasting relationship with each club member. Members receive many exclusive benefits and special offers not made to the general public, and they get at least one mailing per month from Royal Viking, including the *Explorer Gazette* newsletter. The newsletter highlights interesting features of upcoming destinations. It is accompanied by highly targeted announcements promoting specific cruises.

Royal Viking found that segmenting members by their expressed choice of a future vacation spot didn't work. But when Skald members who had sailed on a specific ship got a letter from the ship's captain, a $75,000 mailing generated more than $1 million in revenue. Another benefit of Royal Viking's mining its 100,000-member worldwide database to generate passenger bookings is that it has been able to avoid open discounting in its trade advertising.

BUILDING AND INCREASING LOYALTY

The growth and development of customers' loyalty, nurtured by a CIF, can be well represented by the "loyalty ladder," a construct created by Considine and Raphel.[9] This paradigm illustrates the process that marketers should use to *intensify the customer's relationship with the company.* The notion is that potential and current customers should be advanced up a ladder or progression of steps in terms of the intensity of their loyalty to the marketer.

Considine and Raphel describe the following steps:

- *Suspects:* the universe of people (or organizations) identified as potential customers.
- *Prospects:* individuals who have heard of a marketer's products or services but have not yet purchased.
- *Trial buyers:* first-time buyers; those who are trying out a marketer's products or services; their judgement is withheld.
- *Repeat buyers:* a buyer who is beginning to make a mental commitment to the marketer by buying the marketer's product or service again.
- *Clients:* people who buy a variety of products and services from a marketer over time, selecting the marketer's brands over those of other competitors and thereby exhibiting loyalty.
- *Advocates:* repeat buyers (clients) who are active proponents of a marketer, recommending the marketer to their friends or business associates.

Bickert observes that too often marketers stop short, being satisfied with converting a prospect into a repeat buyer.[10] The real value in establishing a CIF is the advantage the database gives a marketer in nurturing the customer further up this loyalty ladder. The goal of aftermarketing in terms of this paradigm is to transform as many trial buyers into advocates as one possibly can.

Because a customer information file facilitates tracking the purchases of prospects and current customers, it is a unique tool with which to implement the loyalty ladder. Forearmed with information from the CIF, consider the likely

EXHIBIT 3–3
Example of a Coupon Personalized through the CIF

Artist: Julie McWilliams.

difference in redemption of two coupons: one a generic, impersonalized coupon that is mass distributed, and the other a personalized coupon acknowledging the information known about trial and repeat buyers (see Exhibit 3–3).

PURCHASING TRIGGERS

One of the most effective ways to use a customer information file, it is claimed, is to incorporate information about lifestyle changes. Changes are believed by many to be more compelling for marketers' purposes than straight lifestyle information.

Consider the substantial purchases that occur as the first child enters a family household (the start of the "full-nest" stage) or the changes in consumption as a worker retires from the workforce. There are numerous major and minor lifestyle changes that can be identified for customers:

High school or college graduation.

First job.

Entering or leaving the armed forces.

First car.

Marriage.

Buying a house or renting an apartment.

Birth of a child.

Job promotion.

Turning 30, 40, 50, or 65 years of age.

Retirement.

Changing careers.

Divorce.

One list maintenance company, Lifestyle Change Communications, organizes its entire list offering by major lifestyle changes, including the ultimate lifestyle change, death.

Richard Black suggests that a marketer adopt a matrix approach such as that demonstrated in Exhibit 3–4, whereby customers are cross-referenced in terms of both their position on the "loyalty ladder" and their stage in their family life-cycle. The resulting matrix does two things. It profiles a marketer's total business on these two dimensions, providing input for strategic planning, and it may suggest which of many available tactics to use for each customer in the CIF based on which cell of the matrix describes the customer.[11]

The matrix shows the customers of an upscale home decor catalog marketer. The mix of young singles and solitary survivors is low, as the marketer had expected. However, the participation of new marrieds, full nesters, and empty nesters was significantly different from what had been imagined. The marketer had considered the more mature empty nesters (who would supposedly be eager to refurbish their homes once they no longer had to worry about children possibly abusing the furniture) to be its primary target. What the matrix showed the catalog marketer was a surprising strength among full nesters as well.

The company responded by aiming a substantial amount of its marketing effort at full nesters. As an additional result, the marketer was able to formulate two very different approaches to the newly married and empty nest segments.

THE ISSUES OF PRIVACY, LEGALITY, AND ETHICS

When Lotus Development Corporation dropped its plans to market a PC database of 80 million U.S. households, MarketPlace: Households™, and withdrew a companion product, MarketPlace: Business™ (a PC database of 7 million businesses), in early 1991, the issue of intrusion into consumers' lives by marketers' databases came under national public scrutiny.

At the same time that Lotus withdrew its database products from the market, Blockbuster Entertainment, operator of the nationwide chain of Blockbuster

EXHIBIT 3–4
Sample Customer Life-Cycle Matrix

Loyalty Ladder	Family Life-Cycle Stages					
	Young Single	New Married	Full Nest	Empty Nest	Solitary Survivor	Total
Suspects	–	3%	2%	1%	–	6%
Prospects	2%	5	5	2	–	14
Trial buyers	2	4	12	7	–	25
Repeat buyers	2	7	9	9	3%	30
Clients	1	3	6	3	2	15
Advocates	1	1	4	1	3	10
Total	8%	23%	38%	23%	8%	100%

Adapted from R. Black, "Life Cycle Marketing," Third Annual Conference on Database Marketing, National Center for Database Marketing, December 1990.

Video stores, quickly dissociated itself from trial plans to sell lists that would have purportedly detailed customers' video rental habits. New England Telephone Company simultaneously dropped plans to sell a proposed computerized database of names, addresses, and telephone numbers of its 4.7 million customers.

Lotus president Jim Manzi openly acknowledged that his company received 30,000 complaints about the consumer product. This appears to be the first grass-roots protest against computerized databases. At least two national organizations appear to have been involved in the dissent: recipients of a newsletter, *Privacy Journal,* and some members of a group called Computer Professionals for Social Responsibility. It is not clear how widely shared are the fears expressed in the campaign against Lotus' product.

The Issue

The issue comes down to this: When are marketers' information needs at odds with our society's inherent respect for individual privacy? Stated even more basically, the issue is one of a direct confrontation between freedom of information versus the right to privacy. Interestingly, the major outcry against Lotus' Market-Place: Households seems not to have concerned the level of detail of the information, but rather its broad market availability. Large corporations hiring data-processing service bureaus and renting the large-scale databases described in Chapter 2 have had such capabilities available for some time. What seems to have concerned people about MarketPlace: Households was its availability to virtually anyone with a PC and a few thousand dollars.[12]

MarketPlace: Households was a set of 11 databases providing names, addresses, age ranges, gender, marital status, dwelling types, income ranges, and lifestyles for 80 million U.S. households. One group of opponents of the product, Computer Professionals for Social Responsibility, contended that the database contained "a great deal of information obtained without the consent of the people listed." Lotus defended its actions saying that some "privacy safeguards" had been built in: for example, the system was not designed to allow examining individuals' profiles but rather identifying consumers in the aggregate who matched a specific predefined profile.

Some suggest that there can be no problem with databases provided that consumers are made aware of what use will be made of the information they supply in various applications and surveys. Lists-On-Disc™ is a computer software package with factual information on millions of private and public businesses. The producer of Lists-On-Disc, American Business Information of Omaha, says that all the businesses listed were first identified from their listings in 5,000 Yellow Page telephone directories, and then each business was contacted to verify the information and to be informed of its inclusion in the file.[13]

In another example, customers of U.S. Shoes' retail stores including Petite Sophisticates, Caren Charles, August Max, and Casual Corner are readily volunteering information at the stores' cash registers. The information collected by U.S. Shoes' cashiers feeds its database, which tracks over 100 customer attributes. "Privacy hasn't become an issue," says Thomas Noether, director of sales, "because customers don't mind giving the information as long as it's being used *to provide an extra service*."[14]

It is apparently not clear whether current invasion of privacy laws would apply, should one marketer or researcher—having obtained the information that John Q. Public on 123 Main Street has a dog and a Porsche, drinks Johnny Walker Black, smokes cigars, and goes to the Caribbean once each year—sell that information to another.

The Degree of Concern

Equifax, Inc., the partner of Lotus Development in the construction of Market-Place: Households, had commissioned a survey of Americans' attitudes toward issues of privacy and customer databases prior to the public outcry against the database. Equifax confirmed the increasing distrust Americans feel toward their institutions but found little proof of any database violations of privacy:

Americans are becoming more concerned over issues of privacy and this parallels their rather general increasing distrust of business and government institutions. From a baseline concern of only 31 percent in 1978, the proportion of Americans "very concerned" over invasion of personal privacy has risen to 51 percent in 1994![15]

In the 1994 wave of its survey, Equifax found Americans were distinguishing who they might trust or distrust with confidential information. The medical profession (doctors and nurses) was most trusted—43 percent said doctors would use confidential information in a "proper manner". Businesses (companies selling by telephone and mail) were least trusted, only 5 percent thought they'd use information in a "proper manner."[16]

Regarding marketing uses of large-scale consumer databases, Equifax's 1990 survey showed two somewhat contradictory findings apparently related to how the questions were worded:

When asked if it is a "good or bad thing" that "businesses are now able to buy from mailing list companies information about your consumer characteristics, e.g., your income level, residential area, and credit card use," two-thirds said this is a *bad* idea.

Yet, when the potential customer advantages are identified within the question, "Increasingly companies are marketing goods and services directly to people by mail. Companies try to learn which individuals and households would be the most likely buyers of their product or service. They buy names and addresses of people in certain age groups, estimated income groups, and residential areas with certain shopping patterns so they can mail information to the people they think will be most interested in what they are selling. Two-thirds said they find this practice "*acceptable*." The percentage increases as two protective measures are added: No financial information is provided to a company (acceptance rises to 75 percent) and consumers wishing to have their names removed could do so (acceptance rises still higher to 88 percent).[17]

At the time of the Blockbuster Video announcement, a survey conducted by the Gallup Organization revealed that three-quarters of a national sample said they "would take their business elsewhere" if they learned that a store or chain was selling information about their purchase habits.[18]

Other polls suggest that the American consumer will not be upset by databases if they are given opportunities to have their name removed from lists. But that is a questionable option, difficult to implement on an industry-wide basis, and virtually unenforceable even within, much less outside, the information industry. (The Direct Marketing Association in New York currently maintains a file—the Mail Preference Service—of some 3.3 million consumers who have asked to be removed from all circulated databases.)

The question of compensating consumers for the use of their name and information has also arisen. It could be argued that compensation has already been provided consumers by the premiums and coupons now sent out in exchange for completed questionnaires. Some industry observers believe that ultimately consumers will be paid on a per-use basis for their names and purchase data. There is also the possibility that consumers will become much more wary about releasing information about themselves. Radio Shack, one of the marketers who are today aggressively exploring the benefits of databases, is known for capturing certain information at its stores' cash registers, nationally. Recently a sign appeared at each Radio Shack counter explaining the value of the practice and guaranteeing customers their privacy:

We Respect Your Privacy

I've heard customers ask, "Why does Radio Shack need my name and address?" Simply put, we value you as a customer! We add you to our private mailing list in order to inform you of upcoming sale events and special offers, and to send you important product updates. Printing your name and address on every receipt also helps to speed up warranty work, returns and adjustments.

Rest assured that this information is held in strict confidence. Our mailing list is never sold to other companies. We want you to think of Radio Shack as more than just a store! Thanks for helping us to serve you better.

Leonard Roberts
President

But even without fully voluntary compliance, any firm can compile significant data on the purchasing habits of its customers through observation alone. There are also marketers who, without much solicitation, receive significant information from eager customers. Nintendo, for example, gets hundreds of thousands of "volunteered" letters and phone calls about its electronic games. Each letter and call is logged and analyzed and is entered into the company's extensive database.

Where the Data Come From

The source of the information contained in the databases is obviously the most sensitive issue. In Chapter 2, a four-category description of the possible kinds of information that a marketer might possess about a customer was described. Each information source has relevance to the implied ethics of the information:

- *Declared information:* information volunteered by customers, ostensibly with the knowledge that it was being recorded. This use seems totally ethical.

- *Implied information:* inferences about customers through correlations in declared information. Consumers have no basis for complaint here.

- *Overlaid information:* using a "key" for a customer (perhaps the customer's Zip code) to identify the customer's likely income level. This is simply utilizing information, however sensitive, that has always been in the public domain.

- *Appended information:* matching two different data files available to the marketer (two internal files or an internal with a commercially available external file such as Polk's X-1 file). When two internal files, presumably both containing volunteered information, are combined, the application seems ethical. It is only when an internal database is *enhanced* with a proprietary external database, the contents of which may exceed the specific information needs of the marketer, that consumers have some justification for feeling "exposed."

AFTERMARKETING WORKING
Individual Marketing

Database marketer Robert M. Smith has outlined four "commandments" that he views as central to achieving good relationship marketing through a customer information file.

Commandment #1: Identify Your Customers

- *Build a customer database.* Use questionnaires, computer warranty disks, a 900 number, sweepstakes, and so forth.
- *Add relevant information.* Match available demographic and behavioral data from commercial lists.
- *Continually update.* Develop an internal company culture that appreciates the value of customer data.

Commandment #2: Learn More About the Customers Who Drive Your Business.

- *Profile your customers.* Use multivariate analysis to determine the predictive characteristics that identify high-value customers.
- *Develop models.* Create predictive models of customers with different values and purchasing behavior that will permit you to focus your marketing test resources.
- *Clone high-value customers.* Invest marketing resources in high-value prospects and reduce investment in low-value consumers.

Commandment #3: Tailor Individual Messages to Individual Consumers.

- *Focus on their needs.* Customize your marketing messages and offers to the needs and interests of the individual customer.
- *Provide relevant information.* Facts about your product or service that are relevant to each customer individually are often the most powerful incentive.
- *Begin a dialogue.* Inviting a customer to respond with comments, suggestions, and so on is the most effective way to integrate a sales message.

Commandment #4: Deepen Customer Loyalty.

- *Communicate regularly.* Stay in touch with your customers; update them with new information on your products or services.
- *Involve customers.* Give them opportunities to critique the product, attend a briefing, or come to an opening, all intended to build a personal relationship (it's easy to switch brands but difficult to break a personal relationship).
- *Up-sell, cross-sell, and begin again.* This permits you to reap the rewards of the building relationship and it helps deepen the relationship further.

Source: R. M. Smith, "Customer-Driven Marketing: The Competitive Edge in the 1990s," Third Annual Conference on Database Marketing, December 1990. The National Center for Database Marketing Inc., 14618 Tyler Foote Road, Suite 888, Nevada City, CA 95959-8599, Telephone: (916)292-3000.

KEY POINTS OF THE CHAPTER

Opportunities to Establish CIFs.

For Service Marketers:

Application forms.   Letters, telephone calls.
Memberships.   Customer surveys.
Program participation.

For Durables Marketers:

Owner warranty/registration.
Financing applications.
Letters, telephone call.

For Consumer Packaged Goods Marketers:

Coupon, offer redeemers.
Contest entrants.
Letters, telephone calls.
Club memberships.
In-pack or on-pack questionnaires.

Customer loyalty ladder. A way of classifying customers based on their degree of repeat purchasing and their attitudes about the marketer. Groupings range from prospects to trial buyers to clients to advocates. The "ladder" reminds the marketer that not all purchasers are totally committed to his brand and reiterates the importance of cultivating a lasting relationship with each customer.

Sources of data about customers.

- *Declared information.* Information that customers supply the marketer themselves.
- *Implied information.* Assumptions the marketer makes about customers by making inferences based upon their declared information and generally held beliefs about it.
- *Overlaid information.* Using a "key" variable that exists both in the customer's declared information and in an external database to add some information to the database. (Postal ZIP codes are a convenient and frequently used key.)
- *Appended information.* Adding the contents of another, often proprietary, database, to the marketer's existing customer database.

Consumer privacy. This is an issue that is expected to become increasingly important in the future and that could constrain the marketer's aftermarketing opportunities. However, because aftermarketing focuses on *current* customers, there is a better opportunity to collect the desired information first-hand with customers' permission, and to use the data to serve them better. Data in aftermarketing would never be used to solicit business from new customers, a practice that could risk losing their goodwill.

NOTES

1. Goodwill is the one asset: R. M. Smith, "Customer-Driven Marketing: The Competitive Edge in the 1990s," Third Annual Conference on Database Marketing, National Center for Database Marketing, December 1990.
2. Examining the resulting structure: P. Hawkin, "The New Di-Economy," *Marketing Communications,* March 1987, pp. 43–48.
3. According to Donnelley Marketing's annual survey: Donnelley Marketing, *Thirteenth Annual Survey of Promotional Practices,* Stamford, CT, 1991.
4. Coupon redemption increased during the promotion: "Wacky Warehouse Builds Kool-Aid's Market Share," *Direct,* January 10, 1990, p. 4.
5. Adapted from: L. Egol, "Sherwin-Williams Paints a Database," *Direct,* June 1994, pp. 11, 26.
6. About 7 to 10 percent of the cards were returned: "How Five Companies Targeted Their Best Prospects," *Marketing News,* February 18, 1991, p. 12.
7. Nintendo's customer interaction: S. Rapp, and T. L. Collins, *The Great Marketing Turnaround,* (Englewood Cliffs, NJ: Prentice-Hall, 1990), pp. 246–247.
8. Royal Viking has built its database: L. G. Coleman, "Database Masters Become King of the Marketplace," *Marketing News,* February 18, 1991, p. 13.
9. J. Bickert, *Adventures in Relevance Marketing* (Denver: National Demographics & Lifestyles Inc., 1990) (Bickert credits Considine and Raphel).
10. Bickert observes that often: Bickert, *Adventures in Relevance Marketing,* p. 4.
11. Black suggests a marketer adopts: R. Black, "Life-Cycle Marketing," Third Annual Conference on Database Marketing (NCDBM) December 1990.
12. What seems to have concerned people about MarketPlace: Households: P. H. Lewis, "Why the Privacy Issue Will Never Go Away," *New York Times,* April 7, 1991, p. F4.
13. The producer of Lists-On-Disk : P. H. Lewis, "Why the Privacy Issue Will Never Go Away."
14. Privacy hasn't become an issue: H. Schlossberg, "Marketers Moving to Make Databases Actionable," *Marketing News,* February 18, 1991, p. 8.
15. Americans are becoming more concerned over issues of privacy: Equifax, Inc., *Equifax-Harris Consumer Privacy Survey,* 1994, Atlanta, GA, p. 1.
16. *Equifax-Harris Survey,* pp. 6–7
17. Equifax, Inc. *Report on Consumers in the Information Age,* Atlanta, GA, 1990.
18. At the time of the Blockbuster Video announcement: "Consumers Target Ire at Data Bases," *Advertising Age,* May 6, 1991, p. 3.

Chapter Four

Blueprinting Customer Contact Opportunities

The primary mechanism for building long-lasting customer relationships is to increase customers' satisfaction with interactions with the marketer's organization, both in quality and number. In order to monitor interactions, the marketer needs to have a complete understanding of how customers currently purchase his products or services and how they interact with his organization. Regarding interactions with the organization, the marketer should know when, how, under what conditions, for what purposes, and with whom customers interact in his organization. A convenient way to identify specific interactions with customers is called *customer blueprinting*.

Blueprinting is an objective process for flowcharting a marketer's customer contact opportunities. As each current contact opportunity is identified, the marketer is better able to understand how the contact is currently handled, with what degree of success, and by whom. Understanding the process and the roles in a contact point allows the marketer to consider how customers' satisfaction might be further enhanced.

A detailed blueprint can help marketers spot key opportunities for improving their service or identifying untapped opportunities at which aftermarketing activities could be rendered.

CUSTOMER INTERACTIONS: MOMENTS OF TRUTH

Jan Carlzon, president and CEO of Scandinavian Airlines System (SAS), was one of the first marketers to popularize the importance of customer contacts in fulfilling the promise of a product or service. He describes in his book, *Moments of Truth,* how he recognized the importance of focusing on contacts with his customers.[1] He realized that SAS' 10 million annual customers each came into contact with approximately five SAS employees during a flight on SAS. With each contact lasting approximately 15 seconds, he concluded the following:

> Thus SAS is "created" 50 million times a year, 15 seconds at a time. These 50 million "moments of truth" are the moments that ultimately determine whether SAS will succeed or fail as a company. They are the moments when we must prove to our customers that SAS is their best alternative.[2]

Carlzon had recognized that interactions with employees were a very obvious way for customers to judge the quality of the service that SAS provides. With his focus on customer contacts (and other aspects of his business as well), he turned SAS around from its status as an $8 million a year loser to a $71 million a year winner! A substantial part of this turnaround came from managing the encounters his employees had with his customers and thus more completely fulfilling customers' expectations. Carlzon's goal was to imbue every aspect of a customer's contact with SAS with quality.

But quality in a product or service as judged through customers' eyes is a highly subjective issue. No matter how objective the marketer considers the quality of her product or service, it is open to *interpretation*. Customers actively seek "evidence" or clues to help them ascertain the quality of the products and services they buy, and even this evidence can become quite subjective.

For example, another airline executive, Donald Burr, chairman of the now defunct People Express airline in the United States, concluded that, from the passenger's perspective, coffee stains (negative evidence) on flipdown trays could suggest that engine maintenance might also be shoddy. As Tom Peters has said, "Perception is all there is. What customers perceive [in their experiences with products and services and their contacts with employees] is real; it must be listened to, [understood], and acted upon."

Customers' perceptions of the quality in products and services is a key correlate with building long-term relationships. Aftermarketing's goal of increasing loyalty requires the marketer to fully understand her customers' opportunities for assessing the quality of her products and services. Whereas some of these opportunities will consist of physical evidence (the clarity of a TV picture, the appearance and helpfulness of booklets and printouts prepared by a life insurance company, the rich decor of a bank's lobby), other opportunities will consist of interactions with a company employee or dealer's salesperson. It is in these transient moments of truth that the company really shows its true colors. This is when customers formulate much of their impression of the quality of the product or service they have acquired.

Services, because of their basic impalpability, are probably most in need of support evidence—a recognition all too frequently ignored by service marketers. Customer contacts become very important sources of evidence about the quality of the service contracted for. Aftermarketing is even more important for marketers of services than for marketers of physical, tangible products—where the product itself can supply substantial evaluatory evidence.

Carlzon's and Burr's valuable insight was that customers seize on *any available information or interaction* (such as Carlzon's moments of truth) to help them evaluate the quality of the product or service they've purchased. To fully manage the contact evidence surrounding his product, a marketer must do the following:

EXHIBIT 4–1
A Moment of Truth Model

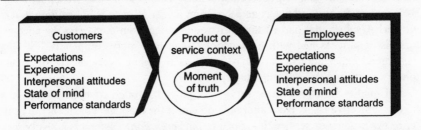

Adapted from K. Albrecht and L. Bradford, *The Service Advantage* (Homewood, IL: Dow Jones-Irwin, 1990).

- Identify customers' possible contacts with his employees.
- Instruct (and motivate) his employees on how to satisfy customers.
- Monitor the quality of service that customers actually experience.

Moments of truth are, of themselves, neither positive nor negative. It is the quality of the *outcome* of a moment of truth that is important. Identifying moments of truth forces the marketer to be conscious of outcomes. Was the shopper satisfied with the salesperson's description of the product's features? Did the counter person treat the customer rudely? Can representatives on the 800 telephone lines authorize exchanges and solve other problems by themselves for expedient solutions of customers' problems?

Not all moments of truth are equal. Some are far more important than others. Those that have a critical effect on customers' perceptions must be known and should receive a disproportionate share of managers' attention.

As in any interpersonal encounter, each party to the moment of truth (the customer and the employee) will bring his own set of values and expectations. Both will be subjected to the product or service context of the interaction. A moment of truth can be modeled as shown in Exhibit 4–1.

A satisfying or productive moment of truth requires congruence among the three components: the context, the customer's frame of reference, and the employee's frame of reference. However, congruence may be difficult to achieve. Consider how different each party's frame of reference may be, as demonstrated by Exhibit 4–2.

The moment of truth is another way to talk about the extent of "servicing" the customer requires or anticipates from the marketer. This has led some writers to speak of moments of truth as "service encounters."[3] But the opportunities within a moment of truth are really much broader. These customer interactions ought to be considered "marketing encounters." And ensuring success in these encounters ought to be considered a major marketing responsibility.

EXHIBIT 4–2
Difference in Frames of Reference

	Customer	*Employee*
Expectations	I don't expect anything more than courtesy and helpful assistance.	Our customers just can't be satisfied. They want everything.
Experience	Service has been good (in this store) in the past.	Management says they want satisfied customers, but do they have to give the store away?
Interpersonal attitudes	This salesperson looks uninterested in my questions.	The customer already looks mad. I'll bet he's had a bad day and will take it out on me!
State of mind	I'm in a hurry, and must purchase something quickly.	I've been on the floor all day without my break because two people didn't show up.
Performance standards	The other stores I shop at hire only professional people who are articulate and charming.	I'll be polite and responsive, but he's using the wrong terms for some simple product features!

The Servicing Outcome

Levitt was one of the first marketing theorists to conceive of products as composed of several component products. Modifying Levitt's idea (according to Kotler) produces a three-level structure. Exhibit 4–3 shows the resulting components.

The lowest-common-denominator product (within any category) is defined as the *generic product.* This is the fundamental, rudimentary "thing" or service. The next level, the *expected product,* has added to the *generic product* all of the features customers want and expect. The *augmented product,* the third and final level, brings with it additional unexpected servicing and benefits, which can help distinguish one company's offering from others'.

The augmented product is the physical product imbued with the added value and assurance of aftermarketing services.[4] This model appears extendable to services (as marketing entities) as well as physical products. Several service marketers adopted Levitt's ideas and depict all marketable entities (tangible goods as well as intangible services) as composed of both physical components and servicing aspects (the augmented product component). The inescapable conclusion is that, whatever marketers sell, it is likely to be an amalgam of both hard evidence (tangible elements) and soft evidence (intangible events from the augmented product level). And both types of evidence are sought by customers to help them evaluate the quality they have received.

In both the case of the marketing of services and the marketing of products, the *servicing* that customers expect will be rendered by many different individuals interacting with the marketer's customers. Recognizing the likelihood that

EXHIBIT 4–3
The Components of a Product

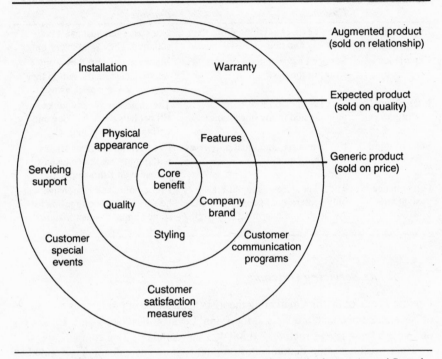

Adapted from P. Kotler, *Marketing Management: Analysis, Planning, Implementation and Control,*
7th Ed. (Englewood Cliffs, NJ: Prentice-Hall, 1991), p. 430.

servicing will be performed by employees of an agent or dealership, rather than
by the marketer's own employees, increases the importance of identifying all of
the moments of truth involved in the sale of one's products and services. Having
identified the interactions and the participants in each allows the marketer to
attempt to better manage these contacts with customers.

The fragility of these customer interactions is underscored in a book written
by two psychiatrists, Zunin and Zunin. They postulate that there is a short
moment in time, a four-minute window of opportunity, during which the satisfaction of a human contact will either be established or denied.[5] Zunin and Zunin
describe the basics leading to good contacts in terms of "four C's":

- *Confidence.* At least one of the parties must convey a certain degree of
  self-confidence; a self-demeaning or apologetic attitude will not elicit a
  receptive reaction.
- *Creativity.* One must find a way to tune into the feelings of the other party;
  this requires a sensitivity to a wide variety of people.

- *Caring.* It's important to show personal interest and total attention. Avoiding distraction and staying with the train of thought has surprising results.
- *Consideration.* Establish and radiate a concern for the other person. Consideration entails being sensitive and aware of the relationship with another person who is unique and also has fears, dreams, hopes, and insecurities. Consideration also invokes the art of being a good listener.

The four-minute threshold sets a demanding standard for all marketers to meet in managing their customer contacts. Not only must contacts be supportive overall, but they must establish an immediate tone of compassion and express a desire to achieve a mutually satisfying relationship with the customer. The four C's suggest skills in which customer contact people should undoubtedly be trained.

In a similar vein, Karl Albrecht and Ron Zemke emphasize the tremendous importance of controlling (managing) customer contacts:

> From many of our everyday experiences..., we can draw a fairly mundane conclusion, one that we believe can be stated as an out-and-out principle of service management: *When moments of truth go unmanaged, the quality of service regresses to mediocrity!*[6]

The difficulty of the marketer's task (in managing customer contact points) is even better understood when it is considered that, paradoxically, it is very often the *lowest-level employees* in any organization with whom customers will have the most contact.

CUSTOMER INTERACTION BLUEPRINTING

Because they understand the importance of good customer interactions, marketers in service industries have become very alert to interaction points with customers. One practitioner, Lynn Shostack, has devised a clever graphical method for identifying all of the operations involved in delivering a service. She calls the method "service blueprinting" because of the graphical nature of the tool.[7] For example, the technique helps visualize the service product of a shoeshine in the schematic in Exhibit 4–4.

A method for visualizing a service is important, Shostack says, to better manage current services and to more effectively design new ones. Shostack observes that, as complex as services are, marketers will think nothing at all of implementing a new service with only a verbal description to guide them. They fail, according to Shostack, in anticipating all of the steps and support processes that must be in place *and properly managed* for a new service to function and to succeed. The same accusation might also be made against marketers who, despite the complex supporting relationships that must be established to properly sell their products, naïvely thrust the products out into the marketplace, hoping that the necessary support systems will magically evolve. When support services are not forthcoming, customers become unhappy and products and services fail.

AFTERMARKETING WORKING
Kmart's Efforts to Manage Interactions

Kmart chairman Joe Antonini is spreading the word of Kmart's renewal program to his 350,000 sales associates on a national basis. In his messages, one point that Antonini always emphasizes is Kmart's necessary commitment to customer service. He believes that customer service will become a significant point of difference among retailers in the 90s, and he wants Kmart to be a leader.

To enhance its customer service, Kmart has aggressively reorganized and expanded its efforts within its newly formed Customer Care Network. Assigned to this effort are 17 associates and five regional customer service managers who are ultimately responsible for this critical area of customer communication. Kmart also utilizes a toll-free number (1-800-63-KMART) to accept customer reactions nationwide.

The Customer Care Network is based on 10 commitments to service, which appear to be directed at increasing the satisfaction of interactions between customers and a store's sales associates:

1. *Training excellence.* Kmart's training programs focus on the customer, with the goal of creating confident, knowledgeable, and enthusiastic associates, each ready to exceed the expectations of customers.
2. *Compassionate associate care.* This is an environment-specific program that strives to make the store facilities and environment as comfortable to associates as their own homes.
3. *Sincere customer friendliness.* This starts with the "10-foot rule." That means if a customer comes within 10 feet of an associate, the associate must ask, "May I be of assistance to you?"
4. *Hassle-free service.* If any customer calls or writes complimenting an associate by name, that associate receives the Kmart Chairman's Award certificate.
5. *Effective communication.* Associates are coached to be sensitive to customers' needs, to listen attentively to customers, and to react immediately.
6. *Consistent merchandise availability.* Kmart does its best to make sure that products are available to customers when and where they want them.
7. *Awareness of the competition.* Knowing how the competition is performing establishes goals that allow Kmart to strive to surpass its competition.
8. *Quality store appearance.* Consumers are smart and observant people who make decisions about the retailer's concern for their well-being through how they perceive the store to be maintained. The appearance of a store always sends a message to a customer. Kmart strives to make the message positive.
9. *Effective customer communication.* Associates are taught to seek out communication with customers. Customers should be made to believe that associates really care about their needs.
10. *Leadership by example.* Every Kmart executive is encouraged to be a positive role model for all store personnel.

Source: "Customer Care Network Comprises 10 Credos," *Discount Store News,* December 17, 1990, p. 70; and "Kmart Customer Care Network," a speech by Dick Voss to the National Retail Merchants' Association, June 8, 1989.

EXHIBIT 4-4
A Service Blueprint of a Shoe-Shining Business

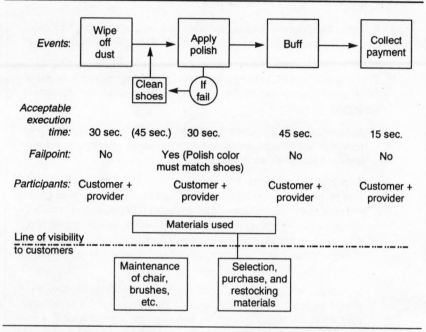

Shostack offers blueprinting as a necessary planning, implementation, and control tool for services marketers. However, it is possible that the technique also has benefit for marketers in general. The more general value of blueprinting may be in *identifying and helping to manipulate interactions with customers regardless of what is being marketed—service or product.* A blueprint may also suggest changes that could be made to the distribution or servicing of a product to increase customer contacts or to enhance the value of current contacts.

Controlling and influencing contacts and interactions is the nature of process control. Unfortunately, in its concerns about delivering quality, marketing theory has generally focused on *production control.* It has not explored the possible values of *process control.* Only two marketing authors, Levitt and Lovelock, have discussed processes as they relate to marketing. Both have characterized processes as existing along a continuum from *standardized* to *customized.* Standardized usually implies highly controlled processes in which steps are executed in a very uniform way. Customized implies bending or modifying the steps to conform to the needs of a particular client, customer, or situation. This is a rather simplistic characterization.

AFTERMARKETING WORKING
A Description of Service Blueprinting

1. A service blueprint is a *planning* tool for visualizing or depicting the service concept in concrete terms, thus facilitating marketing research and concept testing.

2. The service blueprint is an *organizing* tool for assisting managers in assembling appropriate resources for effective implementation of the service concept.

   - *Human resources.* By answering the question "What exactly will service providers do?" blueprints provide a task-oriented basis for job descriptions and employee selection criteria.

   - *Technological resources.* By answering the question "How will the service be provided—that is, using what equipment?" the blueprint guides selection and design of appropriate equipment. In the event that the service system design process begins with innovative technology, the blueprint assists managers with the process of developing rational, systematic human support (work flows and procedures) designed to maximize the technological benefits.

   - *Evidence.* By answering the question "What evidence do consumers require to select the service in the first place, have service experiences consistent with their expectations, and select the service again?" a service blueprint guides the development of advertising and promotion, visual environment, consumer materials, printed forms, and even suggested "scripts" for verbal interactions.

   - *Process.* By answering the question "How does the service work?" a service blueprint is the objective basis for development of service policy, work-flow design, and operating procedures.

3. The service blueprint is a *communication and training* tool that helps service providers relate their specific job to the service overall. By answering the question "How does my job serve consumers?" a service blueprint can foster employee commitment to the marketing task.

4. The service blueprint is a *control* device that makes it possible to structure monitoring and feedback devices at job, system, and management levels. Service blueprints facilitate quality control through analysis of failpoints, which is the first step in identifying meaningful checkpoints for statistical control of quality.

In contrast, Shostack suggests that marketing processes ought to be described in at least two dimensions. Shostack's first dimension, the *complexity* of the process, describes the number of steps and sequences that constitute the process. Her second dimension, the *customization potential* of the process, describes the executional latitude or variability permitted in any one step. These dimensions can easily be used to describe each customer interaction point for a marketing organization.

Because aftermarketing focuses on relationships with current customers, a process like blueprinting could have very real value in identifying aftermarketing opportunities.

THE STEPS INVOLVED IN BLUEPRINTING CUSTOMER CONTACTS

A customer blueprint has three basic elements:

- All main functions to make and distribute a product or to render a service must be identified with the responsible company unit or area specified.
- Timing and sequencing relationships among the functions must be depicted.
- Acceptable tolerances—the degree of variation from the standard that can be tolerated without negatively affecting the customer's perception of quality—must be specified for each function.

It is likely that one or more production functions associated with a tangible product will have been schematized in the way described here, but it is unlikely that any marketing process, including customer interactions at point of purchase and beyond, will ever have been similarly detailed. It is believed that marketers can better form and nurture successful customer relationships with an aid such as customer blueprinting (see Exhibit 4–5).

First, a customer blueprint must clearly identify all steps in a process: in the present case, all contacts or interactions with customers. These are arrayed in time-sequential order from left to right. The blueprint is further divided into at least two "zones": a zone of visibility (steps and interactions that are *visible to the customer* and in which the customer will likely participate) and a zone of invisibility (steps and interactions that, although completely necessary to the proper servicing of the customer, may be hidden from view or otherwise be *invisible to the customer*).

The blueprint also identifies failpoints in the marketing process. Failpoints are steps in the process that are likely to go wrong. (Failpoints are analogous to Carlzon's "critical moments of truth" in that they determine a customer's overall judgment or feeling about a marketer.) As any one of these points fail, the value of the marketing process to the ultimate consumer is diminished. Identifying

EXHIBIT 4–5
Blueprint of the Marketing Process for a Small Appliance

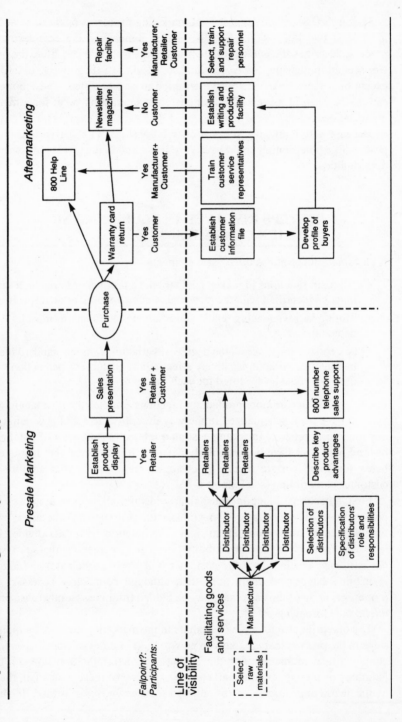

AFTERMARKETING WORKING
Dissecting Service Interactions

Some companies have recently started breaking down interaction points into subparts. These subparts give the company's standards that apply to each employee involved in customer service, either over a long period of time or within any one instance. Some argue against such regimentation, suggesting that this is appropriate for machines but not for human workers. (There is a growing fear that "dissecting" interaction points too much may depersonalize the quality of the interaction.) Not only do such routines deny the service provider any chance for spontaneity, but they often also become focal points, much to the detriment of the real goal—that of increasing the quality of customer interactions.

At L.L. Bean, the job of a telephone customer service representative is broken down into minute parts. Each call—whether it is 30 seconds or 30 minutes long—has four distinct components, and in each component reps are required to meet certain standards.

Opening: This first part of the call is very structured. Reps are expected to use the company's name, identify their department, introduce themselves by name, and offer to help the customer.

Setting the tone: Less rigid, this part includes sounding friendly, actively listening and absorbing the situation, personalizing the discussion by using the customer's name, keeping a positive (rather than defensive) tone, showing understanding for the customer's problem, apologizing for his or her inconvenience, and summarizing the problem.

Assessment and interaction: This includes solving the problem while accepting customer criticism without being defensive, maintaining the company's credibility, and treating the customer as an individual. This section also includes technical components: avoiding "dead air" while flipping from one computer screen to another, thanking the customer for waiting, explaining that customers will be put on hold, explaining the problem-solving actions that will be taken, avoiding the overuse of slang or jargon, and using all resources available to solve the customer's problem.

Resolution and closing: This section encompasses the rep's wrap-up of the call, where he or she emphasizes that the customer and rep have worked together to find a solution, explains to the customer exactly what steps will be taken to correct the problem, and offers his or her department's assistance in the future.

Source: E. Penzer, "Measuring Customer Service," *Incentive,* September 1990, pp. 68–76.

---

specific interaction points as failpoints can help marketers focus their management and quality control attentions on those steps most likely to cause trouble in the marketing process. One researcher, George, characterizes failpoints as either *technically responsive* or *functionally responsive,* delineating those failpoints for which machines versus people are responsible.[8]

AFTERMARKETING WORKING
Creating Better Service Using Blueprinting

A customer interaction blueprint is more precise than verbal definitions and less subject to misinterpretation. It illustrates the dictum of W. Edwards Deming that workers are never to blame for flaws in a process. Process design is management's responsibility.

A customer interaction blueprint allows a company to test its assumptions on paper and thoroughly work out the bugs. A service manager can test a prototype delivery on potential customers and use the feedback to modify the blueprint before testing the procedure again.

A customer interaction blueprint encourages creativity, preemptive problem solving, and controlled implementation. It can reduce the potential for failure and enhance management's ability to think effectively about new services.

The customer interaction blueprint principle helps cut down the time and inefficiency of random service development and gives a higher-level view of service management prerogatives. The alternative—leaving services to individual talent and managing the pieces rather than the whole—makes a company more vulnerable and creates a service that reacts slowly to market needs and opportunities. As the United States moves to a service economy, companies that gain control of the design and management process will be the companies that survive and prosper.

With each step in a marketing process identified, the acceptability of divergence (flexibility) of the step can be specified. Schematically, a step with some or much flexibility is identified with a box with an attached fan shape that denotes the possible flexibility.

The holistic approach represented by customer blueprinting has value because it performs these functions:

- It focuses on the customer and his or her expectations and experiences.
- It shows how the technical procedures relate to the administrative and relationship-building activities of product or service delivery.
- The approach points out activities that may be proceduralized as well as those that must be individualized and thus deserve special attention.
- It provides a basis for identifying gaps in the market that need to be rectified or capitalized upon.
- Blueprinting presents opportunities to increase or decrease customer involvement in the process.
- It shows professional and administrative staff members how their own activities relate to the customer and to each other.[9]

FAILPOINTS EXAMINED: CRITICAL INCIDENTS

A growing number of consumer affairs professionals and marketers are studying the qualitative satisfactoriness of customer contacts with organizations. A technique called the "critical incident" technique has been meaningfully employed in many of these endeavors. The critical incident technique is a procedure for collecting anecdotal descriptions of interactions between customers and marketers. These descriptions are qualitatively clustered based on their judged similarities, and are then quantified in a content-analytic fashion.

Incidents (customer contacts) are defined as discrete interactions between a customer and a marketer. *Critical* incidents are interactions that are especially satisfying or dissatisfying, such that they contribute to or detract from overall satisfaction with the marketer. In addition, because of the retrospective nature of the data collection, critical incidents are also those that are most memorable.

Participants are generally asked the following sequence of questions:

Think of a time when, as a customer, you had a particularly satisfying (dissatisfying) interaction with an employee of ABC Company.

- When did the incident happen?
- What specific circumstances led up to this situation?
- Exactly what did the employee say or do?
- What resulted that made you feel the interaction was satisfying (dissatisfying)?

Three marketing professors, Bitner, Booms, and Tetreault, have described a rather seminal study applying the critical incident technique to the study of customer satisfaction with three service industries: hotels, restaurants, and airlines. From a convenience sample of 375 people a total of 719 incidents were collected. By sorting the incidents according to their similarities, three distinct groups emerged:

- *Employees responding to a failure in the service delivery system.*

  - The service is unavailable.
  - The service was unreasonably slow.
  - Other core support services failed.

- *Employees responding to customers' requests for special needs.*

  - Responses to customers with "special needs."
  - Responses to customers' unique preferences.
  - Responses to admitted customer errors.
  - Handling of disruptive conditions and other customers.

- *Unprompted and unsolicited employee actions.*

  - Extraordinary attention paid to the customer.

EXHIBIT 4–6
Critical Encounters

Nature of the Encounter	Percentage of All Critical Encounters	Odds of Satisfactory Outcome for Customer (Satisfactory:Unsatisfactory)
Independent employee actions	43%	1 : 1
Employee responds to a service or product failure	33	1 : 2
Employee responds to a customer request	24	2 : 1

Adapted from Bitner, Booms, and Tetreault, "The Service Encounter," *Journal of Marketing,* Vol. 54, January 1990, p. 75.

- Employee actions that truly exceed the parameters of their responsibilities.
- Employee actions judged against cultural norms.
- Holistic approval or disapproval.
- Performance under adverse circumstances.

Bitner, Booms, and Tetreault classified the 719 incidents across these conditions and tabulated the proportion of satisfactory versus unsatisfactory outcomes. The results are rather condemning. They suggest a relatively pessimistic picture in terms of service personnel being able to satisfy customers in interactions with them.

For simplicity's sake, the results are substantially collapsed in Exhibit 4–6 to provide an overall perspective. Of all critical incidents collected, the largest number belong to the cluster of *unprompted employee actions.* Among these incidents, there are even odds that the customer was satisfied. The next most frequent critical incident engenders *employees' responding to a service or system failure.* Here the odds are much worse; only one in two times was the employee able to satisfy the customer! Finally, the third but least frequent category is *employees responding to a special request.* Here the odds of satisfying the customer are much better, two to one.

USING EMPLOYEES TO HELP SPOT PROBLEMS

Blueprinting is a convenient way of identifying all of the customer contact personnel in an organization. These employees may often be deeper in the company structure than the typical frontline definition would suggest. Employees who interact with customers can usually provide valuable perspectives on what customers value and how easily the employees believe that they can meet their customers' needs. These employees are often the only company representatives the public ever meets. Among these employees will be represented a range of viewpoints concerning their awareness of their responsibility to the company to maintain and improve customer satisfaction.

The ideal corporate culture would invite contact employees who detect something amiss to report it to their local manager, who in turn would relay it to middle management. But often corporate cultures inhibit contact employees from taking such initiatives. Or they may hold back an observation or comment until they see the problem occur enough times to feel comfortable in reporting it.

A formalized procedure with which to elicit employee feedback is usually a productive process. It gathers information quickly and efficiently and it acknowledges the importance of the interactive role the employees perform. There are three different methods for gathering such information:

- Employee focus groups.
- Employee surveys.
- Alert reports.

Employee Focus Groups

Internal focus groups consisting of customer contact employees and middle managers can help a marketer spot emerging problems before they reach epidemic proportions. Such groups can serve as early warning indicators, alerting the marketer to problems prior to numerous consumers' complaints and often before the problems are noticeable in customer satisfaction survey returns.[10]

Employee focus groups are nothing more than formalized discussions led by a moderator following an agenda of discussion topics. The moderator's role is to attempt to elicit as many different points of view as possible on an issue, and to include all group members in the discussion. When conducted internally, such meetings can be held at lunchtime and may, when deemed advisable, be conducted anonymously by an outside moderator.

Group discussions generally elicit countless suggestions for improvement in service procedures, which are especially compelling because of the first-hand exposure these order takers, repair people, and customer service people have with customers. It is they who are the direct recipients of both the grievances and the gratitude of customers. They know customers and can contribute unique insights to the service process, given the opportunity.

Particularly in service companies, exchanges between company employees and customers may constitute the very service the company sells. The public may form most of its impressions of the company based on the quality of that interaction. Even in nonservice businesses, perceptions of the company and ultimately sales volume can be greatly influenced by the ways in which service and sales personnel interact with customers. Management is well advised to listen not only to recipients of their company's customer service but to those on the front lines who provide it.

Employee focus groups form a privileged and anonymous communication channel from customers through frontline employees to management. Ideas can be sent to management for possible implementation, and criticisms of current practices can be made via the focus group without fear of retribution for any individual employee.

Employee Surveys

Employee surveys can accomplish many of the same goals as focus groups and with their permissive anonymity can make some employees more comfortable, both by easing the conspicuousness of participating in a discussion group—possibly being labeled a "griper" by co-workers or management—and by eliminating the awkwardness of articulating customer service issues among a group of possibly critical co-workers. On the other hand, some believe that the communal group discussion puts many potentially anxious employees at ease, inviting their participation in the discussion. Employee surveys can be conducted anonymously on a periodic basis.

The questionnaire for an employee survey, while pursuing specific issues, should also allow for volunteered issues and information through some open-ended questions. The questionnaire should be kept simple and short. Recipients of the questionnaire can be chosen randomly (and rotated from wave to wave) or a panel of employees can be formed to receive a questionnaire on a regular basis.

Alert Reports

Another medium for information exchange with employees is the alert report. Alert reports are nothing more than the proverbial suggestion box updated to a forum for discussion of customer problems. The process is probably effective for some employees but not for more reluctant or hesitant ones. The main value of the alert report is that it is always ready to receive an employee's warning of a problem without management needing to be aware of it to start the process. It thus serves as a convenient early warning system in the very best sense of the term.

The unfortunate aspect of alert reports is the skepticism that anyone from management will actually review the reports and act on any of them. With no perceived action undertaken, it is easy for employees to decide that reports are not being read; motivation to participate would in that case be greatly diminished.

The Value of Employee Input

Employee focus groups or surveys are generally less expensive, more convenient, and quicker to conduct than consumer research projects because they are usually conducted in-house during work hours. Expensive focus facility rentals are avoided. Also, employee research projects can be convened quickly if a problem is suspected. Probably one of the greatest benefits of such research is the atmosphere it creates. Any outreach to employees for information openly acknowledges their very special role and capabilities. A precedent is set for listening to their ideas and concerns. As a result, they are likely to feel more a part of the marketing program of the organization in the future.

Rather than choosing from among these three procedures, the informed marketer is probably well advised to utilize all three to maximize the effectiveness of his aftermarketing programs.

KEY POINTS OF THE CHAPTER

Managing evidence.   After making a product or service selection or purchase, all too often the customer is unable to adequately assess the value being derived from the purchase or selection. Managing evidence is simply providing the customer with feedback about the value and benefit received from a purchase already made. Supplied evidence reassures the customer that he has made a correct purchase decision.

Moments of truth.   A concept coined by SAS president, Jan Carlzon, this represents the interaction of one of a company's employees with a customer. During this interaction the employee will either live up to the explicit and implicit promises made by the company, or the employee will disappoint the customer. Therefore, no matter how hard companies try to improve their products or services, their futures depend on the interaction of their employees with customers, the moments of truth.

Blueprinting.   Blueprinting is a schematic process for tracing the flow of any product, service, or support activity from production to sale to after-sale servicing. The blueprint process provides a global representation of who and when customer contact people are involved and how they interact with customers. Obviously, interactions can be rated based on who is interacting and what the customer's needs are.

Failpoints.   When a customer contact point in a blueprint is identified as one where things frequently go wrong, the point can be labeled a failpoint. Failpoints are more critical than other contact points because they can determine the perceived quality of the customer's interaction with the company.

Employee focus groups   Customer contact employees can be assembled in internal focus groups to assess what problems they are most frequently confronted with and how easy it is for them to solve these problems. Employee focus groups are an inexpensive method of quickly gathering information about the customer contact process in a business or organization. One must remember that the procedure is far from objective because the same employees who may be delivering poor service are being asked to describe the quality of service being rendered.

NOTES

1. He (Carlzon) describes in his book: According to Karl Albrecht, Carlzon used the phrase "moment of truth" (derived from Spanish bullfighting's *el momento de verdad*—the final moment at which matador and bull face each other, alone) at the suggestion of Richard Normann, a Swedish management consultant who assisted in Carlzon's revamping of SAS. See K. Albrecht, *Service Within* (New York, Dow Jones-Irwin, 1989), pp. 12–13.
2. Thus, SAS is created: J. Carlzon, *Moments of Truth*, (Cambridge, MA, Ballinger Books, 1987), p. 3.
3. This has led some writers: G. L. Shostack, "A Simple Rule for Service Encounters: Do Unto Others..." *American Banker,* December 21, 1983, p. 4.
4. Thus, Levitt's "augmented product:" T. Levitt, *The Marketing Imagination* (New York, The Free Press, 1983), p. 79.
5. The fragility of these interactions is underscored: L. Zunin and N. Zunin, *Contact: The First Four Minutes* (Los Angeles, Nash Publishing, 1972).
6. When the moments of truth go unmanaged: K. Albrecht and R. Zemke, "Instilling a Service Mentality: Like Teaching an Elephant to Dance," *International Management,* November 1985, pp. 61–67.
7. She calls the method "customer blueprinting:" G. L. Shostack, "Designing Services That Deliver," *Harvard Business Review,* January—February 1984, pp. 133–139.
8. George characterizes failpoints: W. R. George and B. E. Gibson, "Blueprinting: A Tool for Managing Quality in Service," in *Service Quality,* ed. S. Brown et al. (Lexington, MA, Lexington Books, 1991).
9. Focuses on the customer: C. A. Congram, "Professional Services," in *The Handbook of Services Marketing,* (New York, The American Management Association, 1991), pp. 479–490.
10. Internal focus groups consisting of "front-line" employees: T. P. Brown, "Internal Research Helps to Define Service Quality," *Marketing News,* February 23, 1991, p. 11.

Chapter Five

Encouraging an Informal Dialogue with Customers

Aftermarketing (like consumer-oriented marketing before it) suggests that the consumer should be the focus of the company as it establishes and modifies its strategic plans. In consumer-oriented marketing, the marketing function is looked upon as the primary conduit for collecting information on consumers to help the company position itself and its products more appealingly to potential customers. In contrast, aftermarketing identifies a range of activities to help the company increase satisfaction with itself and its products among current customers. (Conventional marketing exhibits a more blasé attitude regarding activities to be directed at current customers.) In organizations currently performing such activities, these activities will generally be conducted outside of the marketing function. In addition to their value in maintaining customer relationships, these interactions are also a rich source of additional information about customers. Unfortunately, many of the departments currently handling these interactions are not organizationally within the marketing area, and some are not even in daily contact with it.

Much of the feedback companies receive from customers will be customer-initiated. Therefore, astuteness on the marketer's behalf is required to recognize these contacts as important sources of marketing information. To fully utilize this information the marketer must institute a process to *receive, analyze, acknowledge,* and *act* on the information voluntarily submitted by customers. In doing so, the marketer achieves an open and active dialogue with his customers.

To fight competition, knowing what's on the customer's mind is the most important thing we can do.

Richard E. Heckert, Past-Chairman, DuPont

Dialogue with customers can accomplish the following:

- Tell you if you are doing something wrong and how to do it better.
- Give you ideas for new products and ways to present existing products.
- Make the prospect more interested and less wary, annoyed, and frustrated.
- Make the customer feel more loyal and more committed to doing business with you.
- Provide impressive customer endorsements for your advertising.
- Add value to your product or service.

Direct customer contact is one of the best ways to build lasting customer relationships.

MAKING AN ORGANIZATION ACCESSIBLE TO CUSTOMERS

"I could get my job done if it weren't for all the time I waste talking to customers!" Thus spoke a frustrated employee of a service organization. The employee's concern is obviously misplaced, but this sentiment unfortunately is all too typical of the attitudes of many frontline and middle management executives. In some companies such an attitude may even be held by some top-level managers!

If this attitude is characteristic of people at the lower strata of an organization, then the organization is anything but aftermarketing oriented. Aftermarketing focuses on *maximizing* interactions with customers, *not* avoiding such contacts.

Customer contact has traditionally been shunned by many marketers. They fear the outcome of too much "exposure" among customers. There are four different perspectives that embody many of the fears causing marketers to distance themselves from customers:

• *The ostrich syndrome.* Many marketers seem to feel that customer problems, if left alone, will somehow take care of themselves. Thus, like ostriches, they avoid customer contact. They are really only fooling themselves. Dissatisfied customers will vent their dissatisfactions one way or another. The enlightened marketer will attempt to defuse customer aggravations by actively seeking out dissatisfied customers. Through conversations with these customers, a mutually satisfying solution can possibly be achieved. But avoiding contact can only result in losing the customer to a more "compassionate" competitor.

• *The invited target syndrome.* This perspective could also be labeled the "pump-priming" syndrome because it stems from the fear that *any* dialogue with customers will only stimulate criticism. In fact, it is feared that a dialogue about satisfaction may prompt even mildly satisfied customers to become overly critical and hence ultimately dissatisfied. This perspective also holds that monitoring satisfaction implies to some customers (who might never have considered it beforehand) that not everyone else is as satisfied as they may be. With such a seed of suspicion planted, it is feared that a brush fire will ignite in the grass roots of a marketer's franchise, generating a substantial number of dissatisfied customers. Such a backlash would be considered the result of the marketer's having raised the issue of satisfaction in the first place.

• *Falsely raising expectations.* Some believe that by the very nature of corresponding with customers there may be an implied contract to fix all problems. If a marketer is not truly committed to acting on the problems discovered in conversations with customers, then customers are best left alone. Discussing issues that are not immediately targets for improvement may, indeed, cause some customers to expect change, and when none occurs, their dissatisfaction will possibly escalate.

• *The controller's nightmare.* Many marketing firms worry about the costs involved in conducting a dialogue with customers. Some of these firms, while believing in their obligation to be accessible to their customers, nevertheless worry about these issues:

- The costs of offering such accessibility in a professional manner.
- Inviting a deluge of only mildly unhappy customers to take advantage of the offered dialogue (which is intended for only the severely dissatisfied).

Inherent in both of these concerns is a bottom line mentality. *Why should one invest substantially in any activity which will not proportionally increase the bottom line?* This is obviously a short-term perspective which needs to be replaced with a dedication to the long-term survival of the organization by truly satisfying customers.

Marketers oriented to aftermarketing accept communication with customers as a natural part of doing business. This acceptance is based on the recognition of the following factors:

- An increasingly *sophisticated (and educated) customer,* who is no longer in awe of national marketers but is comfortable speaking to a marketer as an equal and demanding fair and just treatment.
- A *more cynical customer,* whose trust in institutions and businesses has been severely compromised by discoveries of wrongdoing in government; abuses of the ecology by major corporations; the failure of many financial institutions through poor management; and general schemes of exploitation of customers in all areas of business.
- *Consumer ombudsmen* preaching the "caveat emptor" sermon to consumers from most major media, including local newspapers, radio and TV stations, and national organizations such as Ralph Nader's group.
- A *more expectant, critical customer* whose expectations may have been heightened by the highly competitive claims and counterclaims in a product or service category.
- Increasing evidence that *customer outreach contributes to the bottom line*[1] A series of studies by TARP appears to substantiate this.

A satisfied customer will tell four or five friends about a product or service, but a dissatisfied customer will tell twice as many about her problems. Each time a customer contacts a company, the contact represents another opportunity to increase the customer's satisfaction. Direct contact can be the beginning of a strong customer relationship, even if the original reason for contact is negative.

Engaging in dialogue with customers tells them that they are important. It assures customers that their opinions are sought and that the company is interested in serving their needs. Dialogue also can ease a wary customer's mind, soothe an angry customer's temper, or reaffirm a satisfied customer's purchase decision.

Listening to customers is a value-added service that only some companies offer, but it is a posture that more and more customers expect. In fact, it is virtually impossible to hide from customers, and avoiding them is *not* a desirable tactic.

Opening a dialogue with customers affords a five-step process (the "five A's" of aftermarketing) to occur:

- *Acquaint* yourself with your customers, get to know them and their needs;
- *Acknowledge* your customers showing them you know them personally;
- *Appreciate* your customers and the business they give you;
- *Analyze* what customers tell you in their correspondence;
- *Act* on what you learn from your customers—showing them they count!

RESPONSIBILITY FOR CUSTOMER OUTREACH

With the adoption of customer-oriented marketing during the 70s and 80s, most firms acknowledged that the marketing department or marketing executive ought to have the responsibility for identifying and interacting with *potential* customers. Marketing's sovereignty in prospecting for customers was thus established. The problem is that these same enlightened firms failed to enlarge marketing's responsibility to include actively caring for *current* customers!

The goal of marketing's contemporary focus on understanding customers appears limited to creating better advertising and offering better products and services. *Today's marketing is not oriented to building better relationships with customers.* Few marketing departments will be engaged in handling after-purchase correspondence with customers, in establishing a customer database, or in providing 800 telephone center product support.

In fact, it is very likely that no single department or function is properly or fully sanctioned as having "stewardship" responsibilities for current customers. Current customers thus exist much like orphaned children, acknowledged but largely fending for themselves.

It is all too typical in today's business organization to have current customers handed off from one area to the next, with no uniform treatment given them, no collective dossier assembled on any individual customer's plight, no marker in the company's CIF (customer information file) to document a customer's unhappiness. Instead, customer contact is all too frequently relegated to "specialists."

Normally, handling by specialists means better treatment. But, consider the possible result of many different customer requests being handled by different areas within an organization (see Exhibit 5–1).

Is it possible that any of the departments involved are recording their interactions with customers in a central CIF? Most likely they have each solved the customer's problem insofar as their domain allows, and then have forgotten the identity of each customer with whom they have interacted. And it is even more

EXHIBIT 5–1
How Customer Contacts Are Currently Routed

Type of Customer Contact	Corporate Department Involved
Request for recipes, product use information	Home economists, customer relations (P.R. function)
Request for company magazine	P.R. department, corp. publications
Inquiry about nearest dealers	Sales area
Complaint about product, packaging	Quality control (under manufacturing)
Complaint about retailers, dealers	Sales area
Questions about billing, charges	Accounting, accounts receivable
Suggestions for new product	Production, marketing
Volunteered anecdotes/experiences	P.R. department

unlikely that any of these departments have reflected on the potential marketing value of their interactions with customers.

In contrast to the disjointed way in which customers are currently responded to, aftermarketing suggests that current customers ought to be handled with a more coordinated, holistic approach. All contacts with customers ought to become a part of the marketing department's mission. In Chapter 1, a broadened operational perspective for the marketing function was identified. It was suggested that marketing's 4 P's be expanded to include

- Product.
- Place.
- Communication:
  - With prospective customers.
  - With present customers.
  - With noncustomer stakeholders.
  - With noncustomer members of the public.
- Customer satisfaction.
- Servicing.

These definitions all suggest an expanded role for marketing—more than simply winning customers, the role would be *customer management*. As such, a number of operations that are not generally within the current aegis of marketing should be unified within marketing. These areas are

- Public relations.
- Customer relations.
- Quality control.

AFTERMARKETING WORKING
How to Run an 800 Number Facility

A firm which has raised customer service to new heights is the GE Company. Acknowledged as "world class", its GE Answer Center® boasts a well-trained staff of 250 to answer questions about GE consumer products and services. Given GE's giant size—among the Forbes 500 companies it ranks first in market value and fifth in profit with over $60 billion in revenues—that job is quite difficult.

"GE and other large firms can be faceless," says Merrell Grant, manager of the GE Answer Center, Louisville, KY. "At the Answer Center, we try to give GE a face."

The center was developed with a $2 million investment in 1981–82. To develop that "familiar face-to-face" feeling with customers over the phone, GE executives originally traveled to Disney World to observe how Disney trained their people. Disney employees are called cast members, and customers are guests. In constructing the Answer Center, these important nuances were taken to heart. And today at GE, "our calls are all 'face-to-face calls'," she says. "We don't have 12,000 calls a day, we have 12,000 visitors a day."

Grant is extremely careful in screening job applicants. Since candidates have to learn 120 product lines and be conversant with over 8,500 models, a college degree is helpful. After six weeks of training, new service reps are put on the phones with another 50 hours of training a year to keep them up on their jobs and to boost morale.

Grant is proud of the center's service level: 85 percent of calls are answered immediately, only 13 percent of calls experience an average delay of 30 seconds, and only 2 percent of callers receive a busy signal.

Such service reaps great benefits. According to Grant, since GE instituted the center its image has been enhanced; customer satisfaction increased to 93 percent, increasing purchase impact 67 percent; warranty costs have been reduced; production and quality have improved, and dealers/distributors are happier than ever with GE products.

To show Grant that her crew in not just "window dressing," GE has been pumping millions of dollars into the Center to improve conditions and to facilitate superior customer service.

What puzzles Grant is why other companies don't take consumer complaints more seriously. "Most of them don't understand that inquiry handling is an opportunity to build loyalty and to get sales. Most of them think that if they hide from consumers that they'll go away," she says. "Well, they don't. Those with questions left unanswered will go to the competition."

And that's not a good thought to ponder as direct marketing continues to grow in popularity. As the market gets more and more saturated, those who ignore customer complaints may end up in the red. Grant sums it up this way, "Excellence in customer service is the competitive weapon of the future, by retaining the customers you have, increasing productivity and providing sales growth, you'll survive and prosper in the market of the new millenium!"

Perhaps the most controversial of these recommendations is the suggestion that quality control be moved within marketing. Manufacturing or production most likely currently manages this function and views it as necessary feedback from customers on its manufacturing processes. However, the opportunities that these interactions with customers represent suggest very real *strategic marketing value* to which manufacturing is probably not prepared to react. It seems far more beneficial to put marketing in charge of the quality control outreach program, relaying quality feedback information to manufacturing or production and simultaneously exploiting each customer interaction opportunity for its aftermarketing value. Aftermarketing promotes the belief that the marketing department can enhance the long-term relationship with customers better than other areas within the organization whose primary function is something other than customer contact.

HOW REPRESENTATIVE ARE LETTERS AND TELEPHONE CALLS?

In many cases today, those customers who take the time to write or call a business are disregarded as a "biased, self-selected sample" whose opinions, satisfactions, and dissatisfactions cannot be generalized to the larger customer-body. Even marketing research departments (who by now ought to know better) will disavow themselves of the opportunity to use data from self-initiated contact customers, and likely as not will deny the importance of the information contained in these contacts.

If intuition alone is not sufficient to repudiate these assumptions, there is a growing body of data and information which demonstrates the very real importance of those customers who care enough to contact a company. The emphasis here ought to be placed on "care enough," since it is certainly easy for most consumers nowadays to find an alternate brand or source of supply for an unsatisfactory product or service. The fact that a customer spends his or her own time to contact a marketer seems to suggest a desire on that customer's behalf to stay affiliated with the marketer, if only the marketer will rectify the experienced problem.

There is hard evidence to show the value of resolving customers' comments. The Coca-Cola Company commissioned TARP (Technical Assistance Research Programs) to conduct a study tracking 1,717 persons who had filed complaints or inquiries with the company's Consumer Affairs department.

The study shows that Coca-Cola was able to satisfy a majority of its complaining customers (85 percent). But the more important news is that nearly 10 percent of those customers actually increased their reported subsequent purchases of Coca-Cola! And the "gossip factor" (word of mouth comments) paid healthy dividends as well. Coke's satisfactory handling of the complaints netted an estimated 1.5 new customers for every one customer lost because of negative word of mouth.[2]

READ YOUR MAIL

Although customer telephone calls outnumber customer letters today, most companies nevertheless receive a substantial volume of mail. Letters can produce a number of different reactions. Most often they are perceived as a burden, an obligation that has no direct bearing on future profitability. The customers writing the letters will probably be stereotyped, most likely as "classic malcontents" or even "kooks" who have nothing better to do than to bother corporations with mail.

There are indeed some facts that apply to most letter-writing customers:

- They are *generally older* (only today's generation thinks nothing of making a coast-to-coast telephone call).
- They are *more likely to be women* (perhaps almost exclusively), who until recently were perceived to have more free time than men.
- They will be *less economically advantaged*.
- They may *desire a record or documentation* of their dissatisfaction. In this respect the letter writer may be somewhat more serious and litigious in nature.

Very few companies accord their mail the importance it should be given. Some companies that have a government-granted monopoly (such as the television networks) may consider it in their own best interests to maintain a good understanding of the attitudes and content of the letters they receive. But even this posture is defensive, not imaginative.

During the 1970s the National Broadcasting Company maintained a very efficient audience communications department. It was the responsibility of this department to prepare a weekly report on

- The primary targets (programs and personalities) of the week's letters and calls.
- The qualitative direction of the correspondence (supportive, neutral, opposed).
- The presence of any organized campaigns or continuing themes of response.

The report was circulated to the president and chairman each week, as well as to program producers. Not only did it inform all levels of management as to the basic approval or disapproval of viewers, it offered a cornucopia of other information about viewers. For example, it linked levels of reaction to various regions of the country. Though motivated by defensiveness, the program is exemplary of the types of information that can be extracted from customers' voluntary communications and then incorporated into strategic planning.

Many marketers who receive letters will pass the letters along to their telephone facility as a first attempt at responding to complaints. If the letter writer can be reached through telephone directory assistance, resolution will be attempted by phone. Some marketers respond to customer letters by mail only as a last resort.

COMMUNICATING WITH CUSTOMERS BY TELEPHONE

The telephone provides a medium for communicating with large customer bases unlike any other. First, communication is better and more complete when conducted by phone. Emotionality can be neither easily concealed nor overlooked in a telephone conversation. The customer's anger, pleasure, frustration or indifference can be sensed by the receiver, who can then deliver an appropriate response to help create satisfaction.

And there is instant feedback to each conciliatory effort, allowing the marketer instant feedback on the success of his efforts. For this reason, telephone calls have a higher success rate at soothing frayed tempers and reinforcing brand loyalty.

Second, the telephone allows for immediate response and problem resolution. As our society becomes more and more accustomed to "instant gratification," communication channels that can offer immediate resolution will be more favored and effective.

Telephone communication provides other advantages. Answering phones can be cheaper than replying to customers' letters. (Industry sources report processing costs for a typical telephone call average $8 to $10, while processing a letter can cost as much as $18.)[3] Telephone communications also increase employee productivity, as it takes less time to respond to a telephone call than it does to answer mail. (Some marketers reportedly attempt to keep their customer contact calls to 3½ minutes in length.) And, while turnaround on a phone call is instantaneous, getting a written response delivered to a letter-writing customer can take three to five days or longer.

There are three ways in which a customer can initiate contact with a marketer through telecommunications (see Exhibit 5-2): A toll-free 800 number, a conventional telephone number, and the newer 900 number.

Marketers face two different obligations with regard to their telephone "outreach":

- The obligation to make sales data and information readily available to potential customers.
- The obligation to support current customers with answers to operational questions and other product-use related questions.

Which of these obligations is strongest is truly a matter of judgment. However, from the after-sale customer support perspective of aftermarketing, the marketer's

EXHIBIT 5–2
Types of Telephone Calls

800 Telephone Number	Regular Telephone Number	900 Telephone Number
Company pays for call	Customer pays for call	Customer pays for call
Company pays for staff	Company pays for staff	Customer pays for staff

AFTERMARKETING WORKING
How Do Corporations Handle Their Mail?

To find out firsthand how companies handle small gripes, a *Wall Street Journal* reporter sent complaints on plain stationery to 10 companies on October 1, 1990. This was not a scientific survey, but responses to the letters, which were based on real consumer complaints, are probably typical of how many companies handle consumer grievances. Corporate America seems to have one thing in common—companies answer all complaints, no matter how small. Here is a sampling of their letters.

Dear Kimberly-Clark
　　Can you explain why the big national diaper brands all sell for the same price? Why is it so much more than the Pathmark diapers?

In a letter dated October 30, the nation's No. 2 manufacturer of disposable diapers explained that the three national brands are all "premium products and often carry a higher retail price than some other disposable diapers." Why? Because of their "premium quality" and "unique features." Not that the store brands are not quality products, the letter added generously.

Kimberly-Clark's response contained nary a word about why all the national brands were priced identically, but the company did provide a short-term solution: two $1 coupons.

Dear Liz Claiborne
　　I like the dress, but the buttonholes keep unraveling.... It didn't even last one year.

Apparel giant Liz Claiborne Inc. was "chagrined" to receive reports of a faulty buttonhole. "We're sorry to have disappointed you even once, and will strive in the future to deserve your trust," gushed a letter dated October 4. No matter that the complaint letter admitted the dress was well-worn and wasn't particularly expensive in the first place. "Loose buttons or imperfect buttonholes are unacceptable," the letter stated emphatically. The company included instructions to have the dress fixed by any tailor, along with assurances that reimbursement would be forthcoming.

Dear Campbell Soup
The nutrition information is misleading, I doubt anyone gets more than two servings from a can of soup. Why don't you just list the calories in a total can?

In a letter dated October 10, the company thanked the writer for her concern but added that "we have found the recipe, the size of the serving and the container to be the most popular." Though the letter said Campbell had previously considered making changes of the type suggested in the letter, it added that it does not believe that "modifications are desirable at this time." Nor did the company deem the suggestion worthy of coupons, it sent a leaflet of recipes that require Campbell's cream of broccoli soup instead.

Dear Health Valley Foods
The flakes were fine, but the box hardly contained any raisins at all.

Responding to consumers can be a big challenge for small companies, but this California manufacturer of natural foods seemed downright pleased to hear of the perceived raisin shortage. In a two-page letter, dated Oct. 3, George Mateljan, the company's president, thanked the writer for being "concerned, enlightened and loyal enough to write." "A situation like this distresses me deeply," he wrote, "and I deeply regret any inconvenience you may have been caused."

Mr. Mateljan didn't stop there. The company sent a replacement box of cereal, an Oat Bran Jumbo Fruit Bar, a packet of herb seasonings and $1 coupon for higher-fiber cookies, muffins or bars. The parcel also contained a questionnaire about the samples, a small card to give to retailers requesting that they carry Health Valley products, and information about how the company's Oat Bran products fit into a cholesterol-busting diet.

Source: K. Deveny, "For Marketers No Peeve Is Too Petty," *The Wall Street Journal,* November 14, 1990, pp. B-1, B-8; by permission of *The Wall Street Journal,* ©1990 Dow Jones & Company, Inc. All rights reserved worldwide.

obligation to current customers is the most important. The decision the marketer must make is to determine which type of telephone support is most appropriate for each situation.

As telecommunications technology becomes increasingly sophisticated, another choice is presenting itself to marketers—whether a customer's call will be answered by a person or receive an automated response. Although in the early 90s automated telephone systems still appear to aggravate many people, it is likely that they will increase in acceptance. They are efficient answering and routing systems, and with ANI (automatic number identification) they can instantly capture considerable information about a caller, thereby minimizing labor in an otherwise intensive application. If used sparingly and only in situations where information capture is more important than issue resolution, their future seems bright.

New telephone company services like AT&T's InfoWorx Interactive Voice service let businesses use voice response units for automated answering and call processing without having to invest in the equipment and its maintenance. This capability promises new efficiency in designing aftermarketing activities.

Answer Your Phones: 800 Numbers

In early 1991, there were as many as 300 major marketers offering customers 800 numbers for complaints, questions, or compliments.[4] Another source places at 200,000 the total number of 800 lines that are "directly related to customer service." And the number of lines is reportedly growing at 30 percent per year![5]

AT&T's reports show a dramatic increase in the number of 800 lines and calls. Of the 50 billion or more calls made on AT&T networks per year, over 13 billion—almost one-quarter—are 800 calls.[6] A 1992 survey conducted by the Society of Consumer Affairs Professionals in Business shows that two-thirds of the 400 companies surveyed use 800 customer service lines, a dramatic increase over the 38 percent identified in a similar survey a decade earlier.[7] The survey showed that one of the reasons given for using 800 numbers was to "boost customer loyalty."

For more and more successful companies, 800 lines are the customer contact medium of choice. The philosophy underlying the use of 800 numbers is to make the company as accessible to customers as possible and never make the customer pay for after-sale service.

But how are 800 numbers used? *Target Marketing* magazine reported in 1991 that over 75 percent of all 800 number calls are for customer sales or service. Firms are learning, the magazine reported, that the "comfort level" of customers rises with their ability to keep in touch with a company. ("Comfort level" can be correlated with "repeat sales.") Currently, 800 telephone numbers as a medium of customer interaction are being experimented with by marketers for a number of applications:

- *Information line.* As consumers read advertisements they frequently have additional questions. A telephone number placed in the ad gives them the opportunity to get more information 24 hours a day, either from a "canned presentation" or from a live operator. (If a canned presentation is used, the brand's actual spokesperson or celebrity can be used to make the response even more enjoyable.)
- *Coupon or sample requests.* Allowing consumers to call the marketer requesting either coupons or samples saves the tremendous amounts of money required for FSI distribution or national household sampling programs. And the distribution will produce much higher redemption and use rates since the sample of consumers is self-selectedly predisposed toward the product.

- *Polling or opinion lines.* Customers are always willing to offer their opinions and sometimes marketers can profit from such a listening post. Levi's 501 jeans advertised an 800 opinion line, asking customers to tell what they liked to do while wearing their 501 jeans (they were encouraged with the promise that their story might be used in a future 501 TV commercial). In one month the company received 800,000 calls and more anecdotes than could ever be collected in a marketing survey!

- *Dealer referral.* When consumers are really interested in a product or service, they need to know where to purchase it. An automated telephone service into which callers key their zip code can efficiently steer them to a nearby retailer.

- *Sweepstakes and games.* More and more marketers are experimenting with sweepstakes and games in which customers call special numbers to enter or to see if they have won. Quaker's Cap'n Crunch "Find LaFoote" sweepstakes is a landmark example. The company drew 24 million responses in a four-month period![8] A telephone sweepstakes held in conjunction with the TV quiz show "Wheel of Fortune" generated 4.7 million calls in 21 days!

- *Surveys.* Marketers with clubs or membership programs have experimented with automated telephone surveys as an economical method to learn about the current interests and needs of their members as well as for collecting demographic and psychographic information.

- *Retail applications.* Point-of-purchase displays have been used by some marketers to distribute "take one" pads with individualized PINs. Customers are invited to call an 800 telephone number to see if they are winners of merchandise or a prize.

Toll-free 800 numbers have given many companies a competitive edge, providing a value-added service with none of the downside risks. Exhibit 5–3 shows an actual usage report from a major packaged goods manufacturer's operation.

In general, this breaks down to only about one-quarter of the calls received being complaints (taste, product quality and packaging) with the remaining 75 percent being marketing-related (usage questions, clarification/education). And a TARP study collaborates this data, attributing 50 percent of toll-free calls to product information requests that conceivably represent new sales opportunities.[9]

Benefits of 800 Numbers

The two most common uses for a toll-free 800 number are to handle customer complaints and to provide sales information. But most companies do not realize the depth to which these two objectives can be pursued, nor do they see the multitude of other benefits from 800 numbers.

Here are a few examples of how some companies are already using 800 telephone numbers to build relationships with their customers:

EXHIBIT 5–3
Issues Addressed by Customers Calling an 800 Number

Complaints	27%
Product complaints	22
Complaints about promotions	6
Product usage/availability questions	43%
Questions about productivity availability	19
Questions about nutrition	13
Questions about usage/preparation	11
Other questions/concerns	26%
Inquiries about promotions	11
Testimonials	5
Education-related questions	5
All other	5
Unfinished, previous calls	3%
Follow-up from previous calls	3

- *Problems in the service.* Burger King Corp., Miami, has instituted a 24-hour hotline called "Your Comments Count." Of the 4,000 calls received each day, 60 to 70 percent are complaints, 20 to 30 percent are compliments, and 10 percent are questions or requests. If enough of one complaint is registered, the system triggers a warning. Ninety-five percent of all calls are resolved with the initial call. The remaining 5 percent are directed to a restaurant manager or franchisee. Twenty-five percent of customers calling the service are randomly recontacted within one month to ensure their satisfaction with the handling their call received.[10]

- *Problems in product quality.* The General Electric Company's GE Answer Center in Louisville, Kentucky, is probably one of the most ambitious problem detection centers in the country. Operated 365 days a year, the center receives daily reports about the satisfactoriness of GE's products and servicing, allowing the company to modify both continually. Appliance returns are often avoided by the center by a simple explanation to a customer of how to operate the appliance.

- *Problems in performance.* Many automotive companies have recently announced roadside assistance or service programs. Cadillac, Mercedes-Benz, and Rolls-Royce have led the way in this important statement of commitment to automobile owners. Cadillac's ads for its service contained the following description:

Professional help is a toll-free phone call away—24 hours a day, 365 days a year. When you phone the Cadillac Roadside Service Hotline at 1-800-882-1112, you speak with a phone advisor who knows your Cadillac intimately. The advisor will ask specific questions to help diagnose the problem and, in many cases, give you instructions over the phone to get you back on the road.

On-the-spot service when you need it the most—nights, weekends, holidays. If necessary, a service advisor will dispatch an authorized Cadillac dealer's technician in a specially equipped vehicle, well stocked with special tools and genuine GM parts. The technician will even provide you and your passengers with courtesy transportation to your home, a hotel, or another local destination if more extensive service is required.

- *Problems in packaging.* Kraft General Foods has reportedly found information from its 800 number operation useful for redesigning some product packaging and the way promotional offers may work in requiring UPC codes.

- *New product opportunities.* Warner Lambert reports (with uncertainty as to how it will use the information) the number of compliments it receives on the effectiveness of its denture cleaner, Efferdent, in cleaning toilet bowls.

- *Answering customer's product-use questions.* Employers Health Insurance, Green Bay, Wisconsin, has assembled a complex computer database of scripts that employees can use to answer policy holders' questions over the telephone. The employee keys in the caller's name, location, and type of health insurance question. The computer then pops up a question and answer format that can be read verbatim. "We know that 75 percent of the calls we get are standard questions," says Sterling L. Phakides, an Employers Health assistant vice president. "Because our telephone people stick to the scripts, they are giving the most up-to-date information possible without consulting technicians. Questions not covered in the scripts are referred to specialists."

- *After-sale assistance.* Both Sharp Electronics and Sony staff sizeable telephone operations to help answer questions of product owners. Sharp actively advertises its service in magazine ads with the following copy.

If you have a question or problem with an electronics product, who do you call? If it's a Sharp consumer product, you can call Denise Martin, Mike Bosanti, Paul Moore or another of the professionals standing by in the Sharp Customer Assistance Center. They're trained to have the answers you need. And authorized to resolve problems quickly. How to install a CD player. What a VCR limited warranty does and does not cover. Where to find a replacement battery charger for a lap-top computer.... If you have a question regarding any Sharp consumer product, please call 1-800-237-4277.

Toll-free lines are also used for sales, taking telephone orders and telling people where they can purchase the product. But even sales-dedicated 800 lines can help improve aftermarketing if the staff is taught that its primary responsibility is to assist either present customers or future ones.

The benefits a company can reap from toll-free telephone information go beyond solving complaints and making sales. Callers' opinions can identify up-to-the-minute changes in trends, fads, and consumer tastes. Companies spend thousands of dollars on marketing research studies to collect many of the same opinions that consumers voluntarily offer during their calls to the companies. These opinionated consumers can help generate new product ideas, test new product concepts or prototypes, or even participate in focus groups or other customer research projects.

By asking the caller a few strategic questions, a company can build a powerful database identifying various target markets for specially focused promotions. This information can help increase a future promotion's impact while reducing its cost.

Most importantly, the two-way dialogue between customer and company generates goodwill and goodwill leads to satisfaction and satisfaction leads to customer loyalty. Can any company afford to tell its customers that they are unimportant or that their opinions are unimportant?

Creating the right 800 operation.   All too frequently companies contract 800 number vendors for their sales and service functions that are inadequate to the task and poorly represent the client's business.

It is critical that a company considering adoption of an 800 line operation understands that it is only worthwhile if it is done right. Many companies establish 800 number operations to join an industry fad and then discover how much of a commitment the operation represents. These operations generally fail. In considering an 800 number facility, there are some basic questions a company must ask itself:

- *Are adequate resources and capacity available to handle the number of calls expected?* Many companies do not have the resources of personnel or phone lines to handle the vast number of calls they will receive. These companies may ultimately try to minimize the call level by concealing their number from customers rather than making it easily accessible. This can obviously frustrate customers who want to contact the marketer.

- *Is a system available that will keep callers from waiting, so that callers aren't further frustrated?* In this day and age, speed is crucial. A wait can frustrate an otherwise satisfied customer or further infuriate a dissatisfied customer. Twenty-seven percent of customers who cannot get through on the telephone will either buy elsewhere or skip the transaction altogether. There are many ways to combat the waiting problem. Most 800 facilities have as an explicit goal answering all calls by the third ring.

- *Has a procedure for handling the calls been created, so that the contact produces satisfaction?* A customer does not call an 800 number with a question to get the response "I don't know if our product does that Mr. Smith." It is important for a company to provide its telephone staff with all of the necessary information and then empower them to make the decisions necessary to satisfy customers.

Most facilities managers will have some very definite objectives for the operation of their telephone lines. The Maxwell House Division of Kraft General Foods insists on the following goals:

- Answer 75% (or more) of all calls within 3 rings.
- Abandon less than 5% of all incoming calls.
- Average no more than 3½ minutes per call.

An 800 number operation should not be entered into casually. It carries implicit promises with some rather severe consequences. If a service is to be offered, it must have enough lines and be staffed adequately to meet customer demand.

Costs of a typical 800 number operation.   Costs of a well-equipped, well-staffed 800 number facility could start at $250,000 for a medium-sized firm, though typically companies spend $1 million or more a year.[11] General Electric's GE Answer Center is considered by many to be the epitome of 800 number operations. Handling 3 million calls, it costs GE a reported $10 million a year to operate on a 365-day basis. This expense is defended by GE executives as paid back "multiple times" during each year.[12]

800 operation: On-site or off-site?   Confronted by internal cost structures, some marketers are taking drastic actions to control the cost of their 800 number facilities while guaranteeing the finest in staffing and operation. The Maxwell House Division of Kraft General Foods has contracted AT&T's American Trans Tech subsidiary to operate its 800 number facility totally off-premises.

Contracting to an outside supplier has worked exceptionally well, reports Maxwell House. (A TARP follow-up study with callers shows that they are satisfied with the treatment they received.) "Suppliers are equipped for the long, non-business hours over which you should offer 800 service," says Jerry LaTour, Director of Maxwell House's quality assurance and consumer affairs department. "Nine to five, eastern time operating hours don't impress your West Coast customer who has a question at 8:30 P.M. PST." "And," LaTour adds, "the corporate headquarters' mentality and salary structure just don't allow the 800 facility employees the flexibility they need to have to properly service the corporation's customers!"

Trans Tech is responsible for properly staffing the lines to maintain Maxwell House's stringent objectives. All billing is done on a piece-work basis. Trans Tech handles both telephone calls and letters addressed to Maxwell House. It prepares a monthly report for Maxwell House Quality Assurance management, who prepare internal action plans based on the content of each month's report.

AFTERMARKETING NEEDED
Getting a Message to the Top

A friend of mine whose American luxury car had developed a series of problems in its first 18 months showed me a letter he was writing to the president of the company. "Why write?" I asked. "Why not pick up the phone and speak to him directly?" My suggestion was initially met with a quick dismissal. Yet the idea of once and for all solving his problem became more appealing.

He announced with a sudden burst of confidence and enthusiasm, "I'll do it!"

The first task of obtaining the president's telephone number proved more difficult than I had thought. The switchboard operator asked if he would like to speak with customer service. He held fast, asking to speak to the president. After several minutes wait, he was given an extension and connected.

The person answering turned out to be one of the customer service representatives my friend had coincidentally spoken with earlier. "I was calling for Mr. _____ . Would you please connect me?" he requested. "I am sorry, I can't do that," was the reply. "May I help you?"

"I've already explained my problems to you," my friend explained. "I want to speak with the president."

"I can't connect you!" "Why not?" my friend demanded, getting increasingly miffed. "Well, sir," the reply began, *"Presidents of corporations are much too busy to talk to customers!"*

Since first hearing this (my friend had asked me to listen on an extension phone to the "run-around" he was being given) the words have echoed in my ears. "Presidents of corporations are too busy to talk to customers." I am personally not sure what could be more important for a corporation president than the opportunity to listen to a real customer with something to say about the president's product or company. Now, I will admit that there are a certain number of crackpots in the world who could keep corporation presidents on their telephones indefinitely. I am not advocating total mayhem. However, the facts in this case are clear: The customer service representative recognized my friend and admitted to having his whole dossier in front of her. There was no danger of exposing the president to a crackpot. This was a bona fide owner with real problems!

Even more exasperating was the representative's refusal to even take a message that my friend wanted to speak directly to Mr. _____.

On the basis of *this* incident one could conclude that this car company wants nothing to do with its customers!

Answer Your Phones: 900 Numbers

The newest telecommunications option for aftermarketing applications is the 900 telephone number. With it, customers pay for the service that is provided (anywhere from $.75 to $4.00 per minute). The industry peaked in 1991 with

EXHIBIT 5–4
Revenue and Program Projections, 900 Number Service

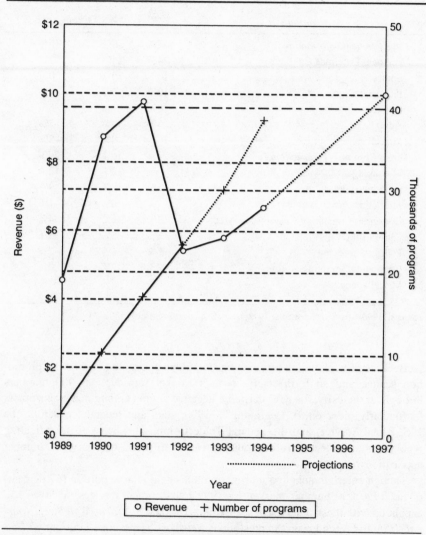

Sources: Strategic Telemedia, December 15, 1990; *Direct,* September 1994.

revenues of $980 million. Tighter federal regulations (on content) have halved the size of the industry. Currently, customer service accounts for only a fraction of 900 number traffic—yet usage is increasing. 13

EXHBIT 5–5
Applications of 900 Telephone Numbers

Application	1990	1993	Change (93–90)
Entertainment/Information	67%	50%	–17%
Personal/Datelines/Gablines	24%	26%	2%
Sports	10%	10%	0%
Financial/Credit	10%	4%	–6%
Games	8%	na	–8%
Adult	5%	3%	–2%
Miscellaneous	10%	7%	–3%
Direct Response/Transactional	21%	50%	29%
Messaging	na	12%	12%
Order entry/Fax	1%	10%	9%
Promotions/Sweepstakes	7%	6%	–1%
Consumer Consulting/Customer Service	2%	6%	4%
Fundraising/Cause related	3%	5%	2%
Polling/Surveying	6%	4%	–2%
Couponing/Sampling	2%	2%	0%
Miscellaneous	6%	5%	–1%

Sources: 1990–Strategic Telemedia; 1993–DMA Statistical Fact Book, 1992–93

Because of exploitation by some unscrupulous operators ("sex lines," promotion scams, and so forth) early in their market introduction, 900 numbers throughout the early 90s have carried a negative stigma among many consumers (particularly older ones). Beginning in 1990, state and federal legislators, the U.S. Postal Service, and the Federal Trade Commission were all investigating regulations to protect consumers against exploitative and unsavory 900 number applications.

Though entertainment and information lines held a large portion (67 percent) of the 1990 900 number market, by 1993 transactional services (at 50%) had caught up with these other uses (see Exhibits 5–4 and 5–5). *The Wall Street Journal, USA Today,* and even the prestigious *New York Times* are all currently offering 900 number services on related topics.

The long-term growth of 900 number services will likely be the result of audiotext service applications and aftermarketing applications. 900 numbers offer considerable potential for innovative aftermarketing applications.

Benefits of 900 numbers.   900 numbers can be used for some of the same purposes as 800 numbers, namely, to immediately exploit the consumer's interest in a product or service at the instant the interest is generated. Information is one thing many consumers do not mind paying for. Some sample applications include:

- *Sweepstakes.* A large number of packaged goods companies have had great success using 900 numbers as the entry or response mechanism for sweepstakes. Generally, the cost of the call is reimbursed (several times) by coupons for the sponsor's products. Such contests are advertised in point-of-purchase displays, magazine ads, and on-package announcements. Besides having the revenue generated help to offset costs of the contest, ANI systems allow easy capture of addresses and other demographics. ConAgra ran a sweepstakes poll in which consumers called to vote on their favorite Healthy Choice meal. By using 900 numbers in sweepstakes or promotions, a marketer can obtain immediate results, measuring the effectiveness of the plan before the promotion is over.

- *Value-Added Services.* Marketers are able to offer their customers or affinity groups information and help on a 900 line without bearing the substantial costs of the service by themselves. For example, *Gardener's Choice,* a cataloger of bulbs, seeds, and gardening supplies, had long used an 800 number for ordering and customer service. Now, they use a 900 number for all questions and requests for tips. *Parents* magazine has created a 900 advice line for parents presenting the views of the magazine's columnists. The expense of the service is offset by a 95-cent-per-call charge and the magazine has generated goodwill as well.

- *Product Delivery.* Digital Publications, a PC software producer, has developed an interesting way to sell its products using a 900 number. Rather than sending software programs to customers in the mail or by Federal Express, the customer simply calls Digital's 900 number. For $1 per minute, a PC program is downloaded (by modem) to the customer's PC. A customer can instantly receive a 266k-byte program for about $35 and Digital is guaranteed payment.

- *Customer Service.* Lotus Development Corporation gives its Lotus 1-2-3™ customers their first six months of support services for free. After that, the customer can either pay $179/year for unlimited use of an 800 number or pay $2/minute for 900 number help. Microsoft, another computer software firm, is also experimenting with 900 number customer support. Both of these applications are examples in which the customer should attribute enough personal value to the call that she will not mind paying for it. This assumes, of course, that the purpose of the call concerns a user's problem, not a problem in the software for which the manufacturer should bear responsibility.

- *Catalog Requests.* A number of catalogers are turning to 900 catalog request numbers to qualify leads and to help pay for the catalog and for shipping costs.

- *Fundraising.* A variety of fundraising groups are experimenting with 900 numbers for quick collection of donations and to help build donor databases. The Red Cross, for example, set up 900 lines to help it quickly raise money for victims of Hurricane Hugo and the San Francisco earthquake. The San Francisco ASPCA added an informational twist to its 900 fundraising line. Callers to a donation 900 PetLine receive the latest tips on proper animal care.

- *Dealer Location*. New audiotext technology makes it possible for callers to access a centralized 900 number to locate dealers and distributors in their immediate local area. Spalding, the sports manufacturer, used a dealer locator device to identify retailers for callers, who then visited the dealer to find out if they had won a sweepstakes.
- *Application Procedures*. Key Federal Savings Bank uses a 900 number to screen inquiries for credit card applicants. Those who become card members are reimbursed the charge of the telephone call.

The real advantage of 900 lines is that they can help a marketer share the cost of an aftermarketing service with its customers. This allows even the smallest companies to offer relatively sophisticated aftermarketing services, if their customers are willing to pay for them. However, customers will only pay for something to which they ascribe value, and for which they do not hold the marketer obligated to supply free of charge. Saatchi and Saatchi research has shown that successful 900 campaigns "were those that offered the consumer relevant information, immediate gratification, or met the need to feel secure, prepared, or competitive."[14]

Marketers are just beginning to explore customers' reactions to 900 number services. For example, Microsoft adopted a 900 number to service its "indirect customers" (purchasers of PCs whose manufacturers have licensed Microsoft software). The PC manufacturers are responsible for handling support for their systems, but some owners nevertheless call Microsoft. To remain available to these customers yet not lose money in servicing them, Microsoft adopted a 900 number operation. The line serves 150 to 200 people a day at a charge of $2 per minute, with the first minute free. The average call lasts about 6 minutes and nets Microsoft $7.50 (after the carrier's fees and taxes). This generated revenue covers approximately one-half to two-thirds of the operating costs of the facility.[15]

Another computer software firm, Buttonware, switched from answering calls for free over a toll line to a 900 number operation. The modest revenue generated (at only $1 a minute) allows the firm to hire better technical people. It was a choice of either increasing the selling price of its software products, or charging for calls for assistance. The line attracts 1,500 to 2,000 calls each month, each averaging 5.8 minutes in length. The revenue generated helps to defray the salaries of two of six technicians.[16]

Today's fast-growing technology makes the 900 number a multidimensional marketing weapon. There are services which can collect marketing information directly from the call itself. One of these is Automatic Number Identification (ANI). ANI service works to provide the telephone center with the phone number of each calling customer. With the caller's number automatically recorded as the call is made, an interactive number–address database can be tapped to provide immediate or after-the-call marketing information on the caller.

For example, the PRIZM 900™, offered at one time by Telesphere Communications and Claritas, used ANI technology to provide the caller's estimated demographics and behavior, including what they likely bought, what they watched on TV, what they read, and where they lived. This system was capable of providing immediate feedback on the types of customers responding to an offer or a service.[17]

Costs of a 900 operation. According to a telecommunications consultant, a 900 number information facility can be set up with as little as a $50,000 out-of-pocket expenditure.[18] And many of the telephone companies (AT&T for one) are offering much of the necessary equipment and services on an off-site, "pay-as-you-use" basis, further easing the start-up costs.

STRATEGIES FOR COMPLAINT HANDLING

Complaint handling is one of the very best examples of active customer relationship management. Unfortunately, no matter how good the established procedures are, only a small fraction of dissatisfied customers ever actually contact a company. Lele and Sheth identify the five things that can happen when a customer is unhappy:

- *The customer suffers in silence.* The next time the customer buys the product or service, he will already have a negative attitude and will be expecting and looking for problems.

- *The customer switches to another marketer in silence.* This is only a problem for the marketer who realizes she has lost a customer, but recognizing the loss provides no information on how or why.

- *The customer tells friends and neighbors about his dissatisfaction.* In this case, the firm stands to lose several customers, the original unhappy one and all the other people he influences.

- *The customer talks to third parties.* This is the worst outcome because it can lead to lawsuits or investigations and increased negative publicity.

- *The customer talks to the company.* This is the only positive outcome. It gives the company a second chance, the opportunity to understand the customer's needs, identify the problem and correct it, and ultimately to win back the trust of the customer.[19]

Studies show that only 4 percent (only 1 in 27) of dissatisfied customers ever complain. The other 96 percent simply go to another company, the vast majority (91 percent) of which will never come back. *However, if a customer's complaint is handled satisfactorily, there is a 90 percent chance that that customer will remain a customer.*[20]

EXHIBIT 5–6
Postures of Complaint Handling

The Company's Reception	The Company's Response	
	Defensive	*Corrective*
Passive	Defensive, deflects complaints	Reacts to needs
Active	Lip service illusionary	Aftermarketing, relationship mangement

Adapted from Millind Lele with Jagdish Sheth, *The Customer Is Key,* (New York: John Wiley & Sons, 1987), pp. 226–227.

Marketers are beginning to understand the importance of good complaint handling. A survey by Organizational Dynamics, Inc. showed that as many as 85 percent of the responding companies reported routinely tracking customer complaints.[21] Good complaint handling obviously increases customer satisfaction, and has been shown to increase brand loyalty and repeat purchases.

Each time a customer contacts a company to complain, the company has the opportunity to convert that dissatisfied customer into a satisfied customer, as well as the opportunity to collect valuable information. In so doing, a company can control problems before they are encountered by many more customers and thus lose market share.

Customers actually have two beliefs regarding a marketer:

- *An expectation of being satisfied.* They believe the marketer's product or service (they have purchased) will adequately satisfy a need or desire they have.
- *An anticipation of being appreciated.* They perceive that because they have supported a marketer by buying his product or service, he will respect them by providing them with aftersale servicing and assistance.

Not every company confronts the opportunities of complaint resolution with an aftermarketing perspective. Four different approaches can be anticipated (see Exhibit 5–6):

- *Defensive* means simply reacting to the customer, getting the confrontation over as soon as possible with a quick pacifier.
- *Lip service* is also a reactive process, soliciting the customer feedback but not taking actions to solve the problems or their causes.
- *Reacts to needs.* Taking a corrective action is good, but it is still reacting to customer-initiated complaints and not encouraging communication.
- *Aftermarketing* puts the company in an active role, encouraging communications and correcting problems.

How to Handle Complaints

Because properly handling complaints is so important, the major steps will be briefly discussed.

- Recognize and deal with the customer as another human being, a person with feelings, anxieties, even nerves.

Don't ever allow another issue or other thoughts to interfere with a concentration on the customer!

- Acknowledge the spirit of the contact without necessarily validating its accuracy. It is important to allow the customer to describe his problem completely. Complaint handlers should not interrupt even if they believe that they quickly understand the nature of the problem.

A 1983 study by Resnik & Harmon showed that consumers are more likely than managers to view complaints as legitimate and that regardless of legitimacy, consumers generally believe that some response is required.[22] Therefore, the first step a company must take is that of acknowledging the complaint and its importance. This affirmation of the importance of the complaint does not have to be an admission of guilt by the company. The complaint could be absurd, but the company should still dignify its customer by acknowledging the complaint.

- Express a sincere concern in the customer's problem and situation.

Companies can also convey the message that a customer's opinion is important by asking questions that generate real responses. Instead of asking, "Is everything satisfactory?" the company can ask, "What *one thing* can we do to make this better?"

- Clearly identify the customer's exact concern and understand precisely what has aggravated him.

The attentive complaint handler will wait until the customer has stopped his explanation. Then it is the complaint handler's opportunity to show she listened by restating the problem to seek the customer's agreement. It is important to let the customer know that his complaint is really being listened to. One way to do this is to let the customer know that his problem is being solved.

- A skilled correspondent should attempt to "neutralize" or "defuse" each complaint by taking the customer's side.

By simply acknowledging the complaint, the company has already begun to neutralize the anger of the complainant. But this response must carry the correct message. Customers want genuine attention, not a token or "form response." Responses must be sincere, and must not talk down to the customer. By taking the respondent's side, it will be clear what must be done and a sincere apology can be offered.

Part of the skill involved here will require getting the customer to focus on the present problem, rather than belaboring what has previously happened to them. By definition, a problem is a situation for which there is a solution. Changing the past is not a feasible solution.

- Offer a solution and get the customer's agreement that this will solve his problem. If the solution will take some time, provide a tracking system so the customer can participate in the resolution of his problem.

Not only should the customer be asked if he agrees that the agreed upon solution solves the problem, he should also be asked if he is satisfied and happy. If not, the complaint has not been satisfactorily resolved. For proper continuity, the customer should be told how to reach the same CSR for additional assistance in the matter, if necessary. These elements all assure proper closure of the problem.

- End with a sincere apology and a request for the customer's future business.
- Recontact the customer one week later to assess his satisfaction with the way his problem was handled and the solution the company provided.

Many companies have adopted a complaint handling monitoring system to check on the adequacy of their company policies and the performance of their complaint-handling personnel. Typical questions include the following:

1. Do you consider the response you received to be satisfactory? If not, why?
2. Did our customer service agent handle your call/letter courteously (and promptly)?
3. Have you ever contacted a company about a problem before?
4. If yes, does our company's response compare favorably to the responses you've received from other companies? If not, why?
5. As a result of our response to you, are you buying our products/services less frequently, more frequently, or about the same?*

The most important aspect of complaint handling is to engender within the organization a willingness to hear complaints. And then, rather than waiting for the 4 percent of the dissatisfied customers to come forward of their own volition, the organization *must actively invite customers to complain,* to help the organization identify and address its problems.

Getting Employees Involved in Proper Complaint Handling

Many employees have a reasonably appropriate fear of eliciting complaints, having been blamed for customers' expressed dissatisfaction in the past. This fear must be overcome and replaced with a commitment to hearing and responding to complaints. No matter how good the complaint-handling system is on paper, it

---

*Adapted in part from Clay Carr, *Front-Line Customer Service: 15 Keys to Customer Satisfaction,* (New York: John Wiley & Sons, 1990), pp. 60–64

will not work if employees don't understand the philosophy behind it and why it is so critical to solve the customer's complaint regardless of the marketer's actual liability.

> Folklore surrounding the Nordstrom Department Store chain includes the story of a Nordstrom customer service representative who addressed an angry customer's complaint about an unsatisfactory set of automobile tires she had purchased at the store. The CSR asked the customer to simply bring the tires in and her account would be credited...even though Nordstrom *doesn't sell auto tires!*

Generally it is useful to employ the following steps:

1. Help employees understand that complaints create opportunities and therefore are desirable. Train them to ask customers questions that will generate more response and to really listen to the answers.
2. Have an effective measurement, motivation, recognition system in place to encourage correct solicitation and collection of complaint information and correct complaint resolution. Reward for excellence in performance.
3. Hire employees who have a customer focus. Look among the employees that currently have a good complaint-handling record, and hire more just like them.

Ideally, every contact with a customer ought to be as personal as possible. Customer contact personnel should be coached to treat each customer as a personal friend in tone, in sincerity, and in seeking a just solution (if one is required). Characteristic of the right way to deal with customers are examples from three widely recognized firms, Stew Leonard's dairy store, the Nordstrom department store chain, and Orvis, a mail-order sporting goods supplier.

Stew Leonard's company policy (carved in a six-ton boulder at the Norwalk, Connecticut, dairy superstore's entrance) reads for both customers and employees alike:

> Rule 1. The customer is always right
> Rule 2. If the customer is ever wrong, reread rule 1.

Having expanded from its origin as a Seattle, Washington, family shoe business, the Nordstrom chain has made news based on its commitment to satisfying customers and its efforts to instill within its employees a similar dedication. Its operating philosophy is

> Listen to the customer; the customer is always right; do anything to satisfy the customer.

Orvis mail-order sporting goods company has a similarly precise policy on how to promote customer satisfaction:

> The customer is always right, even if you know damn well he is wrong. Replace, repair or adjust his [purchase] according to his wishes.

AFTERMARKETING WORKING
Customer Complaint Handling

Marriott is impressive in the way it handles complaints. The writer and his wife were asked to wait in a lounge outside the coffee shop of the Dulles Marriott because no tables were available. Twenty minutes elapsed and other guests were noticed walking in and getting seated. When the writer mentioned this to the host, he and his wife were seated immediately after profuse apologies. Apparently the hostess taking names earlier had gone off duty without leaving her list behind. When the bill arrived the host came over, took it, and said the breakfast was on the house.

During a later stay at the Stamford Marriott, there was a mix-up in the writer's bill which involved a 20-minute wait at the front desk. When no one apologized for the mix-up, the writer protested. Not only did the assistant manager offer an immediate apology, but she later phoned the writer at home to invite him back for a complementary stay. In both cases the Marriott personnel were not aware of the writer's affiliation with a travel magazine.

It is interesting, in contrast, to note how airlines respond to complaint letters. For example, a letter to Ron Allen, head of Delta, about the lack of information and poor arrangements for passengers on a canceled Delta Commuter flight was immediately answered by his vice president of management services. Then followed a letter of apology from the vice president of customer service of Comair, the Cincinnati-based commuter line that incurred the original annoyance.

A letter to Stephen Wolf at United about the inadequate facilities at United's Dulles midfield terminal and the lack of customer direction by its staff there drew a bland apology from a customer relations functionary with no promise to follow up.

Trick number one is to soothe the person who took the time to complain by having the highest-ranking person respond, even if the letter is prepared for him or her. The mere fact that a senior executive is personally interested sends a signal that the company is concerned about its customers.

Trick two is to answer the points raised in the complaint and not dodge the issues by sending out a pro forma apology. Marriott, with its excellent customer relations, not only gives satisfaction but insures repeat business. All businesses could profit from such a complete system.

Source: David Gollan, "Customer Complaints Should Be Promptly Addressed to Assure Their Loyalty," *Travel Agent Magazine,* November 6, 1989, p. 38.

ACKNOWLEDGING COMPLIMENTS

Defensively, most marketers are probably alert and responsive to complaints. After all, when a customer is angry, the enlightened marketer wants to extinguish the furor as quickly as possible. But what about happy customers? Since they are

---

AFTERMARKETING WORKING
How Jaguar Turned Complaints Around

In the 1960s and 1970s, Jaguar held a reputation for producing very unreliable cars. The saying was, "If you're going to buy a Jaguar, buy two—one to drive and the other for parts." In less than twenty years they were able to turn this image around, increasing overall customer satisfaction and repeat purchases.

Jaguar accomplished this feat through four key steps:

1. It acknowledged the problem; making it clear to dealers and customers alike that Jaguar knew their customers were concerned and that these concerns were valid, and that Jaguar had to take the responsibility to make changes.
2. It made necessary changes; changing its design and manufacturing procedures, dropping poor quality suppliers, and investing in new tooling and automation.
3. It communicated its commitment; offering longer, no-questions-asked warranties, doing performance comparisons, and providing individual attention to key corporate customers.
4. It backed up words with actions; bending over backwards to resolve complaints, terminating dealers with inadequate service facilities, setting up extensive testing facilities, and increasing parts warehousing and distribution.

Source: Milind Lele, with Jagdish Sheth, *The Customer Is Key: Gaining an Unbeatable Advantage Through Customer Satisfaction*, (New York: John Wiley & Sons, 1987), pp. 223–224.

---

already satisfied, the marketer's typical reaction may be to momentarily bask in the volunteered satisfaction and then attend to other concerns. After all, the praising customer's letter does not demand a response, and the customer is probably not expecting one.

Few marketers have consciously examined the role and value of compliment handling by American business. One study conducted in 1976 found that American businesses were more likely to acknowledge complaints than compliments (76 percent versus 61 percent).[23] A more recent study by Martin and Smart compares response times and content for compliments compared with complaints.[24] (These researchers actually sent both a compliment and a complaint to the same consumer packaged goods companies and tracked the responses they received.) The study examines speed of response, content of response, and origin of response for both communications.

Speed of Response

Both complaints and compliments tended to be answered to the same extent (about 85 percent, an apparent increase over 1976's levels). Three-quarters of the companies were consistent in their response to both forms of communication. And each type of communication was answered at about the same rate of speed, an average of 21 days.

Content of Response

Almost all responses were personally addressed, but there was significant variation in the specificity of the response depending upon the type of communication. While 73 percent of the responses to a complaint addressed the specific problem, only 21 percent of the compliment responses specifically mentioned the nature of the original compliment. Further, while praisers were universally thanked for their letters, 13 percent of complainers were not thanked. And, few marketers (only 13 percent and 5 percent, respectively) thanked the praisers and complainers for initially buying their product!

The researchers report scant effort to extend the customer's relationship with their organization by recommending additional products or by suggesting other uses or applications of the purchased product. Other characteristics of the responses are detailed in Exhibit 5–7.

Although the letters were addressed to the president or CEO, most responses came from elsewhere in the companies (only two praise letters and four complaints were signed by the president or CEO). The majority of responses (about 70 percent) were from nonmanagement personnel. The most frequent titles were: "Consumer Correspondent"; "Consumer Affairs Representative"; or "Customer Service Representative." Most companies answered both the praise and complaint letter at the same organizational level and by the same department.

THE MARKETING OPPORTUNITY OF SATISFIED CUSTOMERS

Satisfied customers represent a tremendous aftermarketing opportunity. *From an aftermarketing perspective, compliment handling is as critical to maintaining customers as complaint handling!* In the satisfied customer's compliment there may be an anecdote or a piece of valuable research information, or an example of customer language about the category, or maybe even an idea for a new use or usage occasion. Or there may simply be the opportunity to reinforce an already happy customer. *To not follow up on compliments may be as dangerous as not responding to complaints!*

The following procedure is recommended for compliment handling:

• Never allow a customer's compliment to go unacknowledged. Follow up on compliments with as much discipline as complaints are pursued. The only difference is to not impose on the complimenting customer's time to say "thank you." While a dissatisfied customer must be reached at the first available moment (and

EXHBIT 5–7
Nature of Responses to Praise versus Complaint

Response	To:	Compliment Letter	Complaint Letter
Personalized		97%	95%
Specicific to original issue		22	73
Reinforcement offered		92	83
Thanked for writing		100%	86%
Thanked for buying		14	5
Traded-up or cross-sold		32	24
Suggested other uses/applications		19	0
Included brochure		34%	30%
Included quest for information		3	10
Asked to write again		32	30
Suggested 800 telephone number		5	0
Monetary value of coupons		$0.50	$1.99

Adapted from: Charles L. Martin and Denise T. Smart, "Relationship Correspondence: Similarities and Differences in Business Response to Complimentary Versus Complaining Consumers," *Journal of Business Research* 17 (1988), pp. 155–173.

will, no doubt, bend her schedule to communicate with a marketer), a satisfied customer may consider acknowledgment communications less important. So the time and medium of follow-up should be carefully considered. Mail is probably a better choice for acknowledging compliments, though the telephone should not be overlooked, especially if the customer conspicuously lists her phone number. (A telephone call is also a nice way of showing a customer how much the company cares about her—enough to have her phone number, and enough to place a call!)

• Relate to the customer in a very personal, friendly way. Allow him to perceive himself as critical to the business of the company.

• Repeat his compliment and attempt to elicit it back from him. When a customer says something nice, it is important to rehearse him to say it as many times as possible. The more he says it, the more he will believe it and the more he is "innoculated" against future frustrations or peeves with the company.

• Attempt, if possible, to express the company's appreciation of the customer taking the time to forward his compliment. A small gift or merchandise coupon is always recommended *as a token of the marketer's appreciation.* Let him know that others have communicated their satisfaction as well. Do not make him think a compliment is so unusual that it is the reason he is being contacted. Also, explain the value of knowing what is working in the product or service.

• End the communication with an invitation to hear from him again in the future. Keep the door open; happy, communicative customers who feel an allegiance and loyalty to the company are one of the best competitive advantages a company can have.

KEY POINTS OF THE CHAPTER

800 telephone numbers. In 1992, more than two-thirds of all U.S. manufacturer's were offering 800 telephone numbers—a substantial increase from only 40% in the early 80s. The rate of growth was estimated at an amazing 30 percent per year! Because 800 telephone numbers allow customers toll-free communication with marketers, they are a very appropriate tool with which to achieve the accessibility goals of an aftermarketing program. It has been suggested that having access to a company by 800 telephone number reassures current customers about the company's interest in properly supporting its customers.

900 telephone numbers. A newer type of telephone service, the 900 telephone number allows a sharing of revenue from a telephone call between the telecommunications company and the marketer to whose offices the 900 number is connected. Typical costs to the consumer for a 900 number call range from $.75 to $4.00 per minute. Revenues on such calling rates can help considerably to fund many different types of support activities for customers. While 900 numbers were originally exploited by sleazy "date lines," it is believed that the potential of the service for unique support and sales opportunities is substantial. But each application must be well engineered and viewed as worth the charges assessed customers.

Appendix Five
ANALYSIS OF CUSTOMER COMMUNICATIONS

It is not enough to simply read and acknowledge customers' communications on an individual basis. A practitioner of aftermarketing must quantify and track the content and attitudinal direction of the communications received. Content analysis, an analytic technique born out of journalism, is an excellent procedure to use in developing a quantification system for customer communications.

Content analysis is explained by Kerlinger, a social scientist, as follows:

> Content analysis, while certainly a method of analysis, is more than that. It is...a method of *observation*. Instead of observing people's behavior directly, or asking them to respond to scales, or interviewing them, the investigator takes the communications that people have produced and asks questions of the communications.[25]

The basic idea behind content analysis is to try to objectively translate the *intent* and *perspective* of a communication into scores which can then be numerically processed. This requires establishing and identifying the following:

- *Coding units.* The smallest element of the communication which will be quantified. Units can be words, sentences, even paragraphs, depending on the marketer's judgment. (Obviously, the smaller the coding unit, the less sensitive the analysis is to context.)
- *Analytical categories.* Generally something is known of the likely nature of the communications to be received. Marketers will anticipate three general categories of directionality:
  - Positive.
  - Neutral.
  - Negative.

  These evaluations may be affixed to a variety of characteristics of the product:
  - The product itself (taste, aftertaste, freshness, etc.).
  - The price of the product.
  - The packaging of the product.
  - The preparation of the product.
  - Advertising for the product.

- *A coding sheet.* This form prelists all of the responses anticipated for each response to be analyzed. A coder simply reads a customer's comments and then searches the coding sheet to find a match. The numerical identity of the code for the meaning of the comment is entered into the record documenting the nature of the customer's communication. New characteristics can then be added as they appear in customers' comments providing the marketer with valuable contemporary information.

With the coding sheet established, daily or weekly tallies can be instituted to provide a concise summary of the favorableness of communications received, and the specific product characteristics prompting customer comment.

It may also be helpful to link some of the content analysis results with customer demography. Many corporate 800 number facilities will routinely request basic demographics. But even with mail responses, some demographic approximations can be made using a geodemographic database's statistics on a customer's zip code. Such a linkage could show, for example, that a preponderance of complaints about a specific characteristic of a product were related to zip codes with older consumers, with harder water, with more traditional values, and so on.

And although conventional content analysis has been extremely labor-intensive because of the manual coding of communications, computers are beginning to be harnessed for such analyses. Verbatim Analyzer™ is computer software for the personal computer which enables on-screen coding of free-response data.[26] With such computer software, it is conceivable that as a telephone service representative enters a caller's comments into her computer terminal, the program could scan the response for known words, key words, or concepts, and then identify the value-laden adjectives associated with these words or concepts. In such a case, a real-time content analysis would have been performed, and a description of the comments from a day's callers could be available at the end of the workday.

NOTES

1. Increasing evidence that customer outreach contributes to the bottom line: "For Customers, More Than Lip Service," *The Wall Street Journal,* October 6, 1989, p. B-1.
2. The study shows that Coca-Cola: "Resolve Buyer Beefs and Build a Cash Cow," *Industry Week,* November 1, 1982, pp. 72,74.
3. Industry sources report processing costs: personal communication, KGF and Dartnell Target Study, 1991, The Dartnell Corp., Chicago.
4. In mid-1989, there were as many as 300 major marketers: "Toll-Free Feedback," *USA Today,* May 1, 1989.
5. And, the number of lines is reportedly growing: "For Firms 800 is a Hot Number," *Wall Street Journal,* November 9, 1989, pp. B-1–B-6.
6. Over 9 billion or almost 25 percent are 800 calls: E. King, "Integrating Inbound-800," *Target Marketing,* March 1991, p. 20–21.
7. A 1988 survey conducted by the Society of Consumer Affairs Professionals: "More Marketers Using Customer Service 800 Numbers, Survey Shows," *Catalog Age,* May 1989, pp. 19–20.
8. Quaker's Cap'n Crunch "Find LaFoote" Sweepstakes: M.A. McNulty "Phone-In Offers Increase in The Reach Out and Touch Age," *Premium/incentive Business,* September 1988, pp. 28, 30.
9. And a TARP study collaborates this data: L. Liswood, *Serving Them Right,* New York, Harper Business, 1990, p. 58.
10. The percentage of complaints dropped 5 to 10 percent after one quarter: "Burger King Opens Customer Hot Line," *Marketing News,* Vol. 24, No. 11, May 28, 1990, p. 7.
11. Costs of a well equipped, well staffed 800 number facility: "For Firms, 800 Is a Hot Number," Wall Street Journal, November 9, 1989, pp. B-1, B-6.
12. This expense is defended by GE executives: B. Bowers, "For Firms, 800 Is a Hot Number."
13 .in 1991 with revenues of $980 million: "Expectations Lowered for 900 numbers," *Broadcasting & Cable,* October 25, 1993, p. 40 and "Customer Service Will Be a 900 Number Mainstay," *Telemedia News & Views,* November 1993.
14. Saatchi and Saatchi research has shown: "Pay-Per-Call Industry Eyes Marketers for Growth," *PROMO,* February 1991, pp. 23-24.
15. The generated revenue covers approximately one-half: "Pay-Per-Call Customer Support," *Business Marketing,* February 1991, p. 54.
16. Another software firm, Buttonware: "Pay-Per-Call Customer Support," *Business Marketing,* February 1991, p. 54.
17. For example, the PRIZM 900 service: "900 Numbers: Getting Down to Business," *Target Marketing,* February 1991, pp. 22, 25.

18. A 900 number, information facility: "Fun, Facts Fly Over Phone Lines As Market for Audiotext Explodes," *Wall Street Journal,* May 29, 1990, pp. B-1, B-4.
19. Lele and Sheth identify the five things: M. M. Lele with J. N. Sheth, *The Customer is Key: Gaining an Unbeatable Advantage Through Customer Satisfaction,* New York, John Wiley & Sons, 1987, p. 225.
20. Studies show that only 4% will complain: Technical Assistance Research Programs, Washington, D.C.
21. A survey by Organizational Dynamics: L. Liswood, *Serving Them Right,* New York, Harper Business, 1990, p. 6.
22. A 1983 study by Resnik and Harmon: A. J. Resnik, and R. R. Harmon, "Consumer Complaints and Managerial Response: A Holistic Approach," *Journal of Marketing,* Vol. 47, Winter 1983, pp. 86–97.
23. One study conducted in 1976: M. M. Pearson, "A Note on Business Replies to Consumer Letters of Praise and Complaint," *Journal of Business Research,* Vol. 4, February 1976, pp. 61–68.
24. A more recent study by Martin and Smart: C. L. Martin and D. T. Smart, "Relationship Correspondence: Similarities and Differences in Business Response to Complimentary Versus Complaining Consumers," *Journal of Business Research,* Vol. 17, 1988, pp. 155–173.
25. Content analysis, while a method of analysis: F. Kerlinger, *Foundations of Behavioral Research,* New York, Holt, Rinehart and Winston, Inc., 1964, p. 544
26. Verbatim Analyzer is PC software: T. Vavra, *Verbatim Analyzer: Response Processing Software,* Paramus, NJ, Marketing Metrics, Inc., 1988, (201) 599-0790.

Chapter Six

Establishing a Formal Dialogue
Satisfaction Measurement

The typical marketing organization receives enough correspondence from customers and the public to make it appear that substantial outreach is occurring. However, aftermarketing suggests that a stronger commitment be made not only to acknowledge customers' self-initiated reports, but also to establish a formalized satisfaction measurement program to actively assess the opinions of all customers.

On the surface, measuring customer satisfaction would appear to be one of the more simplistic of all aftermarketing tasks. One marketing researcher tells of a store in Minneapolis where the customer satisfaction survey is a simple note to the president, saying, "Hey, Chuck:" with five phrases to be selected from: (a) "I'm very impressed," (b) "I'm pleasantly surprised," (c) "I'm satisfied," (d) "I'm mildly infuriated," (e) "I'm very annoyed."[1] In Hong Kong, the prestigious Hotel Furama invites guests to nominate a hotel staff member who made the guest's stay at the hotel a "shining moment." And then there is the rather inviting card at the Bennigan's chain asking, "If you ran this restaurant, what would you do?" (Despite many a well-intentioned suggestion, the author has yet to hear back from this restaurant chain.)

Beneath the surface, customer satisfaction is very complex. It requires that the marketer know virtually everything about his product or service and how and why customers purchase it. Without this background knowledge, it is impossible to ask the appropriate questions to determine the customer's level of satisfaction.

In an aftermarketing program to build relationships with customers, one of the very first issues addressed with each individual customer must be, "How well are we satisfying you?" Insensitive communications to a dissatisfied customer are a waste of money and may even exacerbate the displeasure. Conversely, communications (even to a satisfied customer) which persist without inviting a dialogue for feedback may create frustration.

A customer satisfaction program has several values:

- It emphasizes *understanding* of the buyer-seller relationship.
- It focuses the corporation's perspective on *customer satisfaction,* not just on competitive offerings.
- It increases inspection of *how employees affect* customer satisfaction.

WHAT IS SATISFACTION?

If asked what would satisfy them most from a product or service, a large majority of consumers would no doubt respond, "receiving quality." But what is quality? Conventional wisdom defines quality as the following:

> "Consistently delivering products and services that fully meet consumer needs and expectations."

Admittedly, the process by which customers operationalize their judgments of quality is more subjective than a manufacturer's rigorous process for quality control. And yet customers' perceptions, no matter how subjective, are the reality of the market with which the marketer must deal. The customer's perception is all there is!

Quality is not only subjective, it is also relative. And competitors are constantly trying to up the ante, making their own products or services even better, and thereby forcing all players in a category to meet higher and higher standards.

Because quality relates to what customers expect from a product or service, it is necessary to understand how expectations are formed. Consumers feel needs or experience problems that a product or service is perceived to solve. Expectations from any particular product or service are established over time through experience. Expectations are a result of more than the product or service itself. The company's culture, advertising, sales, word of mouth information, and aftermarketing activities all help shape expectations (see Exhibit 6–1).

Interestingly, expectations will vary throughout a marketer's served market. They may:

- Vary by *type of customer* (demographic and benefit segmentation).
- Vary by *situation,* depending upon the use context (situational segmentation).
- Exhibit *relative degrees of importance* (hierarchical structures).
- Be *dynamic,* changing over time (tracking analysis).

Research in marketing and the social sciences repeatedly confirms the value of demographic segmentation. It is no less valuable in satisfaction surveys. Younger or more affluent customers have higher expectations than older or less affluent customers. Expectations may differ by other customer demographics as well.

Occasions can also significantly influence consumers' needs and expectations, and therefore their satisfaction. Research in situational segmentation has provided insight into the importance of the situational context in many different products and services.

There is also good reason to believe that hierarchies can exist within a set of needs. The need for peace and quiet in a businessperson's lodgings probably has greater importance than the quality of the breakfast food. Finally, expectations are dynamic; they change over time.

EXHIBIT 6–1
The Formation of Expectations

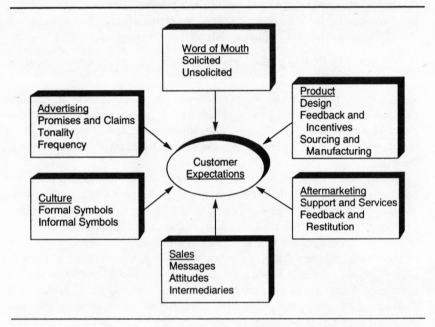

Every marketer who accepts the challenge of aftermarketing must dedicate himself to providing satisfaction. And offering products and services that satisfy requires an understanding of customers' expectations. That is why most good satisfaction measurement programs not only track levels of satisfaction, but provide an understanding of customers' expectations as well. These programs help marketers prioritize customers' expectations, and help to track shifts in their importance and the importance of underlying needs.

With this background in expectations, satisfaction may be defined quite simply as the extent to which customers' expectations about a product or service are met by the actual benefits they receive (perceived delivery in Exhibit 6–2).

Knowing which products and services meet customer expectations and needs has become a critical marketing survival tool employed by successful companies.

But what do customers really expect? Are their expectations realistic or idealistic? How much do customers have to have to be satisfied? Is it possible to maximize customer satisfaction without substantially increasing costs? The answers to these questions are key ingredients to understanding customer satisfaction and dissatisfaction.

There is, perhaps, a hierarchy existing between what consumers fantasize about and what they will actually settle for (see Exhibit 6–3). And there is even

EXHIBIT 6-2
Definition of Satisfaction

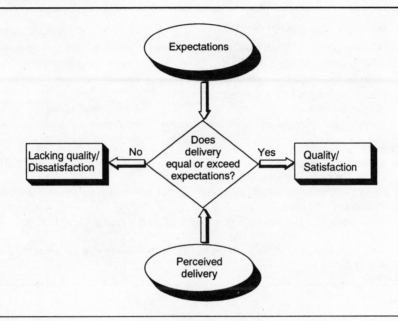

uncertainty about how expectations may influence experienced satisfaction. The naive view would suggest that the higher the expectation, the less likely complete satisfaction. But one of two social psychological theories disagrees with this commonsense understanding:

• *Consistency theory.* This surprising perspective suggests that expectations may be more important than performance, because consumers will try to avoid inconsistencies by shaping their perception of reality to match their expectations. That is to say, if their expectations are high, they will work hard to perceive their experience as satisfactory, rather than face an inconsistent outcome (high expectations; low delivery). This perspective would suggest that marketers need not worry about overpromising because the more customers expect, the more likely they are to try to have reinforcing experiences.

• *Assimilation and contrast.* In this somewhat more expected view, consumers are described as either exaggerating (contrasting) or minimizing (assimilating) differences of experience with expectation. The more involved the consumer, the more likely she is to demand to receive exactly the level of satisfaction she expects. Otherwise a small shortfall will be exaggerated, producing substantial dissatisfaction.

EXHIBIT 6–3
Sequence of Expectations and Goals

a. What customers desire	Customers' needs/expectations
b. What customers think will be offered	Customers' modified expectations
c. What customers perceive is offered	Customers' perceptions
d. What the factory (delivery point) produced	Reality
e. Management's goals for product/service quality performance	Management's goals
f. Management's perceptions of customers' desires	Management's vision

Possible Discrepancies

1. Letter *f* is predicated on management's understanding of *a*, but management's understanding of customers' desires can be wrong.
2. Letter *e* will no doubt include some compromises that management has made for cost or other considerations.
3. What is delivered in *d* will often be something different (perhaps less) from that envisaged in *e*.
4. What customers perceive in *c* will necessarily be different from what is actually delivered in *d*.

A HISTORY OF CUSTOMER
SATISFACTION MEASUREMENT

The ability of a company to satisfy customers may be its most important after-marketing attribute. Because of the importance of satisfying customers, it is critical to have a satisfaction measurement program in place to objectively monitor how well the organization is doing.

A customer satisfaction program may be referred to as *CSM* (customer satisfaction measurement), *CSP* (customer satisfaction program), or *CSI* (Customer Satisfaction Index). CSI is a term that has become widely recognized in the automotive industry. Japanese auto manufacturers are often credited with the emerging focus on consumer interests and satisfactions. Examples given are:

- The sales successes of Japanese automobile manufacturers in the American market.
- Japanese cultural values that place importance on respect for the individual customer.

Customer satisfaction has been most actively marketed in the United States by the consulting firm J. D. Power & Associates. In 1969 Power started conducting and publishing his multimanufacturer findings. The Power CSI is a cross-industry measurement of customers' satisfaction with their new cars within three to six months of purchase. Based on responses from up to 30,000 automobile purchasers a year, Power ranks automobile manufacturers according to how well they score on customer satisfaction.

To supplement the information from Power's industry survey, many automobile manufacturers, including Rolls-Royce, Ferrari, Toyota, Hyundai, and Ford have developed customer satisfaction programs of their own. They recognize that in order to produce a *quality* product, to get customers to become repeat customers, and to get customers to recommend their automobile to potential customers, *they must invite an open dialogue with their customers*.

> The Ford Motor Co. reports that it surveys upwards of 2.5 million customers a year and regularly invites owners to meet with both engineers and dealers to discuss quality problems. Ford has also designed a software system that makes it easier for executives and engineers to use customer satisfaction data.[2] In the words of Ford's former chairman, Donald E. Petersen, "If we aren't customer-driven, our cars won't be either!"[3]

Other industries besides the automotive industry have similarly discovered CSIs and have become very active in customer satisfaction programs:

- Du Pont Company's top management has been trying since the mid-1980s to better adapt the company's technological achievements to customer needs. Du Pont's Chairman, Edgar S. Woolard, has instituted a policy of customer visits by Du Pont technicians and salespeople.[4]
- Marriott spent $5 million in 1993 conducting over 200 different marketing research projects, most directed at listening to customers.[5]

The Value of a Customer Satisfaction Program

Business leaders verbally acknowledge the value of customer satisfaction. From a previous era, the ubiquitous phrase "The customer is always right" expresses a similar commitment. Yet despite these directives, companies truly committed to customer satisfaction may be more the exception than the rule.

In their 1985 book *A Passion for Excellence,* Tom Peters and Nancy Austin investigated the strategy of customer satisfaction. The authors conducted a seminar with 40 company presidents. All the presidents agreed on the importance of long-term customer satisfaction. In fact, it was considered their number one priority. The authors then asked how many of them actually measured customer satisfaction. The answer was surprising. Not one of these 40 presidents had a formal program in his or her company for measuring satisfaction!

This audit was replicated by Peters with a new group of 132 executives, 94 of whom were presidents of small or medium-sized companies. The results were identical; although all 132 ranked long-term customer satisfaction most important, none currently measured it!

AFTERMARKETING NEEDED
A Satisfaction Survey Doesn't Mean You Are Customer Driven

Researcher Bill Neal tells the following story of a client who professed a commitment to customer satisfaction. In a visit to a manufacturing company, Neal reviewed its marketing information systems (of which the president was quite proud). Included was a continuous survey of customers, a kind of warranty follow-up program. The manager of quality assurance received the returned questionnaires and his secretary was assigned to review them and pass on any comments that seemed interesting. All of the questionnaires were then stored in a closet temporarily.

The secretary appeared to carry out her responsibility in the following way. When there was an especially favorable comment, or in some cases when there was a disparaging comment about one of the manager's rivals in the firm, that comment was passed on to the executive vice president, who sometimes passed the comment on to the president. About once every six months a sample of questionnaires was drawn from the growing stacks in the closet and was sent to data processing for data entry and report generation. About two months later, a report was available showing totals and the percent of totals for each of this company's product lines.

Despite the sporadic and biased conduct of this survey, both the president and the executive vice president, who frequently spoke in public, bragged about how they were driven by quality and how they continuously surveyed their customers to make sure their products were of the highest possible quality.

In all too many cases this example typifies companies' "commitment" to customer satisfaction. The company was not really doing a good job of monitoring satisfaction. Its survey was loaded with biased questions, most dealing with competitive information or demographics. Only two questions actually dealt with customer satisfaction at all. One was, "How satisfied are you overall?" and the other was open-ended, "Why are you satisfied, or dissatisfied?"

Source: William Neal, "So You've Done a CSM Survey, Now What Do You Do with the Data?" American Marketing Association and The American Society for Quality Control's Conference on Customer Satisfaction and Quality Measurement, March 11–13, 1990.

In 1988 Dun & Bradstreet determined that approximately half of 5,000 firms they surveyed had implemented some type of customer satisfaction effort. In the 1994 survey reported in Appendix 1, a similar 46% of U.S. businesses reported customer satisfaction surveys as a retention tool they utilize.[6]

Competent aftermarketers must have established programs to measure how satisfied their customers are. More than 90 percent of all dissatisfied customers will not exert the effort to contact a company on their own to express their dissatisfaction. They simply take their business to a competitor. TARP estimates that only 1 in 27 dissatisfied customers will ever contact a marketer of their own volition.[7] However, they are not so silent about their dissatisfaction among their friends and neighbors. In fact, the zeal with which they spread word of their dissatisfaction appears almost vendetta-like. The damage dissatisfied customers cause marketers among other current and potential customers can only be estimated.

There is also some very compelling hard evidence about the bottom-line value of satisfying customers. The Profit Impact of Marketing Strategies project of the Strategic Planning Institute of Cambridge, Massachusetts, shows that financial performance is directly tied to the perceived quality of a company's goods or services. The data also suggest that one of the most powerful tools for shaping the perceptions of overall quality is customer service.[8]

Most business marketers know the 80/20 rule: a small proportion (10 to 40 percent) of a company's customers usually account for a disproportionately large share (60 to 90 percent) of its sales. Although all customers ought to be satisfied, these valuable heavy users must especially be kept satisfied, or a disproportionately large share of business is in jeopardy.

Companies need to have external measures of customer satisfaction for any or all of the following reasons:

- Customer satisfaction is often equated with quality.
- Commitment to a customer satisfaction program demonstrates leadership in a category.
- Internal measurements of customer satisfaction may be inadequate or inappropriate.
- Companies can benefit from listening to an objective voice of the market.
- Many customers do not overtly complain because they may feel that nothing will be done.
- A customer satisfaction program is a powerful tool compelling improvement.
- Competitors may already have successful satisfaction programs of their own.

Some believe that measuring customer satisfaction may be what distinguishes very successful companies from less successful ones. John Brooks, in his book *Telephone: The First Hundred Years,* summarizes the importance of the customer satisfaction movement:

"Talking to customers tends to counteract the most self-destructive habit of great corporations, that of talking to themselves."[9]

Discussed below are some case studies, examples of companies that have successfully measured customer satisfaction and have used what they have learned.

Rolls-Royce Motor Cars. Rolls-Royce Motor Cars has long been associated with superior customer service and therefore strong customer satisfaction. So sure of their motorcar are the craftsmen of Crewe, England, that they proudly boast, "No Rolls-Royce has *ever* broken down!" (They do admit, however, that on rare occasion, one has been known to *fail to proceed!*) Given the mystique surrounding the marque and the admittedly high expectations many people bring to Rolls-Royce ownership, monitoring customer satisfaction has always been given high priority. The format of this monitoring has changed over the years, evolving into its present sophisticated form.

Rolls-Royce Motor Cars has four objectives for its worldwide CSI program:

- To monitor the performance of the motorcar (that is, owners' satisfaction with their motorcars).
- To assess the activities of its dealers in representing the company.
- To track the demographic and psychographic composition of its owners.
- To communicate to its owners its interest in establishing and maintaining an open dialogue with them.

The Rolls-Royce CSI program is conducted by mail, with personalized letters. The program includes two formal measurement points:

- At delivery of the new Rolls-Royce or Bentley (a questionnaire arrives by first-class mail within 14 days of the delivery of the car).
- After six months of ownership.

Once owners' demographic information is entered into its CIF, there are numerous opportunities for informal surveys to collect information of a special nature, for a specific purpose.

The initial delivery questionnaire is relatively short, collecting car ownership information, demographics, and evaluations of the dealer's handling of the sale and delivery of the motorcar. Owners returning this questionnaire receive a Rolls-Royce writing pen and a thank you letter inviting them to contact Rolls-Royce Motor Cars at any time. If an owner expresses any lack of satisfaction with the motorcar or the dealer, a contact operation is immediately begun. This means that a company executive will be assigned to contact and solve the owner's problem. Follow-up will be included at a later time to make sure the owner agrees that the problem has been solved.

The six-month questionnaire is much longer—six pages to be exact! The questionnaire assesses characteristics of luxury cars and asks owners to rate their Rolls-Royce or Bentley against another luxury auto they currently own or have previously owned on these characteristics. (The competitive ratings provide an excellent internal benchmark.) In addition, the questionnaire requests a wealth of psychographic and lifestyle information which has served the company well in numerous different applications.

Owners returning the six-month questionnaire are similarly thanked and sent a Rolls-Royce lapel pin. And any owner stating less than total satisfaction is immediately contacted by a company executive.

Owners who do not return either questionnaire after the first mailing are remailed the questionnaire with a letter pleading for their participation in the program. In all, the program involves about 65 percent of each year's purchasers in either survey and over both questionnaires includes opinions from almost 80 percent of a year's Rolls-Royce and Bentley purchasers!

Twice a year, two management reports are prepared and distributed: the owner profile and the dealer profile. The owner profile describes the typical owner and tracks overall satisfaction with the motorcar and dealers. The dealer profile is a very specific report, specially prepared for each authorized dealership to show how the dealership performed in the eyes of its customers.

One of the reasons for the program's success is the extent to which it has become assimilated into the corporate culture. Rolls-Royce Motor Cars executives have learned the value of the program from two different perspectives. First, they have developed an appreciation for the value of the survey in alerting them to problems at a very early stage. Such information can be quickly fed back to production and can be distributed to field service managers to immediately remedy problems in the field.

Dealers have also developed an appreciation for the value of seeing themselves through their customers' eyes. In a number of test cases, Rolls-Royce dealers have been shown how their customers' opinions of their operations can actually be increased once they have identified their dealerships' shortcomings. (Interestingly, customers' problems are not always focused on the same aspects of a dealership's operations as dealers might imagine, and this is part of the value of the survey.)

While Rolls-Royce Motor Cars Inc. (the U.S. arm of the company) is a relatively small office, a quality assurance department has been adequately staffed since the mid-80s. It is the role of this office to serve as internal ombudsman in disseminating the results of the CSI, and then work with internal areas and dealers to remedy general operational problems, as well as to solving specific instances of owner dissatisfaction.

From an aftermarketing perspective, the openness and accessibility of the company's chief executives to their owners is truly exemplary.

Marriott Hotels. Marriott has established itself as intensely committed to the measurement of its customers' satisfaction with its hotels and resorts. Its Guest Satisfaction Index program is conducted and reported at both a regional and national level.

Satisfaction during a guest's stay is monitored by means of an in-room Help Ideas card. These suggestion cards are strategically placed near the television or telephone in each room to maximize visibility to guests. The card invites the guest to register problems or ideas he or she may have with the room and its appointments. The card is usually returned to the front desk, but may also be returned to the hotel by USPS business reply mail. All returned cards are reviewed by the local guest services manager. When problems are identified, the appropriate department head (within the hotel) will be contacted to take corrective action.

Each current guest raising a problem or concern will be personally contacted by the guest services manager to resolve the issue and to show that the hotel has read and has acted on the problem.

Satisfaction after the stay is measured both through an on-site express checkout Guest Comment Card and by a telephone satisfaction interview later. The Guest Comment Card is distributed to each guest's room on the last night of his or her stay. It invites departing guests to voice satisfactions and any problems experienced during their stay in a Marriott property. The resident guest services manager is responsible for reviewing the cards, taking action on the issues raised, and informing each guest raising a problem or concern of the actions (and, if necessary, sending Marriott's apology).

Each Marriott property has a business plan that specifies GSI goals. Results are posted conspicuously (for employees) throughout each Marriott hotel. For example, current ratings may be posted on the employee side of the front desk. This visibility serves as a constant reminder of the importance of customers' reactions and the goals of the specific hotel. At monthly staff meetings within each hotel, the guest services manager will review results with other department heads. Action plans may be formulated to correct particularly persistent problems. Heads of departments cited for dissatisfaction will be urged to take corrective actions.

On a chainwide level, the MARSHA computerized reservation program periodically selects a random week for each Marriott property per month. A sample of guests from within that week is also randomly drawn. Each guest selected will be interviewed (generally by mail but occasionally by telephone). All completed questionnaires are analyzed at the corporate level with each hotel's standings posted on a three-month rolling average basis. On the basis of these scores, the Marriott hotels are ranked nationally and regionally. Poor performers will be visited by the regional general manager and an executive team. During the visit, the hotel's action plans will be reviewed and modified if necessary.

Guests who express dissatisfaction in the survey are identified to the hotel's guest services manager, who will personally contact them. The letter or contact will be specific to the actual problem mentioned; it will not be a form letter. A unique aspect of the contact is the way the problem will be resolved. The guest will choose the resolution he or she desires. In this way, Marriott maximizes the ultimate satisfaction of each problem.

American Express.   American Express developed a service tracking report for its credit card operations. This system measures the impact of all departments' actions on customers. In addition to these internal measurements, AMEX follows up over 20,000 transactions with customers to see how they rate the treatment they have received. If their reputation as the top credit card company in customer service is faltering, AMEX management wants to know immediately.

WHAT A CSP IS AND HOW IT CAN BE ESTABLISHED

A customer satisfaction program serves an important aftermarketing function by focusing on interaction with customers. In very general terms, a customer satisfaction program usually does several things:

- It establishes a *formal linkage* between the business unit's R&D, production, and managerial functions with customers through a formalized program of *invited* customer feedback.
- It consists of an information collection procedure, usually an *outbound survey,* and often an established mechanism for processing and responding to *inbound customer feedback.*
- The CSP may be overseen by an external consultant or auditing firm.
- It is quantitative in its ultimate form, though it may have qualitative subcomponents.
- It monitors customer satisfaction with the
  - *Product or service.*
  - *Delivery system.*
  - After-sale *service system.*
- The CSP helps to establish goals to increase the satisfaction provided to customers and provides longitudinal feedback for monitoring progress.

The customer satisfaction program is a reality check on the product(s) and business practices of the company. It forms a bridge between marketing management and quality management, providing feedback to support modification of products and practices to put them into better alignment with customers' needs and desires. Exhibit 6–4 shows its role.

A number of prerequisites should be achieved before beginning to actually measure customer satisfaction:

- Get support and input from top management. Getting this support before the program is initiated will help later, when management's belief in the program will be necessary for it to turn the results into actionable strategy. Hyatt president Thomas J. Pritzker emphasizes, "Management has to set a tone and then constantly push, push, push!"[10]

- Define the appropriate customer segments:
  - New, first-time customers.
  - Current customers.
  - Future customers.

EXHIBIT 6—4
The Role of the Customer Satisfaction Program

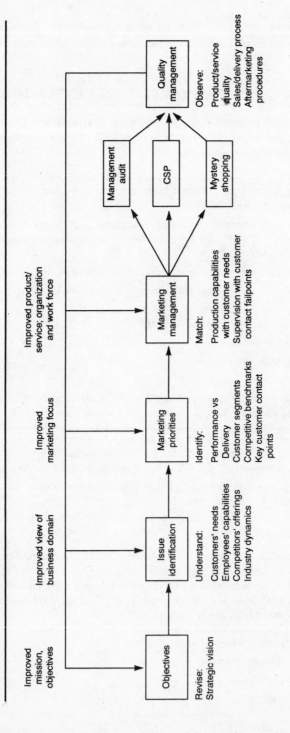

- Lapsed customers.
- Decision makers (from within customers' organizations).
- Users, buyers, influencers, and so forth (from within customers' households).
- Decide how to link the program to internal reward and incentive systems.

DESIGNING THE CSP

A six-step process is recommended that covers the most pertinent steps in establishing an effective customer satisfaction measurement program:

  I. Defining the Objectives for the Program.
 II. Selecting the Fielding Method.
III. Sampling and Timing.
 IV. Designing the Questionnaire.
  V. Pretesting the Questionnaire.
 VI. Analyzing and Reporting Results.

I. Defining the Objectives for the Program

There is nothing more vital to the success of a CSP than accurately identifying the areas and issues to be monitored. Defining the objectives for a program includes the following:

- Identifying the specific issues to be measured and establishing an importance hierarchy among them.
- Agreeing upon organizational operating practices that the survey results will be used to influence.
- Determining who is to be surveyed.
- Identifying who internally will use the data.
- Visualizing how the collected information can most effectively be reported.

It is often true that answers to some of management's questions may already exist in secondary data. Secondary data can include the company's own internal records as well as government and syndicated reports and trade publications. A search through secondary sources is often helpful, as well as cost effective, prior to embarking on primary research.

The perspective: Internal or external? Operational departments within an organization are too often allowed to dictate the informational goals of a satisfaction survey. By allowing this to happen, the resulting CSP may become unfairly myopic, exploring only problems as defined from within, but insensitive to problems and issues from the customer's viewpoint.

The conflict becomes one between a *functional orientation* (an internal perspective) and a *transactional orientation* (a customer perspective). In establishing a CSP, ready lists of questions will frequently be offered by internal managers to assess how well internal programs are functioning. However, these lists can quite often narrow the questioning process, excluding insights identified from a consumer's perspective. Emphasizing consumer input, even at the risk of omitting internal management's questions, is generally recommended.

Methods for identifying the issues. Current customer correspondence (both complaints and compliments) is a rich source of topics for the CSP. Without drawing conclusions on the absolute importance of an issue, it can be judgmentally included or deleted. However, while correspondence can be extremely useful, it should not be the only source of issues to be included.

Focus groups and in-depth interviews are both useful procedures for broadening the list of issues. Focus groups, though subject to the difficulties of group dynamics, are favored by many as the more useful practice with which to generate exhaustive lists of issues. Their selection is based on the positive benefits of focus groups, including synergism among participants, idea snowballing, stimulation of idea exchange, freedom of spontaneity, and the speed with which they can be completed. It is often useful to conduct groups both among customers and among employees (as discussed in Chapter 4).

In sensitive situations or with products or services conveying some social significance, personal in-depth interviews may provide more honest responses. In-depth interviews generally require more effort to conduct and synthesizing their results may require more management intuition.

Once enough issues have been identified, they must be assigned priorities, as it is unlikely that all can be addressed in a single questionnaire. (Very often marketers will design a CSP with several questionnaires, administered at different times, allowing them to collect a greater amount of information than would have been practical in only one measuring instrument on only one measurement occasion.)

The issues must also be scrutinized for the effect of order on results. Some issues if asked before others may influence respondents' answers. Hence, a logical sequence among issues must be devised. This sequence may even specify some questions as lower-priority, to be answered by respondents only if time allows.

Generally, questions should be asked about the following:

• The delivery system for the product or service.
• The performance of the product or service.
• The general image of the company or organization.

EXHIBIT 6–5
Comparison of Field Procedures

	Mail	*Telephone*	*In Person*	*Computer*
Cost	Low	Moderate	High	Low
Turnaround time	Slow	Fast	Moderate	Moderate
Cooperation rate	Low	Moderate	High	High
Geographic coverage	Excellent	Excellent	Difficult	Excellent
Interviewer bias	None	Substantial	Substantial	None
Interviewer supervision	None	Excellent	Poor	Excellent
Quality of response	Poor	Better	Best	Better
Questionnaire structure	Simple	Complex	Complex	Complex
Who's in control?	Respondent	Interviewer	Interviewer	Computer
Obtrusiveness	Low	High	High	Low
Can cope with interruptions	Easy	Difficult	Difficult	Easy
Length of interview	Short	Medium	Long	Long

Source: Marketing Metrics, Inc.

- The perceived price-to-value relationship of the product or service.
- Employees' performance.
- Competitors' strengths and weaknesses.

(There is also the opportunity to capture demographic and psychographic information on customers as well.)

It often helps to organize the questioning procedure very explicitly on these six topics to guide respondents' consideration and answering.

II. Selecting the Fielding Method

There are two basic response formats with which to collect the identified information:

- Self-administered.
- Interviewer-administered.

and there are several methods for fielding large-scale CSP studies (see Exhibit 6–5):

- Through the mail.
- By telephone.
- In person (often at the place of business or as the service is rendered).

Each field method has its own advantages in terms of time, cost, accuracy, versatility, convenience (to the respondent), and resulting cooperation rates.

The element of control is more important than it may appear. There are situations in which information may need to be sequentially revealed. In a self-administered questionnaire there are no sure ways of preventing respondents from looking ahead, and they very likely will do so.

Every study needs to be evaluated individually to determine which of the four fielding methods is best. For customer satisfaction studies, the most frequently used format is the mail survey. This allows for the largest number of respondents at the lowest cost. It is also the least labor-intensive method. However, there are newer methods being devised. One of the more interesting is administering the survey by computer, either where the service is delivered using a specially programmed terminal, or by sending a programmed interview on a computer diskette directly to customers at their businesses or homes.

It is generally believed that the most accurate information is obtained when the interview is completed on neutral ground (for example, the customer's home or office). A hotel chain found that even though in-room surveys seemed the most expedient method for monitoring its guests' satisfaction, the cooperation rate was low; completed questionnaires appeared hurriedly filled out (as guests departed), and guests had not properly organized their thoughts or reactions. Even though it was more costly, this chain decided to conduct its CSP survey after its guests returned home. Interviewers contacted guests a few days later by telephone and asked for their evaluation of the hotel. Responses were considerably more substantive than those from the previous in-room, self-administered version.

However, there are situations when the sheer convenience of having customers assembled in one place makes immediate administration of the CSP logistically unavoidable. It is also possible to distribute the questionnaire when customers are gathered together and to ask them to complete the form later. The only drawback to this strategy is the likelihood of a low response rate.

In designing the CSP questionnaire, the questionnaire itself should be thought of as yet another opportunity with which to interact with customers. This suggests that special attention be given to the appearance and production values of the entire CSP packet:

- The cover letter or verbal introduction.
- The appearance of the questionnaire or the conduct of the verbal interview.
- The wording of questions.
- The reply mechanism (a prepaid USPS business reply envelope, overnight courier service, or telephone interview).

In conducting a CSP by mail, a personalized cover letter, where practical, generally works best. Nothing destroys the goodwill opportunities of a CSP as subtly and yet as thoroughly as a preprinted, general "Dear Customer" cover letter with a facsimile signature. To show concern and interest, the correspondence accompanying a CSP should be as personalized as possible.

An incentive or gratuity is always recommended for CSP questionnaires. An incentive accomplishes two very important goals:

- It acknowledges the respondent's effort in completing and returning the CSP questionnaire.
- It furthers the customer's affiliation with the company both through the pleasure of receiving a gift and, where possible, by receiving a gift with company or corporate identification (affinity merchandise).

When the marketer actually sells affinity merchandise, using the corporate-identified merchandise as an incentive can also make customers aware of the availability of such affinity products for their subsequent purchase.

It is important that the incentive never be positioned as fair payment for the effort involved. It should be offered only as a token of appreciation. Small amounts of money should be avoided. A quarter affixed to a cover letter or to a questionnaire (even a dollar bill to some respondents) cheapens the whole process.

Gratuities also raise the issue of when to present the gift. There are two possibilities: pre-incentivating (sending the gift with the request for information) or post-incentivating (delaying the gift until a completed questionnaire is received). The most cost-effective method is post-incentivating only those who return completed questionnaires. This requires follow-up correspondence (to fulfill the gift). Although it adds expense, this fulfillment should be looked upon as yet another point of interaction with the customer.

Watch the content and tone of the letter accompanying the gratuity. It ought to acknowledge the basic satisfaction reported in the returned questionnaire. (A standard thank you letter that fails to acknowledge the basic direction of the respondent's evaluation will suggest uncaring or, worse yet, inattention to the contents of the returned questionnaire.) On the other hand, if a customer reports real dissatisfaction, the marketer will wish to study the conditions first before acknowledging actual responsibility. So the wording of the acknowledgment must be carefully chosen and noncommittal.

Who should conduct the survey.   It is often a good idea to bring in an objective third party to help in the development and implementation of a customer satisfaction program. Such an external consultant will likely bring extensive experience to the establishment of a program as well as an external, unbiased perspective that might be difficult to obtain from internal staff members. Before selecting a consultant, consider these questions:

- Does the consultant have experience with programs of a similar size and scope?

- Does the consultant have experience with CSPs for both products and services?
- Is the consultant a full-service provider; i.e. qualitative and quantitative, primary and secondary research?
- Can the consultant establish and maintain an intelligent database to drive the interactive correspondence necessary to elicit high cooperation rates?

It is very often the case that a program conducted by an external group will receive a higher response rate. The fact that a third party has been retained may convey a stronger commitment on the sponsor's behalf to potential respondents. It may also suggest a more objective measurement process. Also, respondents sometimes feel that their identity is safer in the hands of an external auditor.

III. Sampling and Timing

Sampling involves two considerations:

- The type and size of the sample.
- The method for selecting the sample.

To decide on the size of the sample, the marketer should carefully consider the role to be played by the CSP. If the role of the program is purely informational (to monitor satisfaction for strategic planning), a statistical sample of customers will be sufficient. If, however, the role of the program is to provide evidence to each customer of the marketer's desire to satisfy all of its customers, then nothing less than a complete census will do.

When a sample is to be drawn, a probability sample is recommended. This requires the marketer to have a database of all her customers to serve as the population. In certain situations, it may be desirable to stratify the sample by model lines, products, or sales regions. In such cases, a prespecified proportion of interviews will be allocated to each model or line (the strata) in proportion to the sales accounted for by the model, line, product, or sales region.

The size of the necessary sample will be influenced by the following:

- Considerations of statistical significance (how large individual subsamples should be to determine the statistical significance of different levels of outcome).
- The size of the budget and the cost of each additional interview.

Costs for interviewer-administered surveys over the telephone (the most expensive procedure other than personal interviews, which are not generally recommended) will probably run $10 to $25 per completed interview. Interviews administered by mail will run much less, probably only $4 to $10 per each completed interview.

Who and when to survey. The design of a survey must be specific about who is to be included and at what stage of customer experience they will be contacted. The sample may contain current customers, past customers, even competitors' customers. Customers sampled should obviously represent all product lines, as well as each organizational and geographic division of the business.

Surveying *new buyers* reinforces their purchase by showing them the marketer cares about them. They are also the best source of evaluations of the product or service purchased and the delivery experience. *Existing customers* should also be contacted at times coincidental with specific conditions in the customer's life (such as at purchase, after six months, or at the end of the warranty period). Some organizations regularly poll a random sample of existing customers in periodic surveys to track how the company and product or service are performing over time.

Past customers and customers of competitors also offer valuable perspectives from which to better understand the opinions of current customers.

Communicating at regular intervals with customers keeps an organization in touch with what is going on and alerts the marketer to any problems that might be arising.

An effective CSP program should be conducted continuously. Surveys should not be mailed in one lump sum once a year, but monthly, quarterly, or at a minimum semiannually. This will help provide a constant reading of changes in the marketplace.

Although a one-time study may be revealing and useful, the ongoing tracking of customer satisfaction levels will:

- Monitor progress.
- Spot developing weaknesses before they become major problems.
- Provide a basis for rewarding consistently good performance.

Experience with any customer group over time will suggest improvements to make the timing of measurements more useful and the type of customers interviewed more relevant.

IV. Designing the Questionnaire

No matter how well planned the CSP, the weakest link will be the questionnaire and the fielding procedure. (This is the stage at which an external consultant's experience will be most helpful.)

The issue of questionnaire design is extremely complex. The major issues can be summarized as the following:

- The *length* of the questionnaire.
- The *organization* of the questionnaire.
- The *type of questions* to be asked.

- The use of *open-end questions.*
- The *appearance* of the questionnaire.

Questionnaire length.   Nothing should be considered more important than controlling the length of the questionnaire. Marketing researchers are repetitively asked, "What is the maximum length of a questionnaire?" The invariable answer is, "It depends." Marketing research folklore holds that a self-administered questionnaire shouldn't exceed two pages, and a telephone interviewer-administered questionnaire 15 minutes. But in actuality, given the right questions and an introduction that identifies the value of the survey to the participant, cooperation can be extended to much longer questionnaires and interviews.

Questionnaire organization.   Regardless of whether the questionnaire is self-administered or interviewer-administered, clear organization and order are critical to eliciting good answers from participants. The questionnaire ought to be divided into informational sections, to help respondents adjust their thoughts to each topic. The division by topics can be shared with respondents in the form of explanatory introductions to questions, such as "Now we're interested in your ideas about different automobile companies." *There is no value in keeping respondents guessing or uncertain about why they are being asked the questions they are asked.*

Skip patterns in a self-administered questionnaire should be kept to a minimum and, when used, should be well explained and implemented with arrows and other visual aids. Questionnaires should avoid use of traditional interviewer instructions because these will only confuse the typical respondent. Data entry codes printed by each response will also serve only to clutter the form and to confuse respondents. The ultimate maxim in the design of a CSP questionnaire ought to be "Keep it simple!"

The type of questions to be asked.   Generally, the easier a question is to answer (such as a yes or no question) the more global and therefore the less discriminating responses to the question will be. In contrast, questions offering finely delineated responses, such as 10-point scales, are more discriminating but are often more difficult for respondents to answer. As the difficulty increases, some respondents may skip a question. The marketer faces a trade-off: specificity versus response rate.

Issues to be measured in a CSP will generally be of two types: *statements of facts* (whether or not something happened or did not happen) and *measures of performance* (how satisfactory something was). Obviously, facts are easier to obtain. Performance measures will frequently require a two-step procedure: how important the item was, and how satisfactory the performance was. For importance ratings it is recommended that a trade-off-type measure be used. A constant

AFTERMARKETING WORKING
Question Types for CSP Questionnaires

The mainstay of most CSP questionnaires is questions describing the product or service being marketed. However, measuring descriptions is not as easy as it might seem. There are at least five different formats for accumulating descriptive judgments. Consider each of the following:

Descriptive format.
My automobile is luxurious. (Check one answer.)

- Strongly agree.
- Somewhat agree.
- Somewhat disagree.
- Strongly disagree.

Qualitative format.
How would you rate the luxuriousness of your automobile? (Check one answer.)

- Excellent.
- Good.
- Fair.
- Poor.

Content semantic.
Please describe your automobile. (First, decide which word best describes your feelings; then decide how much you feel that way and check a space closer to the word that best indicates your opinion.)

- Luxurious O o . = . o O Economical.

Comparative (against expectations).
The luxuriousness of my automobile was...(Check one answer.)

- Much better than I expected.
- Somewhat better than I expected.
- As I expected.
- Somewhat less than I expected.
- Much less than I expected.

Comparative (against competition).
The luxury of my automobile was...(Check one answer.)

- One of the best of all automobiles.
- Better than many automobiles.
- About the same as most automobiles.
- Worse than many automobiles.
- One of the worst of all automobiles.

There is also a range of actual rating scales:

- A five-point school grading system: A B C D F.
- A 10-point numerical rating: 1 2 3 4 5 6 7 8 9 10.
- A verbal scale: Excellent, Good, Fair, Poor.

sum format is ideal. (A constant sum task asks respondents to allocate a fixed number of points across all items, with more important items being given more points.) Respondents, obviously, must be considered capable of understanding and performing this relatively complex task.

It is recommended that customer satisfaction questionnaires utilize at least three question formats:

- Closed-end, categorical questions for *fact-data* and *classificatory* information.
- Six- or ten-point numerical rating scales for *measures of performance* (even-numbered scales are recommended to force discrimination, i.e., a positive or negative response).
- At least two open-end, free-response questions allowing respondents to *volunteer issues and concerns* in their own thoughts and language.

The use of open-end questions.   Open-end questions are harder to analyze, but can be very useful. They elicit a wide range of answers (some delightfully unanticipated) and offer satisfaction to respondents by allowing them to state their own opinion in their own words. At least two open-end questions should be included in every CSP questionnaire. One open-end should probe the respondent's reasons for his scalar satisfaction rating ("Why did you rate us as you did?"). The other open-end may be positioned as an end-of-questionnaire catchall, "Is there anything else you would like to tell us?"

Recently, computer software programs such as Verbatim Analyzer™ have made the reporting and interpretation of open-ends easier and more meaningful.[11] These analytical programs remove some of the burden from the analysis of open-ends and certainly make the results more readily useful.

Questionnaire appearance.   The appearance of the questionnaire is especially important for self-administered CSPs. Unfortunately, most questionnaires produced today fail miserably in this respect. Oddly, marketers don't seem to take the time (or allocate the budget) to add the proper graphic design elements to their questionnaires. Consequently, questionnaires are frequently only typewritten and follow instructional conventions established for interviewer-administered interviews. Expecting customers to follow complicated skip patterns or instructions written in interviewese is futile and frustrates well-intentioned respondents, who may ultimately give up in their efforts to complete the questionnaire.

A layout artist should be consulted to design a professional-looking questionnaire. The CSP questionnaire should be considered as yet another customer-contact opportunity. An inviting and well-organized questionnaire will earn a higher response rate. If it is evident that care and concern have been invested in the construction of the questionnaire, the customer's general opinion about the marketer is also likely to be reinforced.

V. Pretesting the Questionnaire

Ideally, a CSP questionnaire should be pretested as follows:
- Review the questionnaire internally.
- Pretest the questionnaire with a small sample of target customers, using face-to-face interviews or telephone interviews, to see if the questions are being interpreted as intended. It is a good idea to get some feedback from respondents of their understanding of the intent of a question. Asking, "What do you think the question was trying to learn?" or "Could the question have been asked any differently?" will provide excellent ideas of how well a question is communicating.
- Pretest in the field using the field method selected for the ongoing study, with a subsample of the target customers. Study returns to see if the instructions were properly followed in completing the questionnaire.
- Tabulate the responses. The results will show if respondents are interpreting the questions correctly. This field test will also show what response rate to expect and, therefore, how large a sample will be necessary to provide the desired number of responses.
- Refine the questionnaire, rectifying any problems discovered through the pretest.

While pretesting will no doubt delay the start of the customer satisfaction program by several weeks or months, it will be worth the extra effort in the long run. The questionnaire that is ultimately developed will be serviceable for several years!

VI. Analyzing and Reporting Results

How the data is analyzed and presented is as important as how it is collected. The analysis should utilize both cross-tabulations and higher-level statistical procedures. Numerous statistical techniques exist for determining the strength or significance of relationships between the issues measured and customers' overall satisfaction. Analysis presents the opportunity to model overall satisfaction, tracing it back to specific product or service components. Generally, higher-order mathematics (multivariate statistics) will be necessary to conduct such an investigation.

Reporting on satisfaction ratings themselves poses many more problems than might first be imagined. For example, if the ratings are collected on a four-point scale, there are several reporting options:

- Percent of the sample awarding a perfect score of 4.
- A simple weighted average:

$$[(\% \text{ awarding a } 4) \times 3] + [(\% \text{ awarding a } 3) \times 2]$$
$$+ [(\% \text{ awarding a } 2) \times 1] + [(\% \text{ awarding a } 1) \times 0]$$

EXHIBIT 6–6
Illustrations of CSI Results Graphs

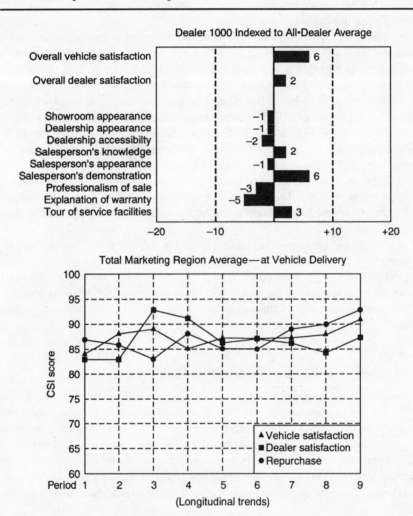

* A judgmentally weighted average:

$$[(\% \text{ awarding a 4}) \times 75 \text{ pts}] + [(\% \text{ awarding a 3}) \times 50 \text{ pts}]$$

$$+ \ [(\% \text{ awarding a 2}) \times 25 \text{ pts}] + [(\% \text{ awarding a 1}) \times 0 \text{ pts}]$$

(Any set of judgmental weights may be used.)

- A percentage measure (how close to a perfect score is the score?):

$$([(\% \text{ awarding a 4}) \times 4] + [(\% \text{ awarding a 3}) \times 3]$$
$$+ [(\% \text{ awarding a 2}) \times 2] + [(\% \text{ awarding a 1}) \times 1]) /100\% \times 4$$

Survey results should be presented in an easily understood format that will allow a management audience of different degrees of sophistication to equally understand the results. Graphical presentations are usually best, if they can be done simply. The thrust should be to identify changes over time. Results should be communicated in a format that even the busiest executive will be able to peruse. Exhibit 6–6 illustrates two graphical reporting methods.

Beyond measuring customers' *perceptions* of the organization's performance, it is essential to study results to learn about customers' expectations and the relative importance they attach to each product or service attribute. The wants a customer brings to a buying situation shape her assessment of the product or service delivered. Knowledge of the consumer's "decision model" helps a company become a stronger competitor in an otherwise confusing market.

Evaluating the relative importance of each attribute is as important as evaluating a company's relative (leverageable) performance in each area. Since it is impractical from a cost standpoint to excel on every attribute, the strategic marketer will decide to focus resources on those attributes customers consider most important. An excellent planning tool is a performance-delivery (or "quadrant") chart (see Exhibit 6–7) which identifies each product or service attribute by its judged importance and performance values.

Management's use of a performance-delivery chart is to learn where to allocate resources. Effort and money should be shifted away from attributes lying in quadrant I (highly effective rating on relatively unimportant attributes) and shifted to quadrant III, identifying attributes of high importance on which the organization may not currently be perceived as excelling.

Benchmarking: Interpreting Survey Results Marketers seeing the results of a CSP will invariably want to know how good their ratings really are. But how does one realistically evaluate customers' ratings of his performance? The scores by themselves are meaningless without a point of comparison or a *benchmark*. There are at least three different perspectives which can be adopted as possible benchmarks:

- Management's own, self-defined performance goals.
- A measure of competitors' current performance.
- Circulated or widely understood industry or category norms.

To establish benchmark data for competitors, the CSP questionnaire could ask respondents to rate competitors' products as well as a company's own products. (Alternatively, some marketers actually conduct their own CSP study, in its

EXHIBIT 6–7
Attribute Ratings, Performance versus Delivery—Supermarket Chain

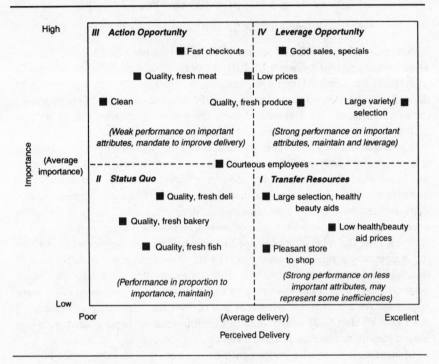

entirety, on a sample of competitive buyers.) Either way, the data on competitors can serve as the benchmark against which one's own performance is gauged.

Competitive benchmarking can help to identify leverageable attributes or gap attributes. Leverageable attributes are important attributes on which a marketer's product or service is rated higher than her competitors' products or services. The attribute identifies a way of winning more customers over to the marketer. For a marketer to aspire to industry superiority on all (or even most) attributes will be impractical. A competitive analysis should be conducted across all attributes, asking the following questions:

- How important each attribute is to current and potential customers.

- How attributes are performing on an *absolute* basis. (A low relative score which is still high in absolute terms may require a disproportionately large effort to strengthen.)

- How is competition doing on each attribute? (Competitively it is ideal to find leverageable attributes on which one can equal or overtake competition, making these attributes one's positioning in the category.)

Gap attributes are reasonably important attributes on which all competitors in the industry are judged as deficient. They identify immediate competitive opportunities. Benchmark data will help to do the following:

- Project trend lines for the organization and its competitors.
- Provide positioning and strategy planning by pointing out the competitive gaps.

The best goal is to aspire to equal or slightly exceed the competition in performance. To aim higher may be astronomically costly, impractical, and unnoticeable to one's customers.

CUSTOMER COMMENT CARDS

Numerous marketers have used customer comment cards for many years. Inserted in their packages or handed directly to customers, such cards have offered an informal and unimposing channel of communication with customers. Unfortunately, often these cards are not part of any formal evaluation program.

This is not so at the Red Lobster restaurants. This chain makes good use of comment cards at each of its restaurants. Frontline managers review the thousands of returned cards on a weekly basis to track the performance of their particular store.[12]

MEASURING CUSTOMER SATISFACTION IN CONSUMER PACKAGED GOODS

Research efforts of packaged goods manufacturers are turning toward the measurement of customer satisfaction. The marketing research area of General Mills, a traditional packaged goods company, has been closely observing the value of customer satisfaction as applied by service marketers. Whereas packaged goods research was once either focused on studying purchase behavior or on product development, today the focus is switching to first-hand experience with customers. The value of measuring customer satisfaction near the time of consumption is becoming increasingly apparent.

But for a packaged food operation, such as General Mills, whose products are consumed daily by millions of households, measuring the satisfaction of each product will be a challenge. General Mills is reportedly contemplating whether its 800 number operations (listed on every package) could become a satisfaction conduit. The company is also exploring large-scale computer-assisted telephone interviewing and customer surveys have even been placed in print advertising. The company even envisions a day when it will be able to use household computers to monitor satisfaction or for "bulletin board" product comments and complaints.[13]

HOW TO INVOLVE CSP RESULTS IN MARKETING STRATEGY

In order to use the results of a successful customer satisfaction program, a "quality action team" should be established. This team should ideally be composed of members from the following levels of the organization:

- *Executive*. Use results to allocate resources and provide direction.
- *Middle management*. Focus on customer priorities and help equip the line functions.
- *Line people*. Examine findings and communicate back to middle management what can be done to improve performance.

The action team should also have representatives of each major functioning department of the organization. This representation assures that all departments will understand the CSP and will rally to support its findings. The role of the marketing area should be overseeing the team as well as participating in it.

The difficult role of the action team is rallying to act on soft *survey data* as opposed to hard *manufacturing or production data*. It is acknowledged that some will have trouble committing resources and plans based only on attitudinal data. It is most assuredly easier to justify a change in operations if one sees hard evidence that a manufacturing tolerance has been breached. It is, however, no less important to the aftermarketing-focused organization of today to react to customer perceptions and desires as monitored in the CSP.

Special techniques have been developed to relate customers' reactions to engineering designs and manufacturing practices. One technique, the "house of quality," will be discussed in Chapter 9.

Adequate communication of results is absolutely essential to a CSP. Beyond circulating results at the corporate level, results should also be distributed to operating units, divisions or branches. CSP results reported at the local level will provide an invaluable picture of the quality of representation provided the marketer by each local dealer, agent, or franchisee. CSP standings have been constructively used in the automotive industry to stimulate competition for high quality ratings among dealers. In mid-1991, BMW significantly increased the importance of its CSI to its U.S. dealerships by announcing that it would award performance bonuses to dealerships based not on sales, but on customer satisfaction scores![14]

Following are some specific management actions taken as a result of a CSP in a company's marketing strategy:

- A system to follow up any customer-specific problems disclosed during a CSP interview should be established. Customers will feel a lot more satisfied if a problem is resolved because they took the time to answer the survey. And response should be rapid.

AFTERMARKETING WORKING
The GTE Business Customer Opinion Survey

Introducing a company-wide program devoted to service quality is meaningless if it does not get company-wide acceptance and understanding. To make sure the business customer opinion survey (BCOS) gained that crucial acceptance, representatives from GTE and its research supplier gave multiple presentations at each of GTE's operating companies at the program's inception in 1986. The survey's internal administrator, Michael English, and members of the supplier firm talked to key managers about the objectives of the program, what it was to do and how to utilize it as a tool to drive improvements in quality. Virtually all of the design and methodology were explained, as well as the calculations.

Meetings were also held to determine in what form the information would be delivered to the GTE employees. "We're treating these people as internal customers of ours within GTE, and as we went around we had discussions about what information would be most meaningful at what time intervals. We got comments like, 'If you put this question in or take this one out, that will make the report more valuable for us', or 'If we could get this information on a quarterly basis rather than monthly, it would be more useful.' That's the participation that led us to where we are today, where we have these three key reports that come out during the month, two of which contain quarter-ending results as well as 12-month-to-date results."

The monthly reports are issued as the following:

- An *advance report* for management, issued within five days of the end of each month, containing the previous month's results.
- A *summary report*, in a more graphical design, showing the results for the key units on key questions.
- *Detailed respondent data* on disk or magnetic tape made available by operating unit.

The research supplier played a key role in designing the reports, working carefully with GTE to make sure the information would get to the right people in the right form. The supplier also established contacts with the service and marketing coordinators at each GTE operating company, as well as personnel at GTE headquarters.

The data can be tailored to meet each group's specific needs, English says. "Our medium and large client results are linked to an account management system, so that the people working on those accounts in a sales capacity get results on them as they occur, for use in conferring with the customers about what they need."

The care and attention paid to making BCOS work for the GTE employees is critical to what English calls the process of "institutionalizing" the program. For a service-quality program to succeed, he says, "You have to integrate it into your fabric and culture of how you do business."

Adopted from J. Rydholm, "GTE Tracks Business Customer Approval with BCOS," *Quirk's Marketing Research Review,* February 1989, pp. 6–7, 56–59.

EXHIBIT 6–8
The Relationship Between Satisfaction and Repurchase

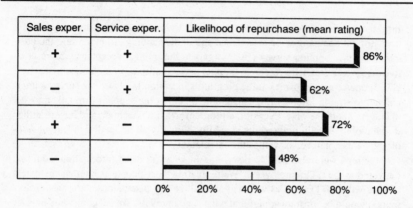

Sales exper.	Service exper.	Likelihood of repurchase (mean rating)
+	+	86%
−	+	62%
+	−	72%
−	−	48%

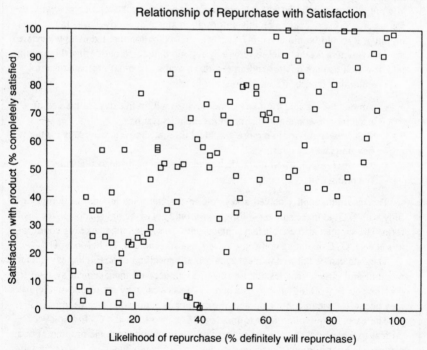

Relationship of Repurchase with Satisfaction

Source: Marketing Metrics, Inc.

• Internal quality control personnel should regularly receive customer input, and should develop internal quality systems to promote the quality aspects most important to customers.

• Data from a consistently administered program may be tied to employee incentive plans. Salespeople who consistently score high marks on a CSP should be rewarded. Low scorers should be encouraged to get further training and be motivated to produce satisfied customers.

• Customers may be segmented into groups based on their satisfaction ratings (high, moderate, low). Identifying the distinguishing characteristics of each segment provides valuable insights for marketing and promotional strategies.

Those customers identified as moderately satisfied in a customer satisfaction program represent the greatest potential. These customers probably characterize the vast majority of owners who will need positive reinforcement to become repeat purchasers. And there is real motivation for increasing customer satisfaction. Numerous studies show that repurchase likelihood is directly related to satisfaction ratings. For example, Exhibit 6–8 is actual data relating satisfaction scores with repurchase likelihood. There is a strong direct correlation. Every effort must be made to interact with the moderately satisfied customers to increase their level of satisfaction, thus encouraging both repeat and referral sales from them.

Expectations of present and potential customers are important too. Managing customer expectations through promotion and advertising, as well as through direct sales efforts, is often handled poorly by American companies. Strategic planning, in addition to other support tools, should also be directed at the management of expectations. Traditionally, firms have overpromised and oversold, creating unrealistically high expectations. Companies also have underestimated nonproduct-related performance and atmosphere factors, such as cleanliness, decor, layout, color schemes, or noise levels. Aftermarketing promotes complete commitment to customer satisfaction in every aspect of customer interaction, from direct experience with the product or service to all after-sale experiences.

In any product or service category, informal networking between customers and clients is always taking place. Consumers actively seek information from other consumers, particularly for high-ticket items such as automobiles. (Study after study shows that the mass media serve to inform, but personal sources confirm purchase decisions.) A dissatisfied customer, through his networking influence, can mean many lost sales. On the other hand, a network of completely satisfied customers is like a sales force. They send out positive endorsements about brands or products, thus actively promoting them. In such cases a marketer's sales efforts and advertising dollars will be maximized!

The overall success of a customer satisfaction program will depend largely on these issues:

• Get commitment and support from all levels of management. Management involvement will help break down any prolonged resistance by middle-level managers who may feel intimidated by such a survey.

• Design the program correctly from the start.

- Tailor the approach to fit the specific information needs identified. There is no single correct method for everyone. Each organization has its own unique requirements.
- Pretest and pretest again the survey instrument until it is certain that it will capture the information needs and achieve the program's objectives.
- Analyze and use results. Do not let questionnaires pile up in an analyst's office waiting to be tallied. Get the results back quickly and accurately.
- Integrate results into management decisions and daily operations, and act upon them. There's no sense in going through the effort and expense of implementing a measurement program if it is not going to be used.

A customer satisfaction program should be undertaken as a journey and not viewed as a destination in itself. It is a process that never ends. The marketer should constantly be communicating with customers, feeding back the results and turning them into actionable marketing strategy.

KEY POINTS OF THE CHAPTER

Customer Satisfaction Program

This is a quantitative system that periodically solicits customers' views on the following:

- What they desire from the company.
- Their expectations of performance by the company.
- Their satisfactions with the product or service as offered.
- Their satisfactions with the service or delivery system.

It is important to note that the program should be a proactive one, soliciting feedback. Besides reports of satisfaction with the marketer's product or service, a CSP also frequently monitors performance of middlemen as they represent the marketer.

CSPs generally provide decision-making information for the marketer and show the customer that the marketer cares. As such, they serve both a marketing-decisions and a marketing-communications role.

Expectations

These are the preconceived notions a customer has about the performance (satisfactoriness) of a product or service; that is, the extent to which the product or service should or will solve the problem for which it is intended. Expectations are the result of possible previous experiences with the product or service, word of mouth, the manufacturer's or provider's reputation, advertising, and so on. It is believed that knowing customers' expectations is the first step to providing complete satisfaction.

Field Methods

The mechanism used for collecting responses to a CSP can be called the "field method." There are currently three popular methods of administering CSPs: by personal interview, over the telephone, or through the mail. Newer methods such as administration by computer promise better data and greater cost efficiencies in the future.

Benchmarking

A reference point from which to read the favorableness of CSP results is often called a "benchmark." There are three types: internal, as judgmentally set by management—often the most demanding; comparative—against specific competitors; and industry wide. Establishing the benchmark for a CSP is an important part of the planning process.

Appendix Six
WHO'S SATISFYING THEIR CUSTOMERS?

Exhibit 6–9 offers a listing of some of the companies which repeatedly are cited for focusing on customer satisfaction and succeeding!

What are the commonalities that industry by industry led the companies in Exhibit 6–9 to be rated highest in customer service? It is thought that these companies are characterized by a culture that embraces customers (both serving them and satisfying them) through many of the following actions:

- They design their products and services to maximize customer satisfaction.
- They create and manage customers' expectations.
- They are obsessive about knowing, even better than customers themselves, what customers want.
- They set themselves impossibly high standards.
- They commit energy and resources to delivering quality products and customer satisfaction.
- They make customer satisfaction the business of all employees, not just the front-line people.
- They hire, train, and motivate employees to serve customers well.
- They constantly ask customers to rate their performance.
- They invest heavily in technology to support customer service.
- They carefully monitor customers' evaluations of their competitors and closely watch their competitors' marketplace actions.

EXHIBIT 6–9

Companies Rated Highest in Customer Satisfaction Industry by Industry

Company	Industry	Rating Soucre
Amdahl Corporation	Computer manufactuer	Datapro
American Airlines	International airline	Poll by the International Federation of Airline passengers of 30,000 frequent flyers
American Express Company	Credit card issuer	*Nelson Report* (1990)
Century 21	Real estate services	Industry experts
Dayton's	Regional department store	Frequency Marketing, Inc. (1994)
Deere & Company	Farm equipment	Customer surveys
Federal Express	Overnight delivery	Industry experts
Fidelity Investor Centers	Discount broker	Payment Systems, Inc.
IBM	Computers and office equipment	Customer surveys
Kodak	Film, office equipment	Industry experts, customer surveys
Kraft Foodservice	Food distribution	Customer surveys
L.L. Bean	Mail order merchant	*Consumer Reports* (1994)
Lexus	Auto manufacturer	J.D. Power & Assoc. (1993, 92, 91)
Maytag	Home appliances	*Consumer Reports*
Northwestern Mutual Life Insurance	Insurance	*Consumer Reports*
Ritz-Carlton	Hotel chain	*Consumer Reports* (1994)
Singapore Airlines	International airline	*Travel-Holiday* magazine
Six Flags	Amusement parks	Trade opinion
WalMart	Discount mass merchandiser	*Consumer Reports* (1994)
Wegmans	Supermarket chain	Consumer Network Panel (1994)
Wendy's	Fast Food Chain	*Restaurants and Institutions* (1994)
Xerox	Office equipment	Customer surveys

NOTES

1. Hey Chuck: J. Pope, "What Are Really the Best Questions for Measuring Customer Satisfaction," Customer Satisfaction and Quality Management Conference, American Marketing Association and the American Society for Quality Control, March 1990.
2. The Ford Motor Co. reports: "King Customer." *BusinessWeek,* March 12, 1990, p. 90.
3. "If we aren't customer-driven: "King Customer."
4. Du Pont Company's top management: "King Customer."
5. Marriott spent over $5 million: Personal Communication, January 1995.
6. By 1988 a survey was conducted: *Dun & Bradstreet Report,* September/October 1988, pp. 8, 51.
7. TARP estimates that only 1 in 27: Technical Assistance Research Programs Institute, "Consumer Complaint Handling in America: An Update Study, Part II, " conducted for the U.S. Office of Consumer Affairs, Washington, D.C., 1986, p. 36.
8. There is also some very compelling hard evidence: B. Uttal, "Companies that Serve You Best," *Fortune,* December 7, 1987, p. 98.
9. Talking to consumers tends: J. Brooks, *Telephone, the First Hundred Years,* (New York: Harper & Row Publishers, 1976) p. 345.
10. Hyatt president Thomas J. Pritzker: "King Customer."
11. Recently, computer software programs: *Verbatim Analyzer: Response-Processing Software,* (Paramus, NJ, Marketing Metrics, Inc., 1989), (201) 599-0790.
12. This is not so at Red Lobster restaurants: G. Dixon, "Keep 'em Satisfied."
13. But for a packaged food operation: G. Dixon, "Keep 'em Satisfied," *Marketing News,* January 2, 1989, p. 1,14.
14. BMW announced in mid-1991: "CSI Will Become Base for BMW Dealer Bonus," *Automotive News,* May 27, 1991, p. 1.

Chapter Seven

Maintaining Customer Contact
Communication Programs

Relationships are built through interaction and exchange. But marketers in the 90s are hampered in their pursuit of interaction. Either the market they serve is removed from them and their customers' identities are unknown, or customers' frequency of purchase is so low as to inhibit an active relationship from developing. Aftermarketing acknowledges these difficulties and suggests the formation of a customer communication program to help establish a better "one-to-one" relationship.

The area of proprietary media (media vehicles produced by a marketer for a specific purpose with a specific audience) is exploding. Marketers are attracted to such narrow-cast media because of the control they can exert over the vehicle. This control manifests itself both in terms of content (editorial and advertising) and in circulation. Proprietary media are usually adopted to accomplish aftermarketing goals such as managing customer relationships. Even though start-up costs are sizable, many marketers have recently instituted their own magazines and appear quite satisfied with the results. Ultimately, such publications become very cost-effective marketing tactics.

Still other marketers have redefined the idea of proprietary contacts and have created proprietary events and gatherings for their customers. This outreach is an equally effective celebration of customership for customers.

Both proprietary media and events evidence an apparent admission by many companies that customer outreach is not only desirable but necessary. And, because of the tremendous waste involved in outreach by mass media advertising campaigns, proprietary aftermarketing activities can be one-thousand-fold more cost effective!

THE NATURE OF PROPRIETARY MEDIA AND PROGRAMS

Beyond the complaint handling and formalized measurement programs (such as CSP) of modern organizations there is the very real opportunity for the organization to reach out to its customers on an everyday basis. Outreach to customers is a very effective means of maintaining customers' loyalty by managing the company's relationship with them. Such is the role of the so-called customer, or proprietary, communications program.

Proprietary communications programs maintain and enhance the relationship between the company and its customers. Customer relationships are equally important for both high-end and low-end products and in both large and small companies. Consider the range of marketers engaged in such programs today: Rolls-Royce Motor Cars, Safeway Supermarkets, Wisk laundry detergent, Deere & Company farm equipment, Mary Kay cosmetics, and the Fox television network. These and other companies are beginning to invest a great deal of marketing funds and supervision in establishing aggressive customer communications programs. Even small companies can venture into communication programs with current clients. If they can't afford glossy paper in four-color bound magazines, they can produce and distribute very informative and effective monthly or quarterly newsletters.

The Communication Goals

Like many company activities, the success of a customer communications program depends on setting objectives. Specifically, what does the company hope to accomplish? These specified objectives should, of course, support the company's overall marketing objectives and strategy. Seven common objectives are as follows:

- *To position* the company or organization. A company can use customer communications to position itself, identifying itself with a particular market, or strengthening its overall image.

- *To inform customers* about current or new products or services. Customer communications can be used to inform customers, notifying them of new products or of new applications for existing products or services.

- *To educate customers.* Customers need to be shown the superiority of a company's products and services. Better understanding the production or delivery process often makes the customer a more astute purchaser, benefiting the marketer. Factory tours and demonstrations can sell very effectively by showing customers what goes into the products they purchase and why the marketer's goods are better than those of competitors. (I was fortunate to tour the factory of Hickey-Freeman Clothiers. As I was guided through the factory it became very clear why the Hickey-Freeman suit is priced as it is and how other suits priced for less were really of far inferior quality.) For far less than the cost of a factory tour, customer communications can accomplish a similar educational role.

- *To stimulate cross-buying.* Encouraging a customer to purchase another of a marketer's products or services is *not* a specific aftermarketing goal. In contrast, as relationship marketing is practiced in the financial services sector, *cross-selling* is the primary motive. However, if cross-buying occurs, it is certainly not an unwanted consequence of an effective customer communications program.

- *To impart a sense of belonging and importance* to customers by making them feel like part of an exclusive or privileged group who receive the customer communications program. This implies real value in the program. Customers will not feel rewarded if the communications have little or no inherent value.

- *To reaffirm the customer's purchase decision.* Post-purchase dissonance, or "buyer's remorse," can be alleviated to a considerable extent by a good customer communications program. No marketer should ever allow herself to believe that it is unnecessary to reinforce customers' brand choice and product or service usage. It is always critical! The materials in a customer communications program can celebrate customership and reaffirm the customer's decision and purchase.

- *To help "manage" issues.* By strategically presenting information to customers at appropriate times, custom publications can help manage their perspective on the issue and to a certain extent "innoculate" them against an opposing viewpoint.

Proprietary customer publications have a number of advantages over other marketing media. Some advantages result from the fact that they are publications, others from their single-sponsor nature. Here are some of the primary advantages of a proprietary customer publication:

Selectivity. Customer publications don't have to reach the whole world. They can be targeted to specific audiences and their interests, zeroing in on prime prospects who are a market for a specific service.

Competition. Customer publications eliminate competition from other advertisers. Only editorials or advertisements for your business and its services appear.

Control. Unlike publications in general circulation, single-sponsor publications offer complete control of editorial material. They also allow coverage of material important to the segmented audience that general magazines might consider too commercial.

Credibility. Editorials in customer publications are considered highly credible. A recent Opinion Research Corporation study showed that almost 100 percent of readers believe editorial content of magazines, whereas only 60 percent rated ads as believable. In contrast, only 40 percent rated TV advertising as believable.

Compatibility. Customer publications do not have to fight for attention in a constantly changing environment. Properly designed, edited, and targeted, they create an environment of their own, building a frame of mind as well as a frame of reference for advertisements.

Utility. In general, customer publications are seldom trivial. They satisfy a need to know. They can cater to special personal or business interests like no other medium.

Depth. Customer publications aren't limited by a stopwatch. A magazine, tabloid, newsletter, or booklet can deliver its selling points in depth in as many words as necessary.

Memorableness. Customer publications aren't as easily forgotten as broadcast media.

Tangibility. Customer publications don't disappear before your eyes. They stay around for a while, and your editorials and advertising are in the prospects' hands to be reread, saved, clipped, mailed, and acted upon.

Long-term results. Customer publications, because of their tangibility, can continue to produce results six months to a year after publication.

Portability. Customer publications are take-alongs that fit into briefcases and tote bags. They can go everywhere—home, hotels, planes, and so forth.

Retention. The life of a well-conceived customer publication typically has a span of 30 days to permanent retention in target households or offices.*

In this chapter, five customer communications tactics will be described as they apply to aftermarketing:

- Proprietary magazines
- Company newsletters
- Special events
- Affinity merchandise
- Corporate videos

PROPRIETARY MAGAZINES

Originating among industrial marketers (for whom customer relationships have always been treated as more critical), company magazines are rapidly being endorsed by consumer marketers as well. More and more organizations, both consumer and industrial, are devoting a greater share of their marketing budgets to customer publications. This trend reflects an acknowledgment that *communication with current customers* is just as important as *advertising to potential customers.* The trend also documents a growing disenchantment with traditional mass media vehicles (for public relations or advertising). As media consultant Joel Book has observed,

In an increasingly cluttered media environment, an effective and innovative solution to this need [delivering properly targeted information that invites action and supports the sales channel] is a database-driven magazine which is custom-tailored to the

---

*Source: B. Winter, "Customer Publications—More Than Just Newsletters," *Bank Marketing,* August 1988, pp. 18–23.

EXHIBIT 7-1
Awareness/Interest in a Proprietary Magazine

Aware of publication title	**96%**
Correct identification by title-aware respondents	77
Aware respondents reporting reading magazine	72
Interest in continuing to receive magazine:	91
Very interested	66
More or less interested	25
Report discussing articles with colleagues	55

Adapted from H. Vredenburg and C. Droge, "The Value of Company Newsletters and Magazines," *Industrial Marketing Management,* Vol. 16 (1987), pp. 175–176.

information needs and characteristics of the company's individual customers and prospects. Properly designed and implemented, a database-driven magazine provides the opportunity for a company to maximize marketing communications effectiveness by maximizing message relevance.

As more companies embrace database marketing as a strategy for "staying close to the customer," the company-sponsored publication is destined to become a "proprietary channel" for building, nurturing, and maintaining that relationship.[1]

Even though company magazines have been around for some time, their effectiveness has generally been held suspect. In a literature search two marketing researchers, Vredenburg and Droge, conclude that, although the scant findings are largely unsupportive of company magazines, the previous research may not have correctly described company magazines and may therefore have been circumspect in preventing company magazines from being fully credited as having influenced decision making. Consequently, Vredenburg and Droge undertook a new study among 1,000 industrial decision makers to investigate the value of company publications. Participants who had been sent at least two copies of a company's proprietary magazine were chosen from the company's database.

Vredenburg and Droge's findings indicate a strong awareness of the company magazine and a considerable level of interest in continuing to receive it.[2] (See Exhibit 7–1).

Although very few respondents (3 percent) reported reading the magazine in its entirety, 26 percent read half or "almost all" of the magazine, and another 38 percent read at least one article. More importantly, 55 percent reported discussing articles with their colleagues, suggesting that this proprietary magazine may have had some considerable impact on its target audience.

In terms of the type of article found most useful by the customers receiving the magazine, descriptions of the sponsor's new products or services were considered most useful. Considered least useful were articles introducing the company's

EXHIBIT 7-2
Perceived Utility of Types of Articles

Descriptions of sponsor's new products/services	80%
How to effectively use sponsor's product/services	68
How to buy sponsor's products/services	62
Descriptions of customer experiences with sponsor	47
Interviews with specialists in sponsor's organization	40
Column about books and articles related to industry	30

Adapted from Vredenberg and Droge, "The Value of Company Newsletters and Magazines," *Industrial Marketing Management* 16 (1987) pp. 175-176.

staff members (perhaps considered too self-serving) and a review of important books and articles in the industry (the readers perhaps are more pragmatic in their interests). Exhibit 7-2 lists the perceived utility of other editorial features.

Under what circumstances should a company consider publishing a proprietary magazine? Several are appropriate:

- *For aftermarketing.* As a major component of an aftermarketing effort to better bond customers to a marketer.

- *When customers are already involved or involvement is desired.* To build or to satisfy customers' involvement in a company or the company's products; this is a superb tactic.

- *For efficient market coverage.* When the served market is so geographically widespread that personal sales calls become prohibitively expensive.

- *In a dynamic industry or for a quickly modifying company.* When the organization makes frequent adjustments (in products and services) to a dynamically changing business climate.

- *To complement sales activity.* When a marketing goal is to try to actively involve customers in the marketing process.[3]

Considering these different circumstances, it is no wonder that so many marketers are experimenting with and committing to proprietary magazines. Exhibit 7-3 provides an incomplete listing of companies currently involved in this new but rapidly growing field.

Deere & Company: The Furrow

Probably the oldest proprietary magazine published, *The Furrow* was first circulated in 1895 by Deere & Company from its Moline, Illinois, headquarters. Today the magazine enjoys a worldwide circulation of 1.6 million customers and is considered the company's primary link with both present customers and dealer-

EXHIBIT 7–3
Proprietary Magazines and Newsletters

Magazine	Company	Details
Aldus	Aldus Magazine	Free to owners of Aldus software products.
All Zipped Up (Ziploc)	Dow Brands	Quarterly newsletter sent to heavy users to retain customer loyalty and gather additional information for the company's segmentation strategies. Each newsletter contains "how tos".
Audi Quattro	Audi (Germany)	Distributed worldwide to all owners of four-wheel-drive Audis.
Baby Care	The Procter & Gamble Company	For Pampers; distributed selectively according to the baby's age.
Barbie Magazine	Mattel, Inc.	Free subscription to all Barbie owners with registration in Barbie's Club.
Bark	Polydor Records	Newsletter written by and for teens, with a circulation of 9,000.
BMW	BMW	Mailed quarterly to BMW owners.
Bricks Kicks Magazine and *Club Newsletter*	Lego	Members of Lego Builders Club receive *Bricks Kicks Magazine* and a *Club Newsletter* four times a year.
Bubble Talk (for Dows Bathroom Cleaner)	DowBrands	Quarterly newsletter sent to heavy users to retain customer loyalty and gather additional information for the company's segmentation strategies. Each newsletter contains "how tos".
Catalyst	Austin Rover Automobiles (UK)	Lifestyles; special feature allows "subscribers" to specify the exact editorial content they are most interested in.
Colors	Benetton	Promotes racial harmony rather than Benetton's product line.
CompuServe	CompuServe, Inc.	Sent to users with account numbers.
Connections	American Express	Targeted to college students.
Craftsman Club Newsletter	Sears	As part of the Craftsman Club, Sears mails a monthly newsletter containing special offers, discounts, a Craftsman calendar, and tool tips.
Customer Access Newsletter (part of Customer Access Program)	AT&T	The *Customer Access Newsletter* is the customer's guide to everything they have access to at AT&T and how they can best use it. The newsletter is mailed three times a year and includes articles about different AT&T divisions, services, and current offers.
Enterprise	Digital Equip. Corp.	A business and technology magazine for executives.
The Enthusiast	Harley-Davidson, Inc.	Harley-Davidson mails to the 256,000 members of its Harley Owners Group a bimonthly magazine packed with listings of regional, national, and international events to encourage them to use their bikes.
Everyday Best (Spray 'n' Wash)	DowBrands	Quarterly newsletter sent to heavy users to retain customer loyalty and gather additional information for the company's segmentation strategies. Each newsletter contains "how tos".

EXHIBIT 7–3 *(continued)*

Magazine	Company	Details
First Word	Saks Fifth Avenue	Members of Saks Fifth Avenue "Saks First" program receive *First Word* newsletter covering fashion trends.
Food Sense	Safeway	Each month members of the Safeway Savings Club receive *Food Sense.* The newsletter contains announcements of specific manufacturers' promotions and offers.
The Furrow	Deere & Company	Circulation of 1.6 million; key communication link with its customers.
Good Times	Kawasaki Motors Corporation	Mailed to Kawasaki owners.
Good Times	Kay-Bee Toy and Hobbie Shops	Mailed to 10 million families nationwide that live within a 10-minute drive of a Kay-Bee store and have children between the ages of 4 and 14.
The InCircle	Neiman-Marcus	Mailed to members of its preferred-buyer club, InCircle.
Insight	Digital Equipment Corporation	For customers interested in technical product information.
Intelligent Decisions	Columbia Audio/ Video	Sent to members of Columbia's audio and video clubs.
Micro-Vax Times	Digital Equipment Corp.	Free to users of Micro-VAX products.
The Miracle Whip Newsletter	Kraft General Foods	Contains recipes and coupons.
Nintendo Power	Nintendo of America	Features on games; monthly sweepstakes; collects game interest information; project is self-liquidating based on $15 yearly subscription fee.
Parents Club Magazine	Sandoz Consumer Products	Quarterly publication distributed to members of Triaminic Parents Club. Articles on children's health issues and offers rebates on Sandoz products
Pool Life	Olin Corporation	Mailed to 1.6 million residential swimming pool owners who have purchased Olin's pool chemicals.
President's Club	R.H. Macy	Sent to customers who spend $2,500 or more per year with their Macy's charge card. *President's Club,* a fashion-oriented newsletter, is sent out every other month.
Pulse	Tower Records	Although sold by subscription, 70,000 copies are distributed monthly to Towers' 70 retail locations.
Queste	Rolls-Royce Motor Cars, Inc.	Mailed to owners of Rolls-Royce motor cars.
Rossa	Ferrari North America, Inc.	Mailed to owners of Ferrari sportscars.
Saab Soundings	Saab	Mailed quarterly to Saab owners.
Tell	NBC & Hatchette USA	Magazine for teenage girls.

EXHIBIT 7–3 *(concluded)*

Magazine	Company	Details
Test	Polaroid Corporation	For professional photographers; uses customers' stories and articles.
Tiffany—The Magazine of Celebration	Tiffany and Company	Mailed to Tiffany customers.
Today's Family	Shop-Rite	Free to members of its electronic card-based frequent-shopper club.
Update	ITT Sheration	Mailed monthly to 600,000 members of Sheraton Club International.
Via	Federal Express Corporation	Extensive database information from customer survey form used for custom tailoring of advertising and editorials as well as promotions.
Waldenbooks' Kids' Club	Waldenbooks, Inc.	Mailed to Kids' Club members.
Your Company	American Express	For holders of the American Express Corporate Card.

qualified prospective customers. The magazine, which has received praise for its editorial content, is published by printing technology called target-market publishing. In all, 28 different editions of each issue are printed—12 for distribution in North America and 16 for distribution internationally.

The circulation for *The Furrow* is driven by the company's CIF, which tracks Deere equipment purchase history and farm operation demographics of customers, collected both from the local dealer and through readership surveys. The CIF also supports targeted direct-mail communications that are product specific.

Deere allocates a substantial proportion of its advertising budget to *The Furrow*. Doug Headley, agricultural advertising manager, refers to the internally published magazine as his "base media buy." The targeting efficiencies represented by the publication cannot be matched in any mass media vehicle.

Nintendo: Nintendo Power

Nintendo Power serves as a two-way channel of information between Redmond, Washington–based Nintendo USA and its U.S. customers. Not only does the magazine distribute product news and information *to* owners: just as important, it collects information about product desires and purchase intentions *from* owners. *Nintendo Power* has given the company an invaluable competitive advantage in understanding a frighteningly dynamic and often fickle market.

The magazine began as a quarterly newsletter sent to owners returning warranty cards. In 1989, burdened with an increasing number of requests for the newsletter, Nintendo turned the publication into a paid-subscription magazine. Today it has secured 2 million paid subscribers for the company and has helped identify an additional 6 million video game players.

Polaroid: Test

An excellent example of a consumer publication that makes the customer feel like he is part of a special group and that encourages interaction from its readers is Polaroid's *Test* magazine. This magazine began as a one-time mailing, but the response was so overwhelming that Polaroid has turned it into a quarterly publication. Sent to professional photographers, much of the editorial content is obtained from the readers, providing a forum in which Polaroid can detail its different films and their uses.

Photographers who receive *Test* are believed to share a feeling of ownership in the magazine because it is full of their stories and their photographs. Articles include such things as how one photographer solved a difficult lighting problem and helpful hints from another photographer on developing techniques. The peer input lends a certain credibility to the articles and creates a definite sense of belonging and self-importance.

An in-magazine reply card collects the valuable database information that Polaroid wants. Reader surveys inquire about new types of film the readers would like produced, current film usage, proofing techniques, and features of interest in future issues of the magazine.

Unique Results of Proprietary Magazines

Proprietary customer magazines can accomplish several aftermarketing goals far more effectively than other promotional options. Consider the following points.

Enhancing the product's image. Marketing researchers have found that growing numbers of consumers perceive products in most categories to be more or less the same (parity products) in quality and value. Many companies have therefore shifted their marketing strategies from product attributes to image attributes and to the unique positioning of their brands.[4] A company publication can reinforce a company's positioning very effectively. Although it is different from a customer magazine, the *Marlboro Store Catalogue* provides an excellent example. For 19 years this program has been very effectively reinforcing the image of Marlboro cigarettes.

The production values of the publication can also affect the company's image, reflecting the personality of the company. Ideally, the content and execution of the publication must be compatible with the communication goals for the brand

and company. Otherwise, the cross-message sent by the publication will ultimately weaken the corporate communication strategy.

A new publication from Benetton, the clothing manufacturer and retailer, is
solely intended to enhance the company's image; there is no direct reference to
the company's clothing products. Named *Colors,* the magazine is filled with articles directed at "creating global understanding and racial harmony." *Colors* aims
to personify Benetton's target customer, an astute, outspoken world citizen of the
90s. The publication reflects Benetton's current controversial advertising campaign, which pleads for greater social responsibility, including greater interracial
tolerance and the practice of safe sex.

Reinforcing the user's self-image.   Companies are also focusing on
the user's self-image rather than concentrating on the benefits of their product or
service. For example, Neiman Marcus both creates a lifestyle surrounding its
department stores and engenders a sense of belonging among its high-value customers (those designated as belonging to its Preferred Buyer Club) with its high-
quality production of *InCircle Magazine.* The publication offers customers (who
receive it quarterly, free of charge) lifestyle articles, tips on clothing and groom-
ing, and ample descriptions of new clothes available at their nearest Neiman
Marcus store.[5]

Similarly, Philip Morris used a magazine, *Philip Morris,* to reinforce its customers' decision to smoke over a five-year period. One alcoholic beverage company reportedly experimented with a similar effort: a magazine romancing the
enjoyment of distilled spirits. Procter & Gamble's publication *Baby Care* provides information that reinforces the consumer's choice of using disposable diapers. Post-purchase reinforcement should not, however, be restricted to controversial products. Though they seem to be the more obvious application,
customers of any product or service can benefit from reinforcement whether
they've purchased a car or cat food.

Encouraging increased usage and more uses.   Admittedly, embell-
ishing a company's image is a somewhat tangential objective for publishing a
proprietary magazine. An objective more directly related to short-term profitability is increasing sales by boosting usage and by cross-selling. An editorial format
magazine offers a company the unique advantage of ample time and space to tell
its customers all of the ways in which they can use the company's products and
services. Customers' satisfaction can be better ensured by describing how to best
use the products and services being sold. The customer magazine, through
proper feedback channels, can also collect and print articles on some of the ways
that customers have used its products. Interviews with field experts can also provide a means of telling customers the many ways in which to use the product.

Cross-selling is greatly enhanced by company magazines. The customer
already uses one or more of the marketer's products; the credibility of the editorial

format can be used to inform the customer about other products or add-on products. The Olin Corporation, in its customer magazine, *Pool Life,* successfully markets its other swimming pool chemicals to purchasers of any of its products who register with the company. Editorially, the magazine provides pool owners with useful tips on how to better maintain their home pools.

Inviting a dialogue. A customer magazine creates an atmosphere of dialogue in which the customer recognizes the marketer's efforts as inviting a free and open two-way flow of communication. The publication thus invites feedback and inquiries that enhance the marketer's relationship goals. The publication can also serve as the vehicle for collecting proprietary information on customers, customers' needs, and specific applications.

A final consideration. It is generally not a good idea to introduce a proprietary magazine simply as a response to what other companies are already doing in a particular industry. Category consumers may already be receiving too many publications for another magazine to have any significant effect. In such a case, another aftermarketing tactic may make more competitive sense.

Target Market Publishing

A special version of the proprietary magazine is a target market publication in which the published magazine is totally customized to the interests of the individual customer. What is revolutionary about target market publishing is its use of four integral components:

- *A smart CIF* that maintains comprehensive information on each customer, including geographic, demographic, psychographic, and product ownership and use information.
- *Multiple versions of the same issue of a magazine,* created by an editorial and magazine production group skilled in producing editorial pieces that can be mixed and matched.
- *Selective binding printing,* in which a printer produces multiple versions of a single issue of a magazine by computer-controlling the particular sections that are bound together to form each customer's unique magazine copy. The computer reads the CIF and then instructs the binding machinery to include only those sections corresponding to certain characteristics of the CIF.
- *Inkjet printing* which allows printing stories or offers in each customer's magazine personalized with the customer's name, city, personalized barcode, or other characteristics.

With database technology companies can place themselves at tremendous strategic advantage. Database-driven magazines can be customized, targeting different geographic and demographic audiences. These highly segmented magazines establish a very personal relationship between the company and the customer, creating an environment that invites feedback and allows more opportunity to address specific needs and concerns.

Consultant Joel Book has estimated the costs of producing a target market published and personalized 24-page magazine for a customer base of 100,000. Using coated paper stock and four-color production liberally throughout, he estimates, at current prices, total creation, production, and mailing costs of approximately $110,000 per issue, or $1.10 per copy.[6] Book's estimate even includes the costs of internal personalization by inkjet printer!

Perhaps the best example of the power of target market publishing comes from a nonproprietary magazine, *Farm Journal.* First published in 1877, at its heyday in the mid-1940s it boasted a subscriber base of 3.2 million. The arrival of television diverted many of its revenues, and in 1958, in a last-ditch effort, the *Journal* repositioned itself to focus on serious farmers and serious farming issues. The *Journal* developed sections on various types of farming: soybeans, hogs, cattle, and so forth. But this meant that conceivably each subscriber would receive sections not directly related to his particular farming interests.

In 1982 R.R. Donnelley convinced the *Farm Journal* to use its Selectronic Binding system. This target market publishing machinery allows the *Journal* to print as many as 8,896 different versions of a single issue to send to its 825,000 subscribers! Each farmer's issue is customized to his particular interests.[7] The *Journal* further capitalizes on the selective binding process by selling selective advertising exposure as well. Advertisements are only bound into issues going to farmers whose interests match the advertisers' products.

The capabilities of selective binding and inkjet printing were introduced to the mass American market with the November 26, 1990 issue of *Time* magazine, the cover of which bore each mail subscriber's name as part of the cover story!

COMPANY NEWSLETTERS

Newsletters give companies that lack the resources to produce a customer magazine the opportunity to cultivate good customer relations through less expensive proprietary customer communications. Newsletters provide many of the same advantages as magazines: maintaining contact with clients, fostering long-term relationships, providing product information, establishing the company as an expert in its field, and cultivating future sales, all at substantially reduced costs.

Perhaps by virtue of their name, newsletters also imply urgency, late-breaking news, and an intent to update the reader for ready action. They may therefore carry a greater obligation than company magazines to convey real news about the product, service, or supplier organization. To succeed and to be read, newsletters must provide customers with relevant news and information. Research shows that self-serving newsletters no longer attract the reader. To be successful, a customer newsletter must provide a payoff for the reader in terms of education, information, or entertainment. Newsletters also tend to be treated as more of a dialogue mechanism, often giving opportunities for customers to air problems, to offer solutions, and in general to interact with one another.

Newsletters, like magazines, have a long shelf life and provide the space to tell a substantive story. A less discussed but equally important advantage is the consistency that a newsletter program provides. If the company's business environment changes often, whether through mergers, turnover, new product development, or new regulations, a newsletter can help keep customers abreast of these changes.

Despite their several advantages, recent increases in the volume of direct mail make high-quality and professional execution of a newsletter critical if it is to break through the clutter of other competing mail pieces received by customers.

Establishing Camaraderie Among Customers

A newsletter can be used to create camaraderie among a company's customers, making them feel privileged to be on a company's distribution list to receive the latest information. Establishing a "club" feeling gives customers a sense of belonging, of being special. In order to best create this sense of camaraderie, the newsletter must be tuned in to the demographic and psychographic profile of the company's customers. A customer-based communications program must always speak to its readers in a manner that acknowledges them as *known individuals,* not as members of a mass audience.[8]

One way to encourage the feeling of camaraderie is to occasionally mention specific customers by name or to regularly list the newest people or organizations joining the company's client list. A broader approach would involve writing an article that targets a very specific group of clients, segmented by need or by geographic or demographic grouping.

Providing a Channel for Interaction

The sense of camaraderie or self-importance the customers feel can be further encouraged by involving them in the newsletter. By providing customers with a channel of interaction, the company has ensured a continued dialog that enhances the customer relationship process. There are many ways to do this:

- Articles on how the company came to the aid of a client or customer.
- Shared information highlighting a particular customer's application of the product or service.
- Articles reflecting how other customers benefited from the product or service.
- Customers' letters of satisfaction showing other customers that the company satisfies many customers and explaining why they are satisfied.

AFTERMARKETING WORKING
Considerations in Producing a Newsletter

1. Define with a professional designer the design parameters such as size, number of pages and ink colors, desired degree of formality, and name. (The name should suit the image to be projected, the business of the firm, and the clientele.)
2. Review "thumbnails"—rough sketches in miniature showing placement and treatment of the various elements of a newsletter. Generally, a designer prepares two or three ideas, each executed on a somewhat different tack.

   Remember that a newsletter is repetitive. A design that is time-consuming to execute may be fine for a brochure but prohibitive for a newsletter. Also look at flexibility. A design with variable column depth, for example, is more forgiving of a shortage of material than a design with even columns. Choose a design that is inviting and easy to read so that it stands out from other unsolicited mail. Also, check the design against post office regulations.
3. Review a full-sized, detailed mock-up based on the most promising thumbnail. Solicit from the designer suggestions for type style, paper, and ink.
4. The designer prepares camera-ready art for the newsletter's flag or nameplate (often mistakenly referred to as the masthead). The flag may consist of type only or include rules or illustration.
5. Set a sample story into the chosen design specifications. The sample will show what the newsletter will look like as a finished product. (Some companies even send this sample out to a few clients to get their reactions and input.)
6. The designer either prepares an actual "dummy," arranging a copy of typeset galleys into pages and indicating where photographs and any illustrations are to appear, or a pencil dummy if desktop publishing will be used to produce it.

   Assign a position priority to all articles (front page, back page, inside). Also note which articles should have a photo or illustration. If a lengthy story must be cut to fit available space, decide how this will be done.
7. The designer prepares camera-ready artwork that is photographed by a printer to make the plates from which the newsletter will be printed.
8. Review a proof copy with the designer before press plates are made. This will be the last chance to make changes.

Source: J. E. Pickens, "The Client Newsletter: Putting It to Work for Your Firm," *The National Public Accountant.* (July 1988), p. 33.

- Testimonials that show that the company's products and services deliver as is claimed.

- A question and answer column hosted by someone in the company.
- A customer forum.

In order to encourage each customer to interact through the newsletter, including a response card is a good practice. The card gives the reader an opportunity to request more information or ask a question, in addition to providing more information about herself and her product or service needs. Inviting readers to respond to offers of free literature, free applications, and so on will show what really interests them. Response cards can also serve as informal readership polls to assess the degree to which the newsletter is meeting its objectives. Subjects for articles should be selected in proportion to their relevance to special interest groups within the customer base.

Computer Bulletin Boards

Computer bulletin boards are fast becoming a new means of information exchange and interaction between customers. Many companies in industries related to PC hardware and software are already sponsoring such electronic forums. These "bulletin boards" may begin to replace traditional print media (newsletters specifically) in the near future. Their primary advantage is their immediacy—the opportunity they provide for customers to instantly communicate with one another and with company representatives.

A company's sponsorship of a computer bulletin board can be interpreted as a fairly passive posture unless the sponsoring company takes an active role in the dialogue occurring on the bulletin board. One way for the sponsoring company to actively participate is by announcing weekly (or daily) discussion topics. In this way the sponsor can "moderate" the direction of dialogue. A disadvantage, of course, is that the more active the role taken, the more time will be required from one or more senior-level people in the sponsoring company. However, no other medium (except the telephone) offers corporate officers a better chance to listen to customers one on one.

SPECIAL EVENTS

For many marketers, event sponsorship is undertaken simply as a substitute for mass media advertising. The event is treated as an outreach, or conversion vehicle. This may or may not be the best use of events in the marketing plan. Event sponsorship can, no doubt, boost awareness of a product or a service, but it seems unlikely that it will prompt a consumer to actually switch brands or suppliers.

Some marketers use event marketing to play both sides of the fence. They invest in event sponsorship because of the visibility that events offer for new customers, but they also leverage participation opportunities (in the event) for their current customers and employees as well.

EXHIBIT 7–4
Growth of Event Marketing

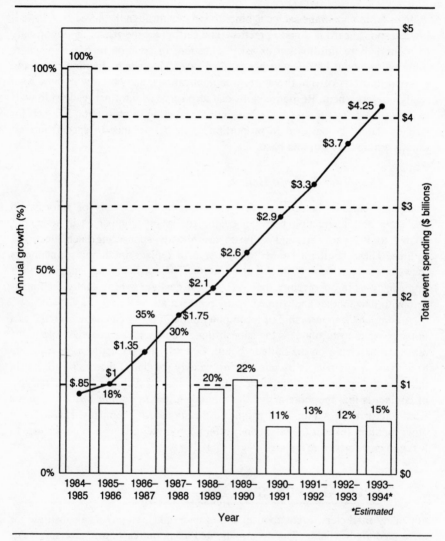

Source: IEG Sponsorship Report, International Events Group, 4/12/93; *Advertising Age* 3/23/92

Other marketers more appropriately use special events for their tremendous aftermarketing value with current customers. Special events directed at thanking customers for their business can send a very positive message, strengthening customer relationships with the company and reinforcing purchase loyalty.

Customer events do not have to be extravagant in order to convey the message of appreciation. They can be simple in design and small in scope by targeting a specific group of key customers.

Use of Special Events in Marketing

Sponsorship of special events is one of the fastest-growing elements of the marketing mix, having grown 300 percent between 1985 and 1994—over 30 percent per year! Sponsorship spending hit $4.25 billion in 1994, boasting a growth rate of 15 percent over 1993's level, or twice that of advertising (see Exhibit 7–4).[9]

For example, in 1994 more than 5,000 companies participated in special event marketing and spent $2 million to $3 million each on sponsorships and support activities. The number of companies spending more than $10 million on event sponsorships grew to 34 in 1994. In fact, companies such as RJR Nabisco and Anheuser-Busch have formed separate departments to plan and administer sports and event marketing. Total spending on sponsorships is currently minuscule compared with advertising and sales promotion, but it represents an increasing portion of corporations' total marketing budgets.

The explosion of event marketing in the past 10 years comes as a direct result of marketers' dissatisfaction with traditional forms of media. "With prices for print ads and broadcast media climbing out of sight and with lower television viewing, marketers are looking for other ways to communicate with a segmented and fragmented marketplace," writes Jim Andrews, senior editor of *Special Events Report.*[10]

Event marketing generally involves tapping leisure pursuits such as sports, music, recreation, and social and political causes as a platform for communicating a marketing message. Such leisure-time activities allow advertisers to meet consumers at a lifestyle level and introduce them to products in a more natural way.

Of the $4.25 billion spent on event marketing in 1994, 66 percent went to sports, 19 percent to music and festivals, and the remaining 15 percent was spent on arts and causes. Auto racing and pro golf received 25 percent and 9 percent of sports dollars spent, respectively (see Exhibit 7–5).[11]

Unlike advertising, event marketing provides sponsors with face-to-face access to their current and potential customers in a fresh and reasonably uncluttered environment. The real advantage of event marketing, however, may be the psychological value of catching customers with their defenses down. Whereas more direct forms of selling tend to raise customers' defense mechanisms, the distraction element of a special event may allow whatever sales message is presented to follow a more open path to customers' minds.

Special events as a marketing opportunity are being quickly acknowledged by most marketing services agencies, including sales promotion and advertising agencies, public relations firms, and corporate marketing executives. Cities,

EXHIBIT 7–5
Distribution of Expenditures by Event Type

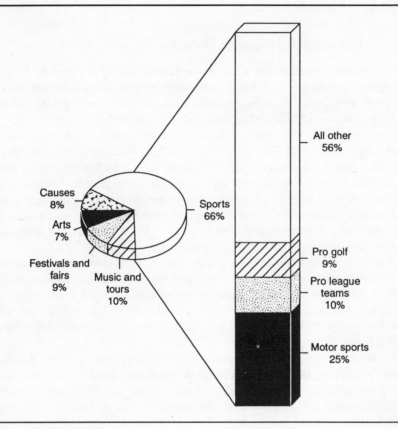

Source: IEG Sponsorship Report, 7/26/93

tourist bureaus, small companies, and large corporations are similarly beginning to understand the advantages of event sponsorship.

In addition, event marketing offers companies with limited media alternatives (such as the tobacco and alcohol industries) a dramatic way to communicate with consumers and stimulate brand sales. Events also provide endless possibilities for combining brands, teaming corporations, or partnering opportunities with the trade or media to offset expenses or even extend a promotion.

A sponsor may buy into an existing special event or create its own special event. The future of corporate event sponsorship, in the opinion of Paul Stanley, an event marketing specialist, is in the sponsor's total ownership of concert tours and entertainment events. Stanley calls this "sponsownership"—an event or sponsorship owned and controlled by the sponsor. Sponsownership gives the sponsor more control and is more cost effective than standard corporate sponsor-ship arrangements. This total control can help ensure that a company achieves its marketing objectives.[12]

Special event marketers may be the sole sponsor of an event or one of many sponsors. Although some companies believe that they must stand alone in the spotlight to benefit from an event sponsorship, others have learned to get good marketing mileage out of cross-promotions and secondary sponsorships.

Such joint-venturing has already produced a good deal of clutter in event mar-keting. An extreme example is the 1990 Indianapolis 500. In this event there were over 176 companies that had a direct relationship with the race. Obviously not all of the 176 companies involved got their money's worth. With all the clut-ter has come the problem of accountability, and, as sponsorship expenditures have increased, so has the demand for accountability. Companies paying higher prices for events, as well as those bracing for uncertain economic prospects, have an increased need to justify expenses.

However, although the value of sponsoring an event can be estimated, there are problems with the methods of estimating the value:

- No single measure is applicable universally. One company may sponsor events primarily to reward current customers; another, to affect the trade; a third, to change consumer attitudes about a product. No single measure accommodates all scenarios.

- Concurrent promotional activities cannot be curtailed. Sponsors usually run other promotions at the same time, making it difficult to isolate which results come directly from event marketing.

- Measurements are borrowed from other areas of marketing. Sponsors fre-quently use benchmarks from other disciplines, such as advertising's CPM (cost per thousand). Yet comparing sponsorship to advertising on a CPM basis is rarely relevant.

It is possible to evaluate sponsorship by measuring changes in awareness or image. By conducting pre- and post-sponsorship surveys, a company can deter-mine a shift in consumer awareness and perception. Spending equivalencies may also be measured. A sponsor can place a monetary value on free media expo-sure generated by determining what it would have cost to purchase comparable advertising.

It is also possible to evaluate sponsorship by measuring a change in sales. There are two ways to make sales analysis easier: to use short-term or localized sponsorships, which aid comparison to control areas, and to design a tie-in using trackable items such as coupons or labels to be redeemed.

Special Events Report suggests the following conditions for measuring the value of event sponsorship:

- Have clear goals and narrowly defined objectives.
- Set a measurable goal.

- Measure against a benchmark.
- Do not change other marketing variables during the sponsorship.
- Incorporate an evaluation program into the overall sponsorship and marketing program.
- Budget for measuring. Most firms suggest that 1 percent to 5 percent of sponsorship spending is adequate for evaluation.[13]

One of the most overlooked areas in event sponsorship is the effect a successful sponsorship has on company employees—those involved in making the product and selling it. Association with a dynamic event will boost the morale of the corporate troops. Seth Martins, special events coordinator for Evian Water, reports that *motivating his sales force* is one of the four goals he hopes to accomplish with special event marketing. His other goals are *encouraging trial, exciting the trade,* and ultimately *increasing sales.*

Media exposure is a major factor motivating companies to pay large sums of money to sponsor events. Volvo International feels that its $3 million investment in sponsoring local tennis tournaments is equivalent to $25 million in advertising because of the extra media value derived. There are also companies that cannot advertise in broadcast media, such as the tobacco and alcoholic beverage companies, which are prohibited from such advertising by law. These companies, as well as companies that cannot afford TV advertising, can obtain TV exposure through event marketing.

Picking an Appropriate Event

"A good fit [of the event] with business and communications objectives is a must," says Alfred Schreiber, executive vice president at Burson-Marsteller, which found in a 1989 survey that 47 percent of corporate sponsors neither prescreen events for appropriate objectives nor measure the effectiveness of an event afterward.

Several factors should be considered in selecting a promotional tie-in:

1. Can the sponsorship be an exclusive one?
2. Do the demographics of the mass media audience and event participants match, as closely as possible, the demographics of the target consumer?
3. The event should receive substantial mass media coverage or participation.
4. The event should in some way demonstrate, evoke, or represent a key attribute of the product or service (for example, a luxury product sponsoring a thoroughbred racing event—"the sport of kings").
5. The value to the sponsored event of the company's association should be no greater than the benefit to the company from the additional mass media exposure from the sponsorship. (This has to do with who is leveraging whom.)

6. The participation should promise sufficient (and appropriate) mass media exposure to offset any real or opportunity costs.
7. The association of the product with the event should ideally offer or suggest a meaningful sales campaign or theme to be run concurrently with sponsorship.
8. Did the company initiate the negotiation or did the event promoters?
9. Is any financial support required?

Using Public (Visible) Support to Reinforce Current Users

By employing a special event, the company has an opportunity to reinforce its current users' brand commitment. Gathering customers (those who are favorably predisposed to the brand or service) provides a valuable public confirmation of their having selected the marketer's products or services. The event is a *celebration of customership.* Polaroid offers several seminars throughout the year, providing professional photographers with a chance to meet among themselves and learn about lighting, developing, and other photography techniques. Polaroid discovered that 30 percent of the attendees reported increasing their use of Polaroid film as a result.[14]

Image Benefits

Special event promotions benefit the company's public image or enhance its current image positioning. Lever Brothers, makers of Wisk laundry detergent, began sponsoring an event in 1987 called "Wisk Bright Nights." The tour involved several months of visiting cities and sponsoring fireworks displays in each city. The promotion was a huge success, with an estimated 3 million people watching the shows and sales of more than 1 million incremental cases of Wisk. Wisk repeated the promotion the following year, thanking its customers for their loyalty and encouraging others to join in their ranks. (Though this promotion was successful at enhancing Wisk's image in the public eye, it lacked a directness with its customers. The fireworks benefited all in the community, without any differentiation for those who used the product.)

Rolls-Royce Customer Events

Rolls-Royce Motor Cars (both in the United States and in the United Kingdom and Europe) has devised an elaborate program of customer appreciation events and activities. Estate tours are events at which the company arranges with the owner of a famous estate or chateau to use the estate for a day. Approximately 20 to 50 owners (sometimes with a few potential purchasers strategically included) will be invited to the estate for a day. In addition to touring the property, participating owners will be hosted to a spectacular meal, a display of clothing fashions, a wine tasting, or displays of other luxury items. Of course, a full complement of new Rolls-Royce and Bentley motor cars will be on display and available for a test drive. In the United States such day outings have also taken the form of special interest days, including trap-shooting, golf, sailing and art shows. To host such an outing, Rolls-Royce identifies owners from its customer database who have an appropriate interest in the activity; are favorably predisposed to rebuy a Rolls-Royce or Bentley; and whose current motor car is approaching the age of replacement. Attendance at these events is usually quite good and, although cultivating relationships is the primary goal of the events, new cars are frequently sold as a result, as well.

Saturn's Factory Homecoming

Another car manufacturer, General Motors' Saturn Corporation, initiated its own special customer event in 1994. The Saturn factory "homecoming" was announced as an opportunity for all Saturn owners to visit the Spring Hill, Tennessee, factory, meet the workers who has assembled their cars, and see the assembly plant itself. Conceived of as a "homecoming," barbecue, and country fair all in one, Saturn was rewarded with visits from 44,000 of its owners during June of 1994!

Such a public affirmation of belief in a US car manufacturer must have been a substantially reinforcing experience for those Saturn owners—many of whom traveled over 2,000 miles to the factory. This event represents the essence of good customer events—it confirms a customer's personal brand choice by allowing him or her to meet other customers who've made the similar brand choice.

Cellular One's Cellular Phone Clinics

The cellular telephone industry is one of the industries most desirous of improving relationships with its customers to reduce the tremendous churn rate experienced by carriers. (It is not uncommon for 25 percent or more of a year's new customers to discontinue service after only 3 to 6 months!) Some of these customers switch to another carrier, and others simply cancel their service.

Cellular One (in the New York–New Jersey market) has developed a tune-up clinic as a customer appreciation event. Customers from a certain geographic area are invited to attend such a clinic, which is set up at a site convenient to the customers (such as a stadium parking lot or civic park). Customers attending have their cellular telephones tested and tuned by the carrier's engineers. In addition, they are frequently offered some sort of special entertainment or display of cellular technology. Often a sports celebrity will be in attendance to meet and talk to Cellular One customers. Customers leave the clinic with better performing equipment, operating problems accurately diagnosed, a better acquaintance with Cellular One executives and technicians, and the feeling that Cellular One truly cares about them.

American Express's Gold Card Theater Parties

In 1988 American Express conceived of a unique reward for its Gold Card holders. Beginning first in New York and Los Angeles, Gold Card Events^SM offer Gold Card members exclusive access to preferred seats for highly regarded cultural, performing arts, and sporting events. American Express has clout with show producers and uses it to secure for its customers good seats with advance purchase opportunity. In 1991 the program was being offered to American Express members in 11 U.S. cities. Members learn about the featured events through their monthly newsletter, by local newspaper ads, and by calling an 800 number. Psychographically, the program is consistent with a major cardholder interest: entertainment. From a positioning point of view, the program truly makes good on the company's slogan: "Membership has its privileges."

AFFINITY MERCHANDISE

Although marketers generally must nurture relationships with customers, sometimes customers go out of their way to establish a conspicuous relationship with a marketer. The popularity of affinity merchandise is evidence of such behavior. Affinity merchandise is any product (other than the company's main product) that bears the company's name, logotype, or trademark or has the company's products pictured on it. Examples of affinity merchandise are T-shirts bearing the Budweiser beer logo, hats with the Ford logo, and umbrellas with the PGA Master's Tournament logo. Affinity mechandise is either purchased by customers at regular or premium prices or may be acquired by redeeming proofs of purchase from the marketer's products. In either case, consumers' desire for the merchandise is motivated by a desire to show an affiliation with the company's brands or personality. Such behavior is truly flattering to the marketer because it testifies that the marketer's company or brand name is associated with values with which the consumer wishes to openly identify.

Affinity merchandise probably has its origins among community athletic teams sponsored by local businesses, which proudly placed their names on team members' shirts, athletic bags, and so forth. Somewhat later, employees of larger companies began proudly wearing jackets and displaying other items identified with the name of their employer. Stamping inexpensive gadgets and toys with corporate logos for use as advertising specialties has been a long-time practice, the idea being that such specialty items would serve, like advertising, to keep companies' names in front of the consumer. Unfortunately, too often the merchandise has been of inferior quality or of such a bizarre nature that it is frequently unwanted or may create a poor impression of the marketer.

Today most American companies have merchandise with their corporate logo conspicuously emblazoned on it. The merchandise may either be offered for sale at the cafeteria or human resources department or kept to be used as incentives or internal gifts. Employees may wear the merchandise because of a sense of pride. Depending upon the prestige of the company, customers and consumers in general are also often eager to own the same merchandise.

This means that companies can now *sell* the same merchandise to consumers! Not only is revenue generated, but additional publicity and advertising are also generated as the merchandise is worn by consumers.

Consumers' willingness (and, in some cases, intense desire) to wear clothes with corporate America screaming from them is rather curious, especially when one considers the amount of criticism directed at the ubiquity of advertising and the cries lamenting our over-commercialized world. Yet customers are proud to wear a Coors T-shirt or a Deere & Co. hat or sport a Green Giant beach towel. Customers' desire for affinity merchandise appears related to several issues:

- Some degree of national pride in successful national companies.
- Recognition of the popularity of a product or brand and the resulting benefit of a bandwagon effect (showing peers that one is "with it").
- Desire to publicly associate oneself with the lifestyle or values attributed to the product or brand through its marketplace positioning and success.

Some marketers have turned their corporate logos into small strategic business units (SBUs) of themselves. Take, for example, the Disney stores, Ringling Brothers and Barnum & Bailey's Circus stores, the Coors Collection, the Marlboro store, and the Lynchburg, Tennessee Country Store. All of these operations are making a profit from corporate-labeled merchandise purchased by affinity-hungry customers.

Companies themselves are still somewhat unclear about the actual value they derive from affinity merchandise. This is true even among those who are offering substantial amounts of merchandise. Anheuser-Busch manager of promotional products, Dan Renz, says, "Our clothes carry real cachet. You can't get the items anywhere else. People who buy our merchandise have a certain affinity either toward our company or toward a particular A-B beer brand." Renz goes on to comment on the merchandise's overall contribution to the Anheuser-Busch marketing program: "We can't say for sure that it sells the beer but it certainly puts our brand name out there. I think it's safe to assume that people who like our beer will have a higher propensity to buy Budweiser than Coors if they're wearing Bud merchandise."[15]

Marketers have traditionally favored affinity merchandise oriented to leisure-time accessories. The goal is to have one's product conspicuously present when

---

AFTERMARKETING WORKING
Affinity Merchandise

Here is an assortment of the corporate merchandise the zealous customer can order today.

- *Coors & Co.* The name of the in-brewery store, which hosts 300,000 visitors each year, has now lent its name to a 12-page catalog. Featured in the catalog are 42 different items of Coors (and affiliated brands) merchandise items ranging from a Coors T-shirt at $18.00 to a Coors Lite "Beerwolf" varsity jacket selling for $250! Judging from the Coors Light bottle bar stool to the Silver Bullet neon sign, subtlety is not what Coors & Co. is selling.
- *United Airlines.* This airline distributed its first catalog of corporate merchandise in the fall of 1989. Twelve hundred different items were offered, all featuring the United corporate logo.
- *Ford Motor Company.* The first issue of the Ford Motorsport catalog was produced in the fall of 1990. The catalog was aimed at two audiences, one ideally motivating the other. Catalogs were mailed to both the owners and parts managers of all Ford dealerships. Dealers were offered special volume discounts to encourage them to buy and stock some of the merchandise. In addition, almost 2 million catalogs were mailed to Ford car owners, segmented by model and year, and to members of Ford Fan Clubs. Five hundred dealers purchased merchandise, and consumer response reportedly exceeded expectations.
- *Brewhaus Gift Shop.* This catalog features licensed merchandise from four breweries (Anheuser-Busch, Miller, Stroh's, and Coors). Distribution of the catalog was increased to 200,000 in 1990, after test mailings to 10,000 and 100,000 generated response rates of 2 percent and 1.5 percent, respectively. Merchandise ranges from clothes to beer steins. The average order was $60 in 1989.

---

customers are having a good time. Consequently, marketers try to place their logos on leisure goods, picnic coolers, ski jackets, sweat bands, caps, and golf umbrellas. The value of the positive association cannot be directly measured, but it seems intuitively appropriate.[16]

Guaranteed Success?

Not all companies experimenting with affinity merchandise are satisfied with the results. Brown-Forman introduced its *Paddle Wheel Shop* catalog of affinity merchandise for Southern Comfort liquor in 1981. The company conducted research to assess what, if any, benefit the brand was deriving from the program. "Our research showed the catalog positively changed the attitude toward Southern Comfort," says the brand's senior manager David Higgins.[17] But the program was discontinued in 1986 because catalog and mailing costs weren't "controllable." Brown-Forman's position is this: "We're not in the mail-order business: we are a distilled spirits business." Brown-Forman apparently concluded that the potential aftermarketing benefits of the branded merchandise did not justify the costs and problems of running a "mail-order business."

But while consumer enchantment continues, and while some marketers profit from it, few marketers are using customers' desire for affinity merchandise for its true marketing value. The current perspective seems short-range at best. The relatively nonstrategic way in which the merchandise is currently being licensed and distributed probably occurs because few marketing departments are actively involved in this part of the business. Licensing and merchandising can frequently occur in corporate areas totally isolated from the marketing department! One would hope that company marketers will ultimately be invited to help determine how to make corporate merchandise work to its full advantage for the company.

CORPORATE VIDEOS

A very new entry in the arena of proprietary company media is the corporate video. Originally used for internal training purposes and then later for communicating with branch offices, corporate videos today are being sent outside the company as another aftermarketing tactic with which to strengthen customer relationships.

For the last year, each purchaser of a new Rolls-Royce has found a well-produced and handsomely packaged "Inside the World of Rolls-Royce Motor Cars" videotape in the glovebox of the new Rolls-Royce. A strange timing for the presentation of basically a selling tool? Quite the contrary! The videotape was developed for the specific purpose of *reinforcing* new owners' decisions of having purchased a very expensive automobile (though the tape also has obvious application as a selling tool, as well).

Industry information and case histories about the effectiveness of corporate videos are almost totally lacking (especially their effectiveness as aftermarketing vehicles). It has been reported that corporate expenditures on video programs of companies including American Express, AT&T, General Motors, IBM, Sears, and State Farm have quadrupled from $1.5 billion in 1986 to an estimated $7 billion in 1990.[18]

A study was conducted by the Wharton School of Business on the effectiveness of video brochures. The study reportedly found that videocassette material was 50 percent better retained than print material, and that it increased buying decisions by 72 percent. The study also determined that three times as many people could be expected to request a video brochure than would request a print brochure, and six times as many people will respond to an offer made through a video brochure than through a print brochure.[19]

A number of personal computer companies have used the video format: Apple, Commodore, and Microsoft have all introduced new products by video or have supplied demonstrations by video. Air France produces videocassettes of its travel packages, offering the videos for free viewing. If the tape is not returned within 14 days, the recipient's credit card is charged $29.95. Air France has received 2,500 requests per week with a 20 percent conversion to the sale of an Air France tour package!

For Christmas 1991, the Hartmarx Corporation produced a 14-minute video catalogue to send to 150,000 of its best customers. Entitled "A Picture-Perfect Holiday," a cast of 24 portrays an affluent suburban Chicago family and their guests celebrating Christmas. In the video they are shown wearing, giving, and receiving classic clothes and accessories available at Hartmarx stores. The effort cost $1 million to produce, package, and deliver.[20] Although the main intent of the Hartmarx video is to show and sell new merchandise, by the very nature of displaying its products in an attractive suburban setting with likable actors and actresses demonstrating an affluent lifestyle, Hartmarx is also reaffirming to current customers the consonance of the Hartmarx brand with their presumed style of living.

The future for customized corporate videos for aftermarketing purposes looks very promising. Corporate videos appear able to enhance the customer's relationship with a company in a more dramatic and vivid manner than any other medium.

KEY POINTS OF THE CHAPTER

Affinity Merchandise

Any product or merchandise other than the company's main product that bears the company's name, logo, trademark, or pictures of its products. This merchandise is often highly sought by customers. The merchandise offers significant strategic value to affirm the value and importance of the marketer's products and image among consumers.

Corporate Videos

A new form of corporate communications, corporate videos can demonstrate the value and quality of a product or service, reaffirming to customers the value of the product or service they are buying. This is management of evidence by electronic means.

Customer Events

Customer events are special events staged either exclusively for customers or events sponsored for the general public in which customers are given special privileges. The event is a very conspicuous way of thanking customers for their business, and also serves the purpose of public confirmation (gathering customers together to demonstrate the following a brand or company has).

Proprietary Media

Magazines or newsletters developed and owned by a marketer can be an effective component of an aftermarketing program. The magazine or newsletter can serve one or more purposes:

Position the company or its products.

Inform customers about new products.

Direct customer attention to various features and enhancements.

Impart a sense of belonging to customers.

Reaffirm the customer's purchase decision.

Help to manage issues.

Appendix 7
SPONSORSHIPS OF SPECIAL EVENTS BY U.S. AND INTERNATIONAL MARKETERS

APPENDIX 7
Sponsorships of Special Events by U.S. and International Marketers

Sponsor	Amount	Event or Party Sponsored
Anheuser-Busch, Inc. (Budweiser)	$400,000+	Title, Superfest, 18 cities*
AT&T	$250,000+	USO Comedy Tour, seven countries*
British Telecommunications	$750,000+†	Assn. of British Orchestras, '94–'96
Cellular One	$250,000+	Title, Summer Nights at the Pier, Seattle*
Chicago Title and Trust Co.	$150,000+	Presentation, Goodman Theatre, Chicago
The Coca-Cola Co.	$3 million+	USA Basketball, '94–'96
	$1.5 million†	Rugby World Cup, '95

APPENDIX 7 *(concluded)*

Sponsor	Amount	Event or Party Sponsored
The Dial Corp. (Dial, Armour Star)	$1 million+	Wynonna, 50-city tour
Drambuie Liqueur Co.	$1.1 million†	Title, Edinburgh Film Festival, '94–'96
Federal Express Corp. (Chevrolet)	$2 million+	USA Basketball, '94–'96
General Motors Corp. (Chevrolet)	$280 million	Major League Baseball, '94–'99 (includes media)
(Chevy Trucks)	$500,000+	Title, World Cup of Fishing
(Cadillac)	$1 million+	Team Dennis Conner America's Cup syndicate*
The Home Depot	$4 million	1996 Atlanta Paralympic Games
Koss Corp.	$500,000	Title, permanent stage, Milwaukee's Summerfest
City of London	$1.4 million†	City of London Festival, '94–'97
Lufthansa German Airlines	$250,000+	Official airline, ATP, '94–'96*
Marks & Spencer	$500,000+†	The Natural History Museum, Scotland
MCI Communications Corp.	$100,000+	Presenting, Penn & Teller, 16-city tour
Miller Brewing Co.	$2 million	Associate, F1's Team Lotus
(Genuine Draft)	$125,000	Presenting, Central Park SummerStage*
Mitsubishi Motors	$1.5 million†	Badminton Horse Trials, '94–'96*
Pepsi/Lipton Tea Partnership	$40 million	Universal Studios, '94–'98
Perry Ellis Int'l	$2 million+	Goodwill Games (includes media)
Phillip Morris Cos.	$1 million	Chinese Soccer Federation
Playboy	$500,000+	Title, jazz festival, 6 cities
Nabisco Foods, Inc.	$1 million+	Beach Boys, 22-city tour
RCA	$750,000	Title, IBM/ATP Tour stop, Indianapolis, '94*
Skandia (insurance)	$3.8 million†	Swedish Tennis Assn., '94–'96
Sears, Roebuck & Co.	$250,000	NBA Jam Session, Canada
Schöller Lebensmittel GmbH	$1 million	Presenting, Cirque Du Soleil, European tour, '95–'96
Shell Oil Co.	$3 million+	Title, PGA Tour stop, Houston, '95–'97
Sprint	$1 million+	Title, PGA Tour stop, Denver, '94–2000
Tipstjänst (Swedish lottery)	$6.3 million†	Swedish Athletic Assn.
Vestfold Kraft (Norwegian electric utility)	$800,000+†	Vestfold Arts Festival

*Renewal.
†Approximate value after conversion into U.S. dollars.

NOTES

1. An increasingly cluttered media environment: J. Book, "One-to-One Marketing Communications," Third Annual Conference on Database Marketing, December 1990, The National Center for Database Marketing, Inc., 14618 Tyler Foote Road, Suite 888, Nevada City, CA 95959-8599, (916) 292-3000.
2. Vredenburg and Droge's research: H. Vredenburg and C. Droge, "The Value of Company Newsletters and Magazines," *Industrial Marketing Management,* Vol. 16 (1987), pp. 173-178.
3. Under what circumstances should a company consider publishing a proprietary magazine? B. J. Altschul, "Market and Monitor Your External Publication," *Public Relations Journal,* March 1986, pp. 36-37.
4. Many companies have shifted their marketing strategy: R. Rothenberg, "Benetton's Magazine to Push Vision, Not Clothing," *The New York Times,* April 15, 1991, p. D-8.
5. Neiman Marcus creates a lifestyle: R. Cross and J. Smith, "Staying in Touch with Private Media," *Direct Marketing,* June 1992, pp. 28–32.
6. J. Book, "One-to-One Marketing Communications."
7. Each farmer's issue was customized: M. deCourey Hinds, "Farm Journal Thrives in Fertile Asphalt Soil," *The New York Times,* December 13, 1989.
8. A customer-based communications program: B. Winter, "Custom Publications-More Than Just Newsletters," *Bank Marketing,* August 1988, pp. 18-23.
9. *Special Events Report* predicts sponsorship spending: Personal communication, International Events Group, Inc.
10. J. Andrews (senior editor), *Special Events Report: The Official Directory of Festivals, Sports, and Special Events,* 1990, International Events Group, Inc.
11. $2.6 billion spent on event marketing: *The Official Directory of Festivals, Sports, and Special Events,* 1990, International Events Group, Inc.
12. "Sponsownership": P. Stanley, "Sponsorships Will Become Standard for Events," *Potentials in Marketing,* June 1990, p. 64.
13. *Special Events Report* suggests the following conditions: Personal communication, International Events Group, publisher of the *Special Events Report.*
14. Polaroid discovered that 30 percent increased their use of Polaroid film: M. Neal, "Polaroid's New Focus," *Direct Marketing,* May 1991, pp. 32-34.
15. Renz comments: "Two Beer Catalogs Offer Dances with Wolves and Clydesdales," *Beverage World Periscope Edition,* December 31, 1990, p. 6.
16. Marketers have traditionally favored: "In the Good Ol' Summertime-Many Companies Bask in the Promotional Rays of Summer," *Incentive,* April 1991, pp. 92-93.
17. The catalog positively changed the attitude: K. Brodsky, "Distiller Finds Little Comfort as a Cataloger," *Advertising Age,* October 27, 1986, p. S-31.
18. Corporate expenditures: W. B. Werther, "Corporate Video Applications," *Leadership and Organization Development Journal,* Vol. 9, No. 4 (1988), pp. 3-6.
19. A study was conducted by the Wharton School: *Direct,* "Video Brochure Cuts Through the Clutter," March 10, 1990, p. 16.
20. For Christmas 1991: L. Petersen, "The 14-Minute Holiday Workout," *Adweek's Marketing Week,* October 14, 1991, p. 9; S. Strom, "For Hartmarx, a Videotape Is Worth 1,000 Catalogs," *The New York Times,* October 9, 1991, pp. D-1 and D-4.

Chapter Eight

What to Do When You Fail
Lost Customer Programs

Scene from a United Airlines TV commercial: CEO enters a small boardroom; executives are seated around (CEO speaks in a disappointed tone).

"I got a phone call this morning from one of our oldest customers.

He fired us! After 20 years, he fired us!

Said he didn't know us anymore."

"I think I know why. We used to do business with a handshake, face-to-face. Now, it's a phone call, and a fax, 'get back to you later,' with another fax—probably.'"

"Well folks, some things gotta change.

(CEO begins handing out airline tickets) That's the reason we're gonna set out for a little face-to-face chat with every customer we have…"

(One executive asks the CEO:) "Ben, where are you going?"

(CEO responds) "I'm going to visit that old friend who fired us this morning!"*

While the primary message of aftermarketing is to establish and maintain relationships with current customers, some more enlightened marketers today are even reaching out to past or lost customers. The philosophy motivating this extraordinary effort is analogous to the "zero defect" philosophy of manufacturing. In zero defect production management, to improve a manufacturing process the manufacturer does not study his *perfect units;* he studies *defective units.* Lost customers are the marketer's defects. These are the customers for whom the marketer's system has failed. To improve his marketing system and products or services, the marketer can contact (and learn from) lost customers. Their opinions about the product or service, the delivery system or personnel, may offer more meaningful and objective information than that provided by current, reasonably satisfied customers.

Another reason for contact with lost customers is that many can be won back! A lost customer survey, besides collecting valuable diagnostic information, can also serve as input to a sales prospecting program by identifying lost customers with high likelihood of repurchasing. Lost customer surveys and win-back programs remind the marketer that customers are not always lost forever.

THE COSTS OF LOSING A CUSTOMER

Losing customers is a costly business:

- The customer of an upscale supermarket will spend $50,000 over the course of a decade.

---

* Used with permission, United Airlines.

EXHIBIT 8–1
The Costs of Losing Customers

Number of accounts lost:	2,000	(167 accounts per month)
	× $1,200	Average revenue per account
	$2,400,000	Total lost annual revenues
Profit loss:	× .12	Profit margin
	$ 280,000	Total lost profit
Account closing costs:	$ 20	Per closed account
	× 2,000	Number of lost accounts
	$ 40,000	Total administrative costs
Total costs:	$288,000	Profit lost
	+ 40,000	Administrative costs
	$312,000	Bottom line annual costs of losing customers

Adapted from L. Liswood, *Serving Them Right* (New York: Harper Business, 1990), p. 93.

- An automobile dealer can expect $150,000 in total income from a loyal customer over his lifetime.
- An appliance manufacturer can count on approximately $3,000 in sales to a satisfied customer over a 20-year period.

Laura Liswood suggests an exercise to appreciate the costs of losing customers over the course of a year for a typical department store in Exhibit 8–1.

Compounding these directly estimable costs, numerous economic studies show that a customer's value to a marketer increases during her tenure with the marketer. Most marketers invest considerable resources in winning a new customer. In Exhibit 8–2, Reichheld and Sasser provide a credit card company as one example. Typically a credit card company spends $51 to win a new customer. Because the new customer uses the card only occasionally at first, profits from the new customer in the first year do not recover the costs involved in winning her. But as the customer becomes more acquainted with the use of the card and satisfied with the service provided by the credit card company, usage and profitability increase.[1]

As the established customer's purchases increase, the company's operating costs decline. The initial credit check never needs to be performed again. And as the company gains more experience with the customer, it can serve her even better. Over time, as the customer begins to rely on the service she receives, she may even be willing to pay more for the credit card than for a competitive card with unknown features and policies. So it is with the costs of acquiring and servicing a customer in most industries and categories.

EXHIBIT 8–2
Profit from Customers Over Time

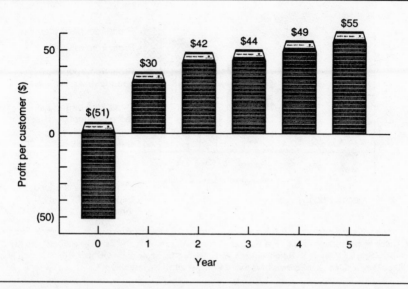

There are other, less concrete benefits from retained customers. For example, they provide wonderful free advertising. Word-of-mouth is not only free, it is oftentimes more effective in the marketplace than paid advertising. For all of these reasons, a customer's real worth appreciates over her life with a marketer (see Exhibit 8–3).

Typically a business will lose 15 to 20 percent of its customer base each year. But as the company lowers the rate at which it loses customers, the average customer lifetime increases and profits increase even more. Exhibit 8–4 shows profits' substantial reaction to decreases in customer defection rates. For example, if a company with an annual defection rate of 10 percent cuts that rate in half, the average lifetime of a customer will double from 10 to 20 years. Profits (in Exhibit 8–4) increase from $300 to $525, and so on.

Customer loyalty, then, has a price. As marketers become more familiar with the idea of a customer's lifetime value, they will begin to calculate it for their own customers. When they reach this level of introspection, they will begin to understand the value of customer relationships in dollars and cents. They will have proof of the profitability of retaining their current customers.

EXHIBIT 8–3
Why Customers Are More Profitable Over Time

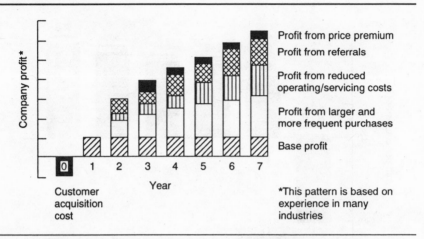

Profit from price premium

Profit from referrals

Profit from reduced operating/servicing costs

Profit from larger and more frequent purchases

Base profit

Customer acquisition cost

Year

*This pattern is based on experience in many industries

Reprinted by permission of *Harvard Business Review.* An exhibit from "Zero Defections: Quality Comes to Services," by F. R. Reichheld and W. E. Sasser, Jr., September–October 1990. Copyright 1990 by the President and Fellows of Harvard College; all rights reserved.

THE STATUS OF LOST CUSTOMERS

Despite the costs and most marketers' sincere efforts to avoid losing customers, customers do not stay with marketers forever. Yet, as customers leave a marketer's franchise, they represent a real marketing paradox. Marketers would probably agree that lost customers could be a source of valuable information (what causes customers to leave), and yet, because lost customers may be considered evidence of the marketer's failures, there may be the tendency to hide, bury, or ignore them. After all, few executives wish to be confronted with their mistakes.

But the marketer is not always directly to blame. Customers will defect from a marketer's business for any of a number of reasons, some under the marketer's control and some out of his control. A customer may leave because the experienced product or service did not live up to his expectations or because a contact person was inattentive or rude. Customers also defect because they move, or are simply offered a better deal by another marketer.

To capitalize on their constructive input, marketers should treat lost customers as learning opportunities. In this respect, they offer valuable information that may be used to identify and remedy problems before the problems affect many more customers.

Some marketing practitioners are campaigning against losing *any* customers. Their goal is to achieve zero defections.[2] This is an admirable but highly idealistic

EXHIBIT 8–4
Profit as a Function of Customer Lifetime

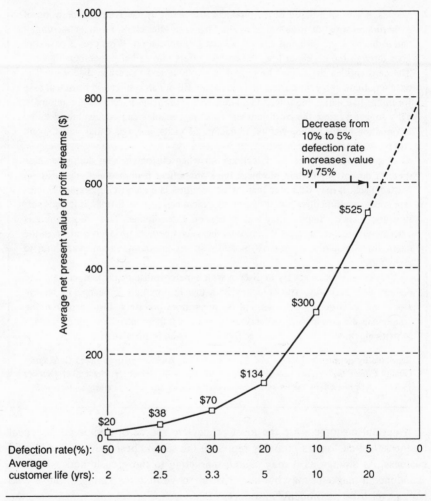

Reprinted by permission of *Harvard Business Review.* An exhibit from "Zero Defections: Quality Comes to Services," by F. R. Reichheld and W. E. Sasser, Jr., September–October 1990. Copyright 1990 by the President and Fellows of Harvard College; all rights reserved.

goal, somewhat out of touch with the exigencies of the real world. In reality, most defecting customers are ignored without ever being asked why they left, or without being told they will be missed. A more realistic and valuable compromise for today's marketers may be to aspire to *reduced defections* and to *zero unacknowledged defections.*

AFTERMARKETING WORKING
How Staples Keeps Defections at a Minimum

Staples is a Boston-based office products discounter. It has done a superb job of gathering information usually lost by the cashier or sales clerk. From its opening, it had a database to store and analyze customer information. Whenever a customer goes through the checkout line, the cashier offers him or her a membership card. The card entitles the holder to special promotions and to certain discounts. The only requirement for the card is that the person fill out an application form that asks for things like name, job title, and address. All subsequent purchases are automatically logged against the card number. This way, Staples can accumulate detailed information about buying habits, frequency of visits, average dollar value spent, and particular items purchased.

Staples constantly tracks defections, so when customers stop doing business there or do not buy certain products, the store notices it immediately and calls to get feedback. It may be a clue that the competition is underpricing Staples on certain goods, a competitive factor that management can explore further. If it finds sufficient evidence, Staples may cut prices on those items. This information is extremely valuable because it pinpoints the uncompetitive products and saves the chain from launching expensive broad-brush promotions pitching everything to everybody.

Staples' telemarketers try to discern which merchandise its customers want and do not want and why. The company uses that information to change its buying stock and to target its catalogs and coupons more precisely. Instead of running coupons in the newspaper, for instance, it can insert them into the catalogs it sends to particular customers or industries that have proven responsive to coupons.

Reprinted by permission of *Harvard Business Review*. An excerpt from "Zero Defections: Quality Comes to Services," by F. R. Reichheld and W. E. Sasser, Jr., September–October 1990. Copyright 1990 by the President and Fellows of Harvard College; all rights reserved.

If current customers are the most productive source of additional or repeat business, lost customers probably represent the second best source of additional business. As strange as it may sound, marketing to those customers who have abandoned a marketer may be more cost-effective than marketing to those who have never tried a company's products or services. The reasons for this are the following:

- With rare exception, customers generally do not totally reject a marketer from whom they have previously purchased products or services. They may currently be out of love with the marketer, but they continue to be *accessible and responsive* to the marketer's efforts.

- Previous or past customers often retain a feeling of loyalty or affinity toward a marketer. After buying a brand for numerous purchase cycles, it becomes an old friend, and it is difficult to dismiss past-used brands.

- Lost customers may have left because they were disenchanted with the marketer's ability to satisfy their expectations. After having sampled the performance of one or more competitors, they may be less demanding or more accepting of the marketer's conduct of business.

- The marketer may have fixed what caused defecting customers to leave in the first place. If the CIF contains a note of why the customer left (from an exit interview), the marketer may be able to win customers back by contacting them when the problem has been fixed.

- The identity and preferences of lost customers are known. The same information about potential customers may be nonexistent or very expensive to acquire.

KNOW WHO YOUR LOST CUSTOMERS ARE

Just as a Customer Information File is critical for serving present customers, so too is it necessary for learning the identities of lost customers in order to win them back. Oftentimes lost customers will be maintained in the main CIF even though they have become inactive. But some data processing operations like to purge inactive records from the CIF to speed daily operations. It is acceptable to allow the data processing people to remove lost customers' records from the main CIF, so long as the records are copied over to an equally accessible file of lost and past customers.

One service marketer conducted a survey among a sample of lost customers to determine how easily they could be won back. The marketer was dumbfounded when she found that although many of her lost customers said they would return, her company was routinely purging their names from the Customer Information File! And unfortunately it would have been difficult to recover the names of customers removed from the file in the interests of efficient file maintenance.

Knowing who defecting customers are is second in importance to preventing them from defecting in the first place. Knowing the identities of lost customers is generally easier for the service marketer than for the product marketer. And in any case it is easier for marketers of frequently purchased products and services to know their defecting customers. Even though a bank has an excellent CIF on its mortgage holders, it may be difficult to discern those who have decided not to reapply to the bank for their next 30-year home mortgage. On the other hand, if a family eats at a restaurant twice a month for half a year and then stops returning, the restaurant should be able to detect their loss within one or two months.

Packaged goods marketers usually enjoy an adequate purchase frequency from their customers, but lack the direct feedback of an interactive CIF to help them immediately spot a defecting customer. Those packaged goods manufacturers with CIFs may have to resort to such approximations as reviewing files of frequent promotional offer redeemers. If a regularly redeeming household fails to redeem in two or three successive offers, it is reasonable to infer that the household is in the process of defecting from the brand.

As supermarkets build their own databases of customers and as packaged goods marketers begin to distribute promotional coupons identifying the recipient households, it will be easier to track sales and redemptions by household or family. For the immediate future, some guessing may be necessary.

CONDUCTING THE EXIT INTERVIEW

When something upsets a customer enough to cause him to stop doing business with a marketer, it is important for the marketer to identify what upset the customer and why. Although some may consider talking to departing customers an example of too little attention, too late, the information to be gained has significant value. It can help to pinpoint problems that are bad enough to cause customers to stop doing business with the company, and can help describe the profile of the high-likelihood defector. Understanding what departing customers did before they decided to take their business elsewhere can help a company to recognize other high-risk customers and can prepare customer service representatives to be more effective in their remedial efforts with them.

It is also important to recognize that, because so few customers ever complain, the marketer should not think that he understands why all customers defect. Those who volunteer dissatisfaction provide only limited information. It pays to attempt to interview all customers who defect.

The goodwill value of showing enough concern to ask why a customer is leaving cannot be underestimated. Though it is unlikely to cause the customer to reverse his decision to leave, it may make the customer more receptive to winback efforts in the future. Why should any customer consider returning to do business with a marketer who never expressed concern over his departure in the first place?

Knowing Who to Interview

Conducting an exit interview requires that the marketer have an up-to-date CIF that interacts with purchase transactions. This is far easier for the service marketer than the product marketer. Services are often rendered on the marketer's premises or involve some amount of registration or information exchange prior to the service being rendered. These conditions make it far easier (and often necessary) for the marketer to maintain a CIF of all active customers. It follows that the service marketer is more able to spot a missing (and presumed lost) customer.

The steps for conducting a lost owner survey include the following:

- Building a database or identifying a source of names of lost owners. (Without an existing source of lost customers' names, the process will be protracted.)

- Contacting the lost customers to administer a questionnaire.
- Assembling a representative tally of responses to be used for strategic planning, for correcting manufacturing problems, and for the improvement of current customer response mechanisms.

Factors to Consider

Factors that will influence the success of a lost customer survey include one or more of the following:

- *The medium of the survey.* The goal in choosing a medium is to maximize response rate while minimizing intrusion into the lost customer's life. Telephone interviews command attention, but often interfere with a customer's work or personal time. Mail surveys are less intrusive but also tend to generate lower response rates. The most common format for lost customer surveys is probably mail.
- *The presentation of the questionnaire.* This is the marketer's last communication with the customer, and how it is presented may influence the customer's long-term remembrance of the marketer. The questionnaire package has two objectives: to acknowledge that the customer has stopped purchasing the marketer's goods or services, and to request information about the circumstances which led the customer to defect. The package containing the letter and questionnaire ought to be as personalized as possible, reinforcing the impression that the customer is known as an individual. Also, any accompanying correspondence must be personally signed and appear to be individually prepared, further demonstrating the marketer's concern.
- *The explanation accompanying the questionnaire.* How can customers who have stopped doing business with the marketer be expected to answer her questionnaire? The answer to this is the marketer's sincere request for *help.* The message delivered to the lost customer must be, "We know you've stopped buying from us," and "We're asking for your help so that we can fix the situation to prevent other current customers from experiencing the same problem." Many customers will be happy, even flattered, to provide their perspective of what is wrong with the marketer's product, service, or delivery system.
- *The structure of the questionnaire.* Customers will provide information, but the marketer must also be realistic. The goal, within five questions, ought to be to identify the problem that lost the customer. Resist the temptation to ask how likely the customer might be to come back, as this appears too self-serving at this point. Wait until the problem is fixed before informing each customer lost because of it, and then ask them to reinstate their business.
- *How completed questionnaires will be collected.* Provide an impartial, third-party auditor or a senior executive of the company to receive

EXHIBIT 8–5
Lost Customer Survey Results

	Year 1	Year 2
Percent responding	39%	45%
Reasons for disconnecting:		
Poor quality/performance	38	35
Poor customer service	25	20
Price/economic conditions	15	19
Lost, sold equipment	10	7
Other reason	12	19
Willingness to resubscribe ("Definitely" + "Probably")	24%	28%

Source: Marketing Metrics, Inc.

completed questionnaires. If prepared for return by mail, the questionnaire should carry business reply postage, alleviating any expense on the customer's side for returning it.

Results of an Exit Interview

Past customers are generally far more cooperative than might have been expected. A surprisingly high proportion of lost customers will generally respond to a lost customer survey. Response rates usually average from 35 to 50 percent, depending on the currency and accuracy of the contact information in the marketer's CIF.

Responses from lost customers are generally constructive and thoughtful, and are rarely disrespectful or angry. And even these disenfranchised customers often express appreciation for the marketer's interest in their needs and opinions.

For example, twice in the last two years a survey has been conducted among disconnected customers of a telecommunications service. In each wave, a sizable sample (1,000 to 2,000) of lost customers were interviewed to determine why they canceled, and what, if anything, the service could do to win them back. Exhibit 8–5 shows the basic results. A large majority agreed to participate in the survey. (Participation has been tested in two conditions: the sponsor's identity concealed and the sponsor's identity revealed. Generally, a slightly higher participation rate has been observed when the sponsor has been identified.)

In a similar investigation reported in the literature, a sizable majority (68 percent) of defecting customers said that they had stopped buying from a marketer for no particular reason. (It appears these customers were detecting indifference

AFTERMARKETING WORKING
A Lost Customer Questionnaire

Sample Cover Letter

Dear Customer:

We pride ourselves in maintaining good relationships with our customers. We hope they will always buy from us. But if something goes wrong, we also hope that they'll tell us and allow us to set the problem right.

We are concerned because your account with us has been inactive for the last three months.

To help us understand your present inactivity and to allow us to correct any problems you *may have* experienced, will you take a few minutes to answer the enclosed questionnaire? Your answers will be held in the strictest confidence and will be used to help us improve the quality of our products and/or service.

When you have completed the questionnaire, simply place it in the envelope we have provided. No postage is required.

Thank you for your assistance. We value your business and hope we may serve you again in the future.

Sincerely,

President

Lost Customer Questionnaire

1. Please indicate the reason or reasons you have stopped ordering from us (Check as many as apply):

    [ ] Moved away from the (city name) area.
    [ ] Your parts are no longer needed.
    [ ] Your company made errors on my account.
    [ ] Your service was slow or inefficient.
    [ ] Your personnel were discourteous or unfriendly.
    [ ] Another (city name) area company is more convenient.
    [ ] Account at another company meets my needs better.
    [ ] Other (specify) _____

    _____

2. Where are you currently buying supplies? (Please check only one.)

    [ ] (Major competitor's name).
    [ ] A (city name) company.
    [ ] Other (specify)
    [ ] Did not replace account.

3. Which of our branches did you use most often? _____

4. How would you rate (our company) in each of the following areas?

	Excellent	Average	Poor
Courteous and friendly personnel	[ ]	[ ]	[ ]
Knowledgeable personnel	[ ]	[ ]	[ ]
Prompt service	[ ]	[ ]	[ ]
Accurate bills/statements	[ ]	[ ]	[ ]
Responsiveness to my needs	[ ]	[ ]	[ ]

5. Please check the statement that best describes you:
   [ ] I give most of my orders to one supplier.
      (Which one?: _____)
   [ ] I give my orders to several suppliers.
   [ ] I no longer have need for the products you sell.
      (Why is that?: _____)

6. Please indicate your age group:
   [ ] Under 25 [ ] 25–29 [ ] 30–44 [ ] 45–54 [ ] 55–64 [ ] 65+

7. Please indicate your annual household income category:
   [ ] Under $15,000   [ ] $15,000–24,999   [ ] $25,000–34,999
   [ ] $35,000–49,999   [ ] $50,000 or more

8. In what ways do you feel we could improve our products or services for our customers? _____
   _____

   Thank you for your help,

   President

from the marketer and were feeling unappreciated.) Fourteen percent left because of a specific complaint that the marketer failed to attend to, nine percent left because they were enticed by competitors, and nine percent left because they moved out of a marketer's territory.[3]

Diagnostic questions in lost customer surveys ought to be asked as open-end questions, allowing respondents to answer in their own terms and as thoroughly as they wish. To provide check categories to speed tabulation of the survey results would be to make two mistakes. The first mistake is the marketer's assumption that he is already aware of all of the reasons why a customer might leave. The second mistake is preventing the responding lost customer from telling as much about the conditions of her departure as she cares to disclose. Obviously, the more that is learned about the conditions of a customer's departure, the more easily (and thoroughly) the situation can be fixed for future customers.

EXHIBIT 8-6
Keyword Search of Open-End Responses

```
Verbatim Analyzer                                          Page 1
Marketing Metrics                               Keyword: TAST*
- - - - - - - - - - -
    #    1    They did not taste very much like homemade.
                They tasted too sweet.
                They tasted stale.

    #    2    The taste of the chocolate was not rich enough.
                The cookies tasted old, as though they had been in the
                box too long. The cookies tasted like plastic, not
                homemade.

    #    3    They tasted like cardboard. I could not taste the chips.
                They tasted like grandma's.

    #    4    The cookies left a funny aftertaste. They tasted stale.
                They did not have enough chocolate chips.

    #    5    The chocolate chip cookies were very plain and tasted
                stale. They were too dry and crumbled too easily. Just
                about any other brand would taste better than these!

        TAST* appeared 13 times in 5 Responses.

        5 Records searched, 5 contained TAST or 100 Percent.
```

Source: Marketing Metrics, Inc.

If open-end questions are used, then they should be reported in as much detail as possible. This is a situation in which a keyword searching routine is invaluable. Exhibit 8–6 shows some survey responses to a diagnostic question processed to search for a keyword. Responses organized in this manner are very compelling evidence. They provide management the opportunity to justify change and to make changes which are appropriate for the problems identified by lost customers.

One of the more tempting questions to ask a lost customer is "What can we do to get you to come back?" Although the informational value of this question is substantial, it approaches an attempt to resell the marketer, possibly causing a true survey to be interpreted as a sales pitch. It is preferable not to introduce a sales message into a communication that is positioned as a research survey. Not only is this practice tantamount to unethical behavior, it could demean the perceived sincerity of the survey in the customer's mind. An increasingly common practice that threatens the survival of the legitimate marketing research community is the so-called "SUGS" activity (Selling Under the Guise of Surveying), practiced by unethical marketing groups as a way to gain attention to their sales pitch.

On the other hand, business is business. The preferable way of handling this situation is for the interviewer at some time within the interview to ask, "Would you like to be contacted by the sales department?" This question, of course, should only be asked of those lost customers who appear somewhat receptive. The CIF record of those customers who answer yes should be marked for a later follow-up by the sales department.

High-Risk Customer Profile

Another fringe benefit of a lost customer survey is the opportunity to build a profile of high-risk customers. For example, in a lost customer survey it was determined that a large proportion of defecting customers had placed at least three calls to customer service during the month preceding when they stopped using a service. An action plan was immediately formulated to contact and resell all subscribers whose records indicated that they had called three times within one month. The contacts to customer service were used as an indicant of a customer who might be likely to stop doing business with the marketer.

Acting on the Information

Lost customer surveys are like any other marketing intelligence effort: they are only as good as the decisions they help support. But if management does not hear the information, the surveys are of little use. MBNA, a Delaware-based national credit card issuer, has taken a rather unique approach to involving company executives in its exit interviewing program. Senior executives at MBNA learn directly from their defecting customers. Each executive spends at least four hours each month in a telephone monitoring facility, listening to customer service reps taking calls from unhappy customers and customers who are calling to cancel their accounts.

This first-hand exposure serves two purposes. First, it builds credibility and reality for the survey mechanism. It is hard to deny findings from a survey that one has actually experienced. Second, experiencing the actual calls may help the executive to better understand categories used in the ultimate report (to economically summarize respondents' comments).

Exit interviews provide some of the most objective information a marketer can collect. Unlike other marketing research surveys that collect opinions or attitudes (which may or may not relate to any future action the customer may take), exit interviews can collect descriptions of actual experiences that were displeasing enough to cause the customer to stop doing business with the marketer. There is no need to "guesstimate" the severity of an issue. Each identified problem warrants the marketer's attention.

Frequently, lost customers responding to an exit interview will describe their previous attempts to obtain satisfaction directly from the marketer. In their descriptions it will become clear to the marketer which existing systems or personnel are inadequately performing their task of remedying customer problems.

Besides being a very provocative source of information for strategic planning, a lost customer survey can also serve as input to a sales prospecting program by discovering the identities of lost customers who indicate that they would repurchase.

In the course of several studies, it has been found that a substantial portion of lost customers indicate that they would repurchase the marketer's brand, product, or service and will describe what the marketer needs to do to bring them back. Their requirements are usually reasonable and often reflect improvements that may have been made already.

Why Customers Leave

The most common reasons that customers stop patronizing an organization include the following:

- *Dissatisfaction with product, delivery, installation, service, or price.* While a customer may excuse any one occurrence of late delivery, inaccurate shipment, even poor quality goods, it is unlikely in today's competitive market that he will remain loyal in the face of repeated instances. A price increase may have the same effect, especially if the customer has not been given much advance notice.

- *Poor handling of a complaint.* This is one instance in which a single incident can lose a customer. If a customer feels that a complaint has been ignored, minimized, or otherwise mishandled, chances are he will search for another supplier. Any arguments with sales representatives over the issue substantially increase the possibility of a lost customer.

- *Disapproval of changes.* Any time a change is made in price, policies, or sales force, customer relationships are vulnerable. Some customers may become so angry that they stop buying altogether.

- *Dissatisfaction with treatment.* Current customers often do not receive the attention and courtesy they deserve. Their familiarity causes them to be treated in an inappropriate (often rude) manner. This is a major mistake—all customers ought to be treated with equal respect and resold on the company and its products.

- *New people or new policies at the account.* Changes in the customer's situation can disrupt the relationship with a marketer, through no fault of the marketer. The best defense is to stay alert to such possibilities and try to anticipate and neutralize their impact.

- *Acceptance of a competitive offer.* No customer, no matter how longstanding, is guaranteed beyond the last order signed. The competition is always there ready to move in, and sometimes they win away an account.[*]

---

[*]Adapted from "How to Make 'Lost' Customers Your Best Source of 'New' Customers," *Profit-Building Strategies,* December 1990, pp. 23–24.

Knowing why a customer has stopped doing business with an organization gives it the opportunity to correct its behavior and possibly win the customer back.

NOT ALL LOST CUSTOMERS ARE EQUAL

Customers differ in their attractiveness to the marketer. Those customers who purchase more, the heavy users, are far more valuable to the marketer than light users. Often demonstrated by Pareto's Rule, the 80/20 Principle, or the Heavy-Half Theory, marketers recognize that a small fraction of their total customers account for a disproportionately large share of their total sales. This phenomenon makes the small group of heavy buyers extremely important in any marketing strategy or plan.

As a campaign or program is planned to win back lost customers, it is important to allocate more attention to the most important lost customers. This is where the purchase history of lost customers can be used to identify those whose past business qualified them as heavy users. They should receive the most attention and should be contacted by the very best and most energetic people.

CUSTOMER WIN-BACK PROGRAMS

Win-back programs can take many forms, from a highly organized, very aggressive effort, to simply maintaining the customer's name on the mailing list to show him he has not been forgotten. As stated earlier, one of the biggest marketing mistakes is removing the names of past or lost customers from the CIF. As this is done, the customer generally stops receiving any communication from the company and her displeasure with it becomes a self-fulfilling prophecy as the company unwittingly breaks off all communication.

Today's marketplace of recently deregulated industries finds many marketers coping with customer loss and win-back for the first time. On the other hand, newer industries, such as cable TV and cellular telephones, have lived with defectors and disconnections from their second day of doing business.

MCI has taken a very aggressive role in protecting its growing share of the long distance telecommunications market. It has converted some sales offices into the new mission of customer protection and win-back. This means that customers are called on a regular basis and asked if MCI's service is satisfactory. It also means that customers who have filed for service change are contacted by very persuasive telemarketing experts whose job is to neutralize and stop defections.

MBNA, the Delaware-based credit card issuer, has similarly dedicated itself to minimizing customer loss. Its defection rate, 5 percent per year, is one half of the average rate for its industry. MBNA has a customer-defection "SWAT team" staffed by some of the company's best telemarketers. When customers cancel their credit cards, the team tries to convince them to stay. They are successful with approximately one-half of the defecting customers they call.

Instituting a Win-Back Program

An effective win-back effort will consist of three steps:

• *Find out why the customer stopped buying.* To plan a successful approach to an ex-customer, the reason the customer left must be discovered. It may be something the company did or did not do, or it may be something out of the company's control.

Lost customer files should be searched for clues of causes for defecting in all records of communication, or the pattern of communication. Check the date that orders began to fall off or ended entirely. Compare it to the date of any change in the company structure or operating practices (or in the customer's).

As the reason for the customer's defection is discovered, design an approach to overcome it. For instance, if late deliveries appear implicated in the loss, the recontact with the customer should emphasize a description of a new system designed to ensure on-time delivery. If a competitor lured the account away, find a special offer to make: samples, a discount, extra service, and so on.

• *Research the customer's present situation.* Do not assume that customers' needs of a year or six months ago still apply. The marketplace changes rapidly and may be making new demands. The customer's internal situation may have changed: budgets may be tighter, offices busier, or specifications revised.

Such circumstances can provide an opportunity to capture the customer's interest. Offer a solution to a new problem, an idea to use now, and quite often customers will listen.

To formulate this kind of approach, it is necessary to know who has buying authority and what are the buying influencers. To determine this information, ask noncompeting salespeople and other company contacts. Some of the customer's own customers are often excellent sources of information. Trade associations and the trade press may also be useful, at least in identifying the latest trends in the customer's industry.

• *Make the Contact.* What is the best way to get in touch with the account: mail, telephone, a cold call? Who should make the contact? Find the answers by reviewing the customer's preferred ways of working. Then put an attack plan into action.

If the research was adequate and the approach is right for the customer, a meeting may be set up. This is a business and not a social situation. The customer's major interest is not in keeping a feud going or in dealing with friends, but simply in getting the best deal. Offering something the customer is not getting—in benefits, services, quality, or any other extra—may provide a new chance.*

---

*Adapted from "How to Make 'Lost' Customers Your Best Source of 'New' Customers," *Profit-Building Strategies,* December 1990, pp. 23–24.

AFTERMARKETING WORKING
A Bank's Win-Back Program

Depositors yanked millions of dollars out of Maryland National Bank in 1990, and the state's largest bank wants the money back.

A personalized letter from company chairman Alfred Lerner has kicked off a campaign directed at hundreds of customers who drew down their accounts after the bank was hit with massive losses in 1990. In the letter, Maryland indicates its intention to lower some deposit minimums and offers special rates to get those customers to bring their business back to the bank.

"The offer you are about to receive comes with my personal thanks for your past business and for your part in making Maryland National strong," Lerner says in the letter.

A follow-up mailing from branch managers offers customers a penalty-free certificate of deposit "when you bring us $10,000 or more from another financial institution." The certificate will pay out 6.88 percent interest, up from the 6.53 rate currently advertised.

The direct-mail offer is part of a campaign that includes increased advertising and incentives designed to pull business and retail customers back into the bank's branches, an observer said.

Adapted from J. P. Pierpoint "MNC Woos Back Jittery Customers," *Baltimore Business Journal,* April 8, 1991, p. 18.

MANAGING EXPECTATIONS

One of the most common reasons for losing customers is the marketer's inability to live up to or deliver on the customer's demanding expectations.

In this respect the practice of advertising and aftermarketing may appear to clash. After all, advertising is accustomed to "selling the sizzle" (not only of a steak but of any product). The more ambitious and fanciful the claims, the supposedly greater the resulting desire for the product created among the target audience. The problem is that ambitious advertising may create unrealistically high expectations. These expectations (which may be so ambitious that no product or service could fulfill them) can actually be responsible for short-term dissatisfaction and customers' resolve not to repurchase the brand or product. (Two opposing perspectives were discussed in Chapter 6.)

It is therefore vital for advertising and aftermarketing not only to talk to each other, but to actually be coordinated with one another as partners, not as possible opponents.

Managing expectations is not much different from managing evidence (discussed in Chapter 4). The only real difference is that evidence can only be managed among current customers, whereas expectations can be managed among potential customers through communications and among current customers through communications and the product or service itself.

Generally, there are four major ways to manage expectations:

• *Through marketing communications.* The product's ads, the promises made personally by salespeople, and the impact of promotional programs should be oriented toward realistic promises.

• *Through the selection and training of intermediaries.* Because these institutions and their employees will often have the greatest interaction with customers, their influence on expectations can be profound.

• *Through literature or instructions.* Delivered with the product or service or sent to customers upon owner registration, such literature can help to focus customers' attentions on the strong points of a product or service. The literature can also help explain aspects of performance which might otherwise be perceived as failures by an uninformed customer. The literature can effectively manage evidence and thereby help control expectations.

• *By monitoring the performance of the product or service.* Know how to underpromise and then overdeliver, maximizing customer satisfaction.

One of aftermarketing's functions is to educate present customers about what to expect or what to appreciate from a product or service, and how to judge the quality of the product or service as received. Everyone is helped by a post-purchase dialogue. If the marketer is delivering fair value by educating customers to appreciate the quality, he gets fair credit for his quality efforts. The customer becomes a smarter customer in the future, and will be more resistant to superfluous claims from competitors. In some situations, customers may be incorrectly evaluating brands or misjudging the quality of products or services using inappropriate criteria. The marketer's aftermarketing efforts will help correct this naïveté, benefiting both the customers and the industry.

The marketer can use a variety of aftermarketing vehicles to help manage expectations:

• Personalized demonstrations.
• Post-purchase correspondence.
• Proprietary magazines and newsletters.
• Proprietary media.
• Special events.

A classic example of managing expectations is the new-car test drive. In this exposure to a new car, the salesperson will generally direct the potential buyer's attentions to appropriate expectation levels in a masterful way, thus avoiding any negative reactions and overcoming any overly ambitious expectations the buyer may have.

One of aftermarketing's more vital roles may be to help manage customers' expectations with products and services. No matter how good a marketer's product is, he should never become so arrogant or blasé as to assume that customers will purchase with an accurate level of expectations. It is the marketer's opportunity to influence expectations and thereby influence the degree of satisfaction customers experience.

KEY POINTS OF THE CHAPTER

Customer Win-Back Program

Marketers are creating special efforts to win back lost customers. A program generally consists of identifying those customers who have been lost, understanding why they have stopped buying from the marketer, and then contacting them to offer assurance that the problem or difficulty they experienced has been corrected. Generally, 15 to 25 percent of lost customers can be won back!

Exit Interviews

Interviews should be conducted with customers identified as no longer buying a marketer's products or services. The purpose of the interview is to determine why the customers are no longer buying from the marketer. Almost one-half of defecting customers contacted in such a survey will normally participate, providing good insights into problems the marketer may be having with his product, service, or delivery system.

Managing Expectations

Because customers' expectations determine how much they acknowledge quality in a product or service, it is to the marketer's advantage to attempt to influence or manage customers' expectations. Customers' attentions should be directed toward aspects of the product or service that are most likely to provide satisfaction.

NOTES

1. Reichheld and Sasser provide a credit card company as one example: F. R. Reichheld and W. E. Sasser, Jr., "Zero Defections: Quality Comes to Services," *Harvard Business Review,* September–October 1990, pp. 105-111.
2. Their goal is to achieve zero defections: F. R. Reichheld and W. E. Sasser, Jr., "Zero Defections: Quality Comes to Services," *Harvard Business Review,* September–October 1990, pp. 105-111.
3. In a similar reported investigation: M. Raphael, "Bring Them Back Alive," *Direct Marketing,* May 1990, pp. 50–51.

Chapter Nine

Building an Internal Organization to Support Aftermarketing

Effective relationship marketing requires an organizational commitment to the aftermarketing techniques described in this book. And it is unlikely to be easily achieved within the conventional organization structure. In fact, one of the worst possible decisions is to institute aftermarketing programs with neither the appropriate staff nor the adequate resources to properly support the programs. To do so is to risk disappointing customers substantially or risk being perceived as basically insincere. It is probably better not to initiate aftermarketing programs at all than to take the first steps and then fail to correctly follow up with each customer.

Relationship marketing is built on providing a quality product or service. The success of Japanese marketing has been attributed by some to how well Japanese management has reacted to quality control programs. The perspectives of zero defects and company-wide quality management have been endorsed throughout corporate Japan, down to the individual factory worker, who regularly participates in a quality control circle with his co-workers.

Although U.S. marketers have been quick to jump on the bandwagon of customer satisfaction and quality production, they have little experience and few success stories in translating such input into product design and production and management strategies aimed at improving quality. At the very least, improving quality requires extreme commitment and substantial resources. For example, Rolls-Royce Motor Cars, Inc. established an entire department to respond to input from its owner contact program. Without such a commitment, many owners probably would have felt that their input was ignored or was not appreciated.

American marketers have the opportunity to fully adopt aftermarketing programs and thus recreate their businesses and their customer franchises. This chapter examines how organizations can act on customer feedback from a variety of sources.

RELATIONSHIP MARKETING BEGINS INSIDE

Developing successful relationships with customers requires constant and unrelenting practice of aftermarketing techniques. One of the more obvious efforts is collecting information from customers. In Chapter 6, the aftermarketing element of a customer satisfaction measurement program was described. This type of program provides customer feedback on the quality of the product or service being distributed and suggests future directions for improvement or change. All of the following aspects must be considered for change:

- The product or service offered.
- The delivery or distribution system.
- Employee actions, attitudes, and values.
- Management's actions, attitudes, and values.
- The organization's structure and culture.
- Employee incentive and reward programs.

But the process of determining how customers feel and what they want and then translating that information into management and employee actions is a tricky process. Perhaps less is known about how to successfully link customer feedback with design and production decisions than is known about anything else in the aftermarketing chain.

J. M. Juran, noted quality advocate, suggests instituting a quality committee or task force to supervise this translation process. Juran describes the role of the quality committee as the following:

- Establishing policies and goals for companywide quality.
- Establishing plans for meeting those quality goals.
- Campaigning for the resources needed to carry out the plans.
- Establishing controls to evaluate progress against goals and to take appropriate action.
- Providing motivation to stimulate management and employees to meet the quality goals.[1]

Whether or not a quality committee is established, a number of informational inputs exist that must be reconciled (they will frequently conflict) and then incorporated into management's planning:

- The customer satisfaction program results.
- Management's perceptions of customer satisfaction.
- Audits by mystery shoppers/customers.
- Observations from customer visitations.

In order to wisely act on the information collected, discrepancies must be resolved. Of the four inputs, it is likely that customers' opinions and management's perspectives may be the most dissimilar. The perspective of the mystery shopper/customer is likely to be closest to an objective view of reality. In this sense, the mystery shopper (if such a program is used) can serve as an arbitrator, identifying which of the two perspectives (management's or customers') is most accurate.

EXHIBIT 9–1
Measuring and Acting on Customer Satisfaction

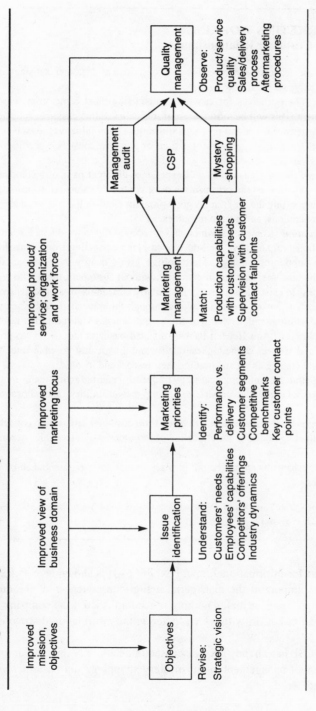

AFTERMARKETING WORKING
Building for Customer Relationships

In discussing the leadership perspective that best fosters customer satisfaction, William Band suggests the following:

• *Intention.* The initiatives for customer satisfaction must come from senior level management. This will be most sincere if it is believed that customer satisfaction offers long-term success and profit maximization. Such initiatives must be on target as identified through good information, and a plan must be specified to achieve what is valued by customers.

• *Integration.* Because customers will experience different parts of a company or organization, all parts of the organization must contribute value to the customer by uniformly supporting the program. A good program requires the combined skills of marketing, operations, and human resources.

• *Implementation.* Companies which have successfully implemented a customer satisfaction program have well-developed plans emanating from a mission statement and supporting strategy. Metropolitan Life's quality assurance credo states, "Met Life customers are our first priority; without customers, there is no reason for a business to exist." Mack Trucks is similarly clear in its mission statement: "We service our customers around the world through the innovative design, engineering, manufacturing, and servicing of trucks and vehicles that meet their needs at low life-cycle cost." And Hewlett-Packard's stated business purpose is "to provide products and services of the highest quality and the greatest possible value to our customers, thereby gaining and holding their respect and loyalty."

Translating strategies into practical steps frequently requires action teams motivating employees behind the project, assigning responsibilities, and allocating resources.

Finally, senior-level management will often form customer satisfaction councils to act as coordinating bodies in the allocation of resources and to recognize accomplishment.

Feedback mechanisms should be put in place to monitor progress and shifts in customers' needs.

Source: W. Band, "The Three I's of Customer Satisfaction Need Your Vision," *Marketing News,* October 23, 1989, p. 17.

The flowchart for informational input (Exhibit 6–4) is shown here as Exhibit 9–1. Notice how important the managerial action consequences of the quality management stage are. Essentially, nothing is accomplished if the company does not have an organized effort with which to act on the information discovered by the CSP.

Because the CSP has already been discussed in detail, only the other informational components (management audit, mystery shopping, and customer visits) will be described here.

MANAGEMENT'S ASSESSMENT OF SATISFACTION

Managers should be encouraged to participate, as respondents, in a survey to assess the quality of the organization's products or services and to estimate the satisfactoriness of the organization's interactions with its customers. This management assessment of satisfaction survey should utilize the same attributes and scales as the customer satisfaction program and may even utilize the same questionnaire. The goal is to have managers participate in a periodic evaluation much the same as customers do in completing a CSP. By objectively assessing the performance of their staff and procedures, they may more readily accept the similar assessment from customers.

The management assessment survey may be conducted by the internal marketing research area or by an outside consultant. Specific outcomes from this evaluation will include management's

- Perceptions of customers' priorities (how management perceives customers' importance ratings across the various product or service attributes).
- Perceptions of the adequacy of the organization's performance in meeting customers' priorities.
- Attitudes toward internal programs for customer satisfaction and quality improvement.

As a result of collecting this information, an analysis can be conducted to see how accurate management's view is of the following:

- Customers' priority rankings of key product or service attributes.
- Customers' satisfaction levels with current products and services.

Exhibit 9–2 shows a case in which management has not totally understood its customers' priorities. This profile is useful information for upper-level management showing just how far off managers' understanding is. In Exhibit 9–2 management has assumed a higher priority for equipment features and a lower priority for sales support than customers express. If introduced tactfully, discrepant profiles like these can help motivate managers to seek a better understanding of customer priorities from the CSP.

Exhibit 9–3 compares customers' ratings of the organization's performance (on key attributes) to management's ratings. This comparison is useful in showing managers how their efforts are really *not* delivering or how customers are not fully recognizing their efforts. Low customer ratings can be the result of *product failure* or a *failure in marketing communications* (customers have not been informed of the product's capabilities or inherent quality). Whenever customers' ratings are low, it is important to determine which failure is to blame so that the appropriate corrective action will be undertaken. Different management reactions will be called for, depending upon the outcome of this determination.

EXHIBIT 9–2
Customer Priorities: Customers' versus Management's View

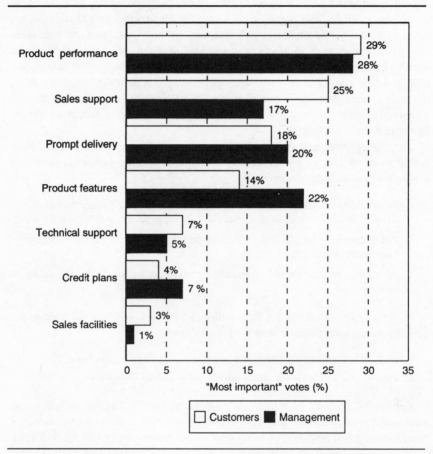

Source: Marketing Metrics, Inc.

THE ROLE OF AN EXTERNAL AUDITOR, THE MYSTERY SHOPPER/CUSTOMER

Willmark, one of the first mystery shopper services, made its name originally by observing salespeople in the burgeoning chain stores of the 1930s and 1940s. At that time, mystery shopping was primarily directed toward assessing employee honesty: were employees putting all of the money in the cash register?

Today, Willmark and other similar marketing intelligence firms send out mystery shoppers to routinely check on customer contact employees in a wide variety of service and product industries. No longer is employee honesty the main

EXHIBIT 9–3
Performance Rating—Customers' versus Management's View

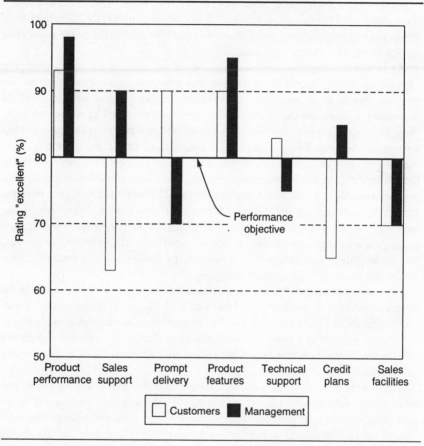

Source: Marketing Metrics, Inc.

goal. In today's mystery shopping, the primary criterion being assessed is employees' ability and willingness to serve as effective aftermarketers. Managers using mystery shopping services seek to improve the quality of both the delivery system and the product or service and to thereby better maintain customer relationships. "A well designed mystery shopper program, with follow-up training and reward programs, can achieve up to a 20 percent improvement in overall customer service," one practitioner maintains.[2]

A company can hire mystery shoppers directly or hire a research firm to develop the observation format, hire the shoppers, and compile the results of the survey. The shoppers, selected to be of different demographic backgrounds, visit, call, or contact stores, branches, or dealerships at different times of the day and different days of the week. During the contact, shoppers inquire about, purchase, or complain about a specific product or service. The main focus of the evaluation is usually on (1) the customer service, (2) the selling, and (3) the complaint-handling capabilities of employees. Other areas, such as the facility or the product or service itself, can also be evaluated.

As in any information program, a company must begin a mystery shopping exercise by setting its specific objectives. Once the objectives of the study are set and the criteria to be evaluated are decided on, the observation form can be assembled. A company can use a standardized form provided by a research company, or it can customize the form (see the accompanying example from the bakery chain, Au Bon Pain). Customized observation forms are generally best, focusing the observation on the specific factors that are central to customer satisfaction in the company's category. Areas for evaluation could be length of wait, product knowledge of customer contact personnel, ability of employees to probe for needs, cross-selling ability, friendliness, and appearance. When specifying qualities for observation, it is important to realize that the mystery shopper's evaluation is limited to what she can see or experience (the "visibles" in the customer blueprint). Such things as company policy or what goes on backstage cannot be measured through mystery shopping.

Once the observational criteria are established, the mystery shoppers study the observation form, familiarizing themselves with the areas to focus on. Sometimes they are assigned a certain product or service to ask for, such as a particular type of account at a bank. Immediately after interacting with the company's employees, they fill out the observation form with as much detail and specificity as possible.

The results from the observations are then compiled and analyzed just as any other survey results would be. It is important to the success of a mystery shopping program that it be conducted systematically and with statistical precision. It should be conducted on a regular basis—every week, month, or six-month period. Specific shoppers must be rotated so that they do not become recognizable to employees.

The results of the mystery shoppers' observations can help to critique just how well relationships with customers are being handled by frontline people. In addition, they can also be used to evaluate all customer-contact personnel. This is why employees should probably be aware that a mystery shopper program is in effect and which aspects of customer interaction will be evaluated.

Mystery shopping programs are often tied to specific corporate goals, with bonus and incentive programs attached. When employees know the criteria for evaluation, with rewards attached, they will generally strive to improve performance in those areas.

However, the information that comes from mystery shopper programs goes far beyond evaluating specific employees. It provides an objective description of

AFTERMARKETING WORKING
Au Bon Pain's Mystery Shopper Observation Form

Courtesy of Au Bon Pain.

aftermarketing efforts that may be compared directly to customers' perceptions and to management's perceptions as well. Mystery shopping studies can identify problem areas, such as whether particular types of customers are treated differently than others. One car dealership, for example, found through a mystery shopping program that women and younger shoppers in its showrooms were not treated with the same degree of seriousness or respect as older, male shoppers.[3]

The studies can reveal how often employee interactions with customers are a positive experience and how able and willing employees are to answer customers' questions. The studies further allow management to track the progress of sales and customer service training. Mystery shopping can also be conducted on competitors for benchmarking purposes. When competitive shopping is undertaken, the results can be used to provide an objective view of comparative strengths and weaknesses that are less biased than the same observations collected from perceptions of loyal customers.

The restaurant chain Au Bon Pain uses its mystery shopper program as a key element in its employee compensation system. The mystery shoppers buy a meal and fill out the observation form (see example). The corporate office compiles the information and provides it to store managers. A scoring system has been established giving points to employees for meeting certain key criteria. Bonuses are attached to surpassing certain score levels. These bonuses and incentives are available to individuals and managers alike. Corrective actions such as retraining result from an employee receiving very low scores. The program is credited with helping to improve customer service at the chain on a national basis. The rate of successful reviews has doubled since mystery shopping began.[4]

MANAGEMENT MONITORING

Perhaps even more controversial than mystery shopping is monitoring by management directly. Various studies suggest that the number of companies using some form of management surveillance or electronic monitoring to determine the quality of customer service delivered by employees could be as high as 40 percent. Service employees, from housekeepers in hotels to stockbrokers, are being monitored either indirectly or directly through the telephones, computer terminals, or other equipment they use.

Despite some worries about the ethics of these practices and the invasion of personal rights of privacy, some managers are successfully using monitoring to improve quality and productivity without alienating employees. The most successful managers follow these sorts of guidelines:

- They make clear to all employees how and why they will be monitored.
- They use monitoring primarily as an aid to coaching and counseling, not as a disciplinary tool. (At car renter Avis's Tulsa phone center, the top

performers work directly with newer agents who ask for help by sitting next to them and taking turns answering calls.)

- They involve employees in setting up a fair system. (AT&T is cooperating with the Communication Workers of America in five pilot projects involving about 1,000 operators. The idea is to set up self-managed telephone call centers where employees will work in teams.)

- The best managers emphasize quality of work over quantity. (At GE's Answer Center, 70 percent of a technician's monitoring score is based on the quality of his response, 15 percent on timeliness and reliability, and only 15 percent on how many calls he handles.)*

THE ROLE OF CUSTOMER VISITS

Somewhat the opposite of mystery shopping is the recently established practice of customer visits. (Though primarily used in industrial marketing situations, there is essentially no reason why a customer visit technique could not be used to similarly study a consumer product or service.) Such visits help management collect information on customers' needs and perceptions in a relatively informal way. This is the case with products or services that are complex, ambiguous, or novel, where personal contact and probing are necessary. Customer visits are also important when the research goals include observation of the customer's environment, exploration of individual customer responses, or the generation of ideas for new products or services.[5]

Though an external research firm can provide a more objective view of a marketer's customers, visits may be better performed by managers and other company personnel to properly probe and fully understand complex issues, examine the customer's technical environment, or understand the customer's varied uses of the product.

For successful implementation of a customer visit program, a company must first set its informational objectives, such as assessing customer satisfaction, identifying customer needs, or exploring new product concepts. Once the objectives are set, the second step is to identify which particular customers to visit. It is important to select a sample that will give the maximum amount of information, reflecting as much as possible the diversity within a company's population of customers. One advantage of customer visit programs is that a wide variety of customers can be hand-selected for visits.

The third step is to select and train the customer visiting team. The team can consist of one person, such as a manager who has a strong impact on the

---

*Adapted from G. Bylinsky, "How Companies Spy on Employees," *Fortune*, November 4, 1991, p. 136.

decision-making process or, as in the case with very complex technology products, a manager and a representative from production and/or R&D. (The direct interaction of the customer with the R&D representative can be quite persuasive in helping to channel R&D's developmental efforts toward specific customer needs.)

The fourth step is to develop a discussion guide that fleshes out the information sought without unduly burdening the customer. The fifth step is to conduct the interviews, which are followed by debriefing sessions. The sixth and final step is to analyze and report the findings.

While customer visits can easily be envisioned by an industrial marketing firm, they also seem feasible for consumer packaged goods companies as well. It seems entirely feasible to send observers into the homes of recruited consumers to collect information or opinions about products and services *during actual use occasions.* (This would follow the roots of focus groups which originated in neighborhood "coffee klatches.") What better time and place to interview a homemaker about a cake mix than when she is in the process of baking a cake in her own kitchen?

It is believed that customer visits offer management relatively objective assessments of the satisfactions delivered by the company and its products or services.

INCORPORATING CUSTOMER INPUT INTO DESIGN AND PRODUCTION

There is no certain best way to incorporate what is learned from customers (specifically in the CSP) into the organization's operating procedures. One method that has found considerable favor among Japanese firms is the House of Quality.[6] This is a graphical flowchart utilized by the quality task force as a tool for integrating the several informational inputs. The graph attempts to relate the following:

• *Consumer attributes.* Requirements of the product or service from the customer's perspective, often identified as either strengths or weaknesses in the CSP. They are usually stated in the customer's words, if possible, although consumer terms may create some ambiguity. (For example, what does a consumer mean by "it closes easily"?) These terms are truer to consumers' concerns than engineering terms.

• *Engineering characteristics.* Design elements that comprise the product or service and that engineers believe affect one or more of the consumer attributes.

• *Relative performance* on each consumer attribute. How does the product's or service's delivery compare with major competitors' performance?

• *Management's priorities.* For positioning the product or service, utilize any and all of the engineering characteristics available.

The process for integrating these disparate points of view is both simplistic and elegant.

EXHIBIT 9–4
Main Floor of the House of Quality

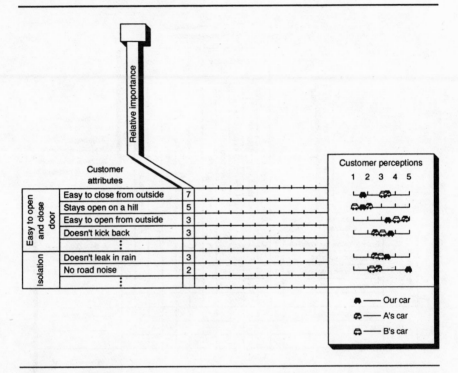

The house of quality starts with a main floor of *customer attributes.* These can be performance attributes or features by which customers judge the quality of a product or service. The attributes may be clustered, either judgmentally or by a statistical procedure like cluster analysis. The attributes are generally rank ordered, with the most important attributes on top and the least important on the lower levels. In addition, the relative performance (versus competition) of the company's product on each consumer attribute is generally shown within the diagram (in a column on the right). The examples in Exhibits 9–4 to 9–6, from an automotive project, concern the design of a car door.

As a second floor, the engineering characteristics are ordered in relation to the customer attributes they most directly match. Each characteristic is accompanied by a + or – sign to indicate engineering's goal to increase (+) or to reduce (–) each characteristic.

EXHIBIT 9–5
Main and Upstairs Floors of House of Quality

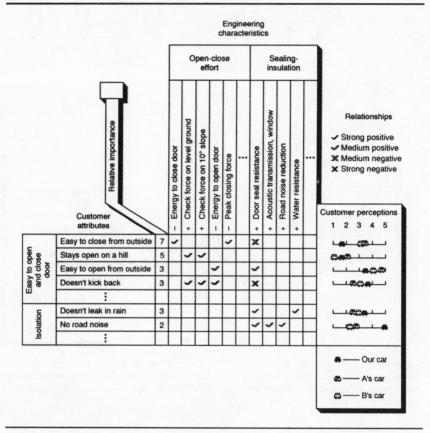

At this point, the quality task force fills in the cells of the house, indicating how strongly each engineering characteristic is related to each customer attribute. Any set of symbols may be used to indicate the strength of the relationship, and binary or scaled judgments are acceptable.

Because oftentimes two or more engineering characteristics may themselves be interrelated, the house of quality utilizes a unique roof matrix to show these interrelationships (see Exhibit 9–6). The same symbols will be used to indicate the strength of the correlations among engineering characteristics.

The quality task force is at liberty to add additional information to its house. For example, it may judgmentally assign importance weights to the engineering

EXHIBIT 9–6
Completed House of Quality

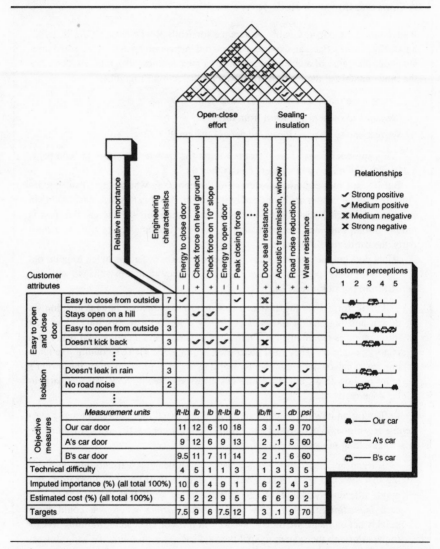

	Customer attributes	Relative importance	Engineering characteristics	Energy to close door (−)	Check force on level ground (+)	Check force on 10° slope (+)	Energy to open door (−)	Peak closing force (−)	...	Door seal resistance (+)	Acoustic transmission, window (+)	Road noise reduction (+)	Water resistance (+)	...
Easy to open and close door	Easy to close from outside	7		✔				✔		✘				
	Stays open on a hill	5			✔	✔								
	Easy to open from outside	3					✔			✔				
	Doesn't kick back	3			✔	✔	✔			✘				
Isolation	Doesn't leak in rain	3								✔			✔	
	No road noise	2								✔	✔	✔		
Objective measures	*Measurement units*			ft-lb	lb	lb	ft-lb	lb		lb/ft	−	db	psi	
	Our car door			11	12	6	10	18		3	.1	9	70	
	A's car door			9	12	6	9	13		2	.1	5	60	
	B's car door			9.5	11	7	11	14		2	.1	6	60	
Technical difficulty				4	5	1	1	3		1	3	3	5	
Imputed importance (%) (all total 100%)				10	6	4	9	1		6	2	4	3	
Estimated cost (%) (all total 100%)				5	2	2	9	5		6	6	9	2	
Targets				7.5	9	6	7.5	12		3	.1	9	70	

Open-close effort / Sealing-insulation

Relationships
✔ Strong positive
✔ Medium positive
✘ Medium negative
✘ Strong negative

Customer perceptions 1 2 3 4 5

🚗 —— Our car
🚗 —— A's car
🚗 —— B's car

characteristics. Or it may guess at the technical difficulties required to overcome each engineering characteristic or the relative costs inherent in each engineering characteristic.

AFTERMARKETING WORKING
A Conversation with Rolls-Royce

Paul Beart is Manager, Quality Assurance for Rolls-Royce Motor Cars in Lynd-hurst, New Jersey. Paul, an experienced veteran in customer satisfaction, is passion-ate about the value of a customer satisfaction measurement program. He describes the fundamentals of the Rolls-Royce Owner Satisfaction Program as:

Desire—we really care about our owners.

We listen to owners and learn from them.

We respond to owners' ideas and needs—we really deliver!

"This approach," says Paul, "builds a thirst for knowledge within the company, a desire to find out why customers feel as they do."

But it's not just customers external to the company who matter; Paul is con-vinced "internal customers" are equally important. And his business has more than its share of internal customers and dependent relationships. "The car business is unique in that both we, the manufacturer, and our customer place trust in a third party, the car dealer," Paul says.

"How do I get the interest of my internal audiences?" Paul is quick to point out that CSI programs require intensive selling when they're first established and may benefit from periodic "reselling":

I look for something that can turn internal audiences on. Information on design and production issues is obviously a top priority. So, too, is the way information is communicated. Verbatims (owners' actual comments) really turn factory people on. They trust the owners' comments. There's nothing like read-ing an actual owner's comments, learning about a problem from the owner's point-of-view to get internal audiences involved in seeing how critical a particu-lar issue really is.

Reflecting on how he, an engineer (with a professed modest trust in many mar-keting techniques), discovered the "truth" in customer satisfaction meaures he describes a long process:

I began noticing trends—confirmation from dealers' warranty-repair spend-ing that matched what owners were reporting in their CSI questionnaires. The major difference was that the CSI questionnaires were identifying areas of con-cern *immediately* and *directly to our headquarters* where we could more quickly act on them. We didn't have to wait for 5 or 10 dealers' warranty reports to pass through the system to spot the existence of a problem; we had informa-tion directly from our owners.

However, Paul sees a danger in the CSIs, being singularly aligned with problem solution. "The CSI shouldn't only be used for 'retro-fitting' designs and solutions but should also be used proactively to implement future designs," Beart strongly believes. "CSI programs also afford a real-time benchmarking opportunity because you can compare new issues with issues you've encountered and fixed before. This helps to 'size' a problem—to determine just how critical it really is."

Paul proudly describes the importance of the CSI within Rolls-Royce Motor Cars today. (Although Sir Henry Royce's precept for starting the company was to provide customers with the ultimate in customer satisfaction—a "worry-free" motor car—this mandate had become "engineering driven." Throughout the 1970s the company's direction had been dictated more by engineering concerns than by customers' requests.) "Now, CSI results help us identify problems and help us assign them priorities for the factory—to tell the factory how critical an issue is relative to other issues they may be working on."

Paul sees a CSI program, if properly integrated into a company's operations, as uniting three groups: customers, designers, and engineers. As such, it "brings the marketplace into the design and engineering stages. It challenges designers and engineers to respond to the question, 'What will the customer get out of this wonderful idea?' A CSI program makes customers' desires a driving force for everyone in the company," Paul observes. And to achieve a true customer focus, typical departmental barriers within a company must give way to working partnerships between areas. This makes obsolescent the parochial way in which departments previously dealt with issues on a sequential basis, relaying problems or solutions to the next department. (In that kind of organization, the customer is the loser.)

Where does responsibility for the CSI function belong? "It's purely 100% marketing!" Paul believes. "Marketing is engaged in outreach to new and existing customers, but it should also be involved in satisfying current customers. That's where the CSI comes in." Paul believes the CSI has real "integrity":

> It's constantly "chipping away," measuring customers' priorities to direct design and manufacturing's attentions, and is thus immune from the preferences and desires of internal politics. My job is the most apolitical job in the company—there are no boundaries, no class distinctions. I daily talk to our president and to the presidents of suppliers. I talk to *anyone* I need to to get complete satisfaction for our owners!

> The CSI also tells us how we're doing at treating our customers, how they are being handled by those "third-party" intermediaries (dealers) who are so critical to the ultimate satisfaction of our customers.

Customer advocates like Paul Beart of Rolls-Royce Motor Cars and his colleagues worldwide are helping redirect the orientation and organization of corporations to better satisfy their customers.

Source: Personal interview with Paul Beart.

THE CHANGING ORIENTATION OF MARKETING MANAGEMENT

As the U.S. economy progresses from a manufacturing economy to a service-based economy, neither efficient production nor product quality will by itself determine from whom a customer buys. Instead, relationships with customers developed through aftermarketing strategies will weigh much more heavily in the selection of a provider. Achieving strong customer relationships will be the primary focus of future marketing management teams.

With this increased emphasis on customer relationships, the organizational structure may need to be changed. Ironically, the existing customer service department (if one exists) will probably be the first victim of a restructuring of the organization. Management will discover that relationship marketing cannot reside in a single department, but rather must exist as a companywide philosophy.

The second victim of restructuring must be the mindset of many current marketing people. Contemporary marketing staffs are unaccustomed to being on the front line, in direct interaction with customers. While the marketing staff is comfortable with its role as counselor and planner, it has traditionally relied on the sales force to directly effect policy with customers. In the aftermarketing organization of the future, marketing will need to adopt a far more customer-interactive role. The marketing department must be ready to assume control over many of the seemingly diverse activities included within aftermarketing (many are not currently supervised by the marketing area). These activities include complaint handling, internal publications, and customer satisfaction.

Some of the service advocates would perhaps see these roles best enacted by a separate *customer service area* headed by a corporate chief services officer.

But a new department would be even less prepared to integrate the expanded functionality with the other operational areas of the organization. Marketing already has a developed expertise for bringing customer information into the firm, but has simply been conducting its work in too narrow a perspective. The marketing department has all of the skills necessary to successfully initiate an aftermarketing effort. It is marketers who should be leading the campaign for customer satisfaction and quality improvement. But often marketers are not in the lead. As one Baldrige examiner discovered, they may even be resisting these movements.

> My role was to talk primarily to marketers and operations managers (within applying firms) about customer satisfaction and what they were doing about it. To my chagrin as a services marketer and Baldrige Award Senior Examiner, I found that the marketers had no real conception of quality improvement or the importance of their role in it. The marketers all agreed they were too busy doing their jobs to worry about quality improvement. They had too many fires to put out, too many advertising campaigns to plan, too many sales projections to make to worry whether customers were satisfied or whether the work the company was turning out was any good.[7]

Marketers must quickly adopt an aftermarketing perspective and use it to better focus their talents on higher-level corporate priorities. At the same time, they must campaign to increase their participation in today's rapidly evolving organizational management. To fully accomplish this new role, the marketing department should reorganize itself to include positions responsible for each of the major aftermarketing functions (see Exhibit 9–7A and B).

EXHIBIT 9–7A
Marketing Organization for Conventional Marketing

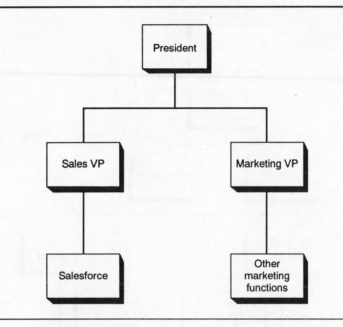

One of the most obvious aftermarketing roles the marketing department can perform is to serve as the translator of customer needs and expectations into corporate priorities. This role jointly serves two interests: that of internal consumer advocate and that of external ombudsman.

None of the new roles should be seen as a conflict of interest for marketing. Indeed, most marketing departments will find their current background of consumer-oriented marketing compatible with the more stringent demands of aftermarketing. They will effectively carry out their ombudsman roles in complete harmony with their roles as strategic marketing planners.

In Chapter 1, a new marketing mix was identified that introduced new concerns into the marketer's traditional scope of inspection. The revised marketing mix included the following:

- *Product:* product quality management, reliability, and features.
- *Price:* price charged, pricing terms, and pricing offers.
- *Place:* accessibility to the marketer's goods or facilities, and customer availability.
- *Promotion (Market Communication):* presale advertising, publicity, and sales promotions.

EXHIBIT 9–7B
Marketing Organization for Relationship Marketing

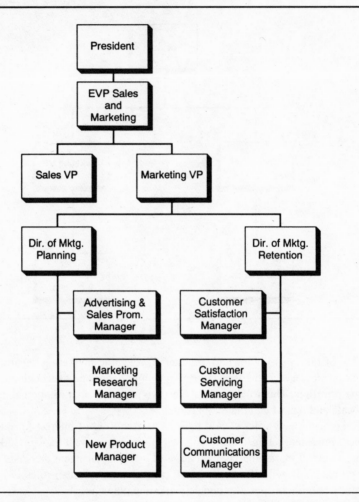

- *Customer communication:* post-sale communication programs (proprietary magazines, events, etc.), 800 telephone center, complaint and compliment handling.
- *Customer satisfaction:* monitoring customer expectations and satisfaction with the existing product or service and the delivery system, striving to improve satisfaction.
- *Servicing:* servicing quality management, pre-sale and post-sale service, and customer convenience activities.

AFTERMARKETING WORKING
Structures Supporting Relationship Marketing

Ron Zemke and Dick Schaaf, authors of the book *The Service Edge,* cite five operating principles that seem to distinguish companies that they view as exemplary in offering quality service:

• *Listen, understand, and respond to customers.* Procter & Gamble's customer service agents, answering 800 telephone calls on washing, tracked an increase in the size of household washloads with a decrease in the average water temperature being used. Additional research confirmed that manufacturers of newer clothes were recommending better control of wash temperatures.

• *Define superior service and establish a service strategy.* Management must not only clearly state its vision of what will comprise quality service, it must also communicate this understanding to both employees and customers. Good internal communication is necessary to maintain a successful service positioning.

• *Set standards and measure performance.* Without standards, a commitment to service is vacuous. Standards must be established that relate to customer-centered measures. Specific standards (with real value to customers) are easily evident in the market: Domino's Pizza's 30-minute delivery promise, Federal Express's guarantee of absolutely, positively overnight, and L.L. Bean's and Lands' End's "satisfaction guaranteed."

Then measurement must occur, formally and frequently.

• *Select, train, and empower employees to work for the customer.* Hiring the correct individuals is critical for providing sincere service. Very often successful service-oriented organizations tend toward nepotism, relying on current employees to find similar-minded individuals.

With the best individuals, both formal initial training and ongoing informal training are necessary. All Disneyland employees go through an extensive training program, during which they are introduced to the Disney organization's view of each day at the amusement parks as a show, with each employee a member of the cast. McDonald's, Wendy's, and Domino's employees regularly go through frontline retraining by watching video instructional programs in their stores.

• *Recognize and reward accomplishment.* When employees do something well, they should be rewarded immediately. The goal is to confirm accomplishment and reinforce the employee's commitment. At Southern Bell, employees can earn a company jacket by saving reward points; Federal Express awards lapel pins.

Adapted from: J. Levine, "Service 101: Lessons from the Best," *Incentive,* March 1989, pp. 22, 24–27; and R. Zemke and D. Schaaf, *The Service Edge: 101 Companies That Profit from Customer Care* (New York, Penguin Books, 1990).

In this mix, customer communications, customer satisfaction, and servicing are the new elements added. These elements are consistent with the expanded role for marketing being advocated.

The Organizational Culture

An organization's culture can have a lot to do with how easily it can adopt after-marketing strategies to achieve relationship marketing. Aftermarketing activities thrive in a *possessive culture,* a culture that covets customers. "Everybody is somebody's customer!" Even employees who never interact with external customers have internal customers. The service they provide their co-worker-customers ultimately affects the satisfaction of paying customers. According to Professor Michael LeBoeuf, "If you're not taking care of customers you'd better be taking care of someone who is!"[8]

But most of all, the commitment to relationship marketing must come from the very top of the organization, and employees must sense that every member of management firmly believes in it. The most important aspect of building relationships with customers is the genuine commitment (easily perceived by employees) of top management. If top management does not demonstrate such commitment by its deeds, its words will fail.

> When a company lacks unremitting pressure from the top to realize a service vision, the daily, unglamourous job of caring for existing customers loses out in competition with sexy projects for winning new customers. It's the old story of grabbing for obvious, short-term profits at the expense of more subtle, long-term gains. As Jay Spechler, who oversees service quality for American Express, explains, "Service is a fragile commodity. You can have it today and lose it tomorrow. *Without senior management behind it, it won't work.* There are so many other things—new products and programs—driving the budget."[9]

Aftermarketing, to be successful, must not be looked upon as this year's marketing gimmick. To stress the bedrock commitment to customer relationship building, it should be incorporated into the organization's mission statement. This helps to remind everyone of its importance.

Corporate culture is composed of the values, beliefs, and roles that employees share. It is partially formal (from training and job descriptions) and it is partially informal (the mode of conduct that employees share and that is not discouraged by management). But culture can also be very difficult to change in the short term.

Davidow and Uttal describe how Macy's department stores in California attempted to "Nordstromize" themselves to become more competitive against the retailing phenomenon. Although they practiced all the trimmings of customer service, their employees still did not *serve* customers. The traditional department store culture was too ingrained within Macy's central organization.

A recent effort by IBM exemplifies the sort of campaign that must be waged within the organization to achieve true change. The company distributed a booklet entitled, *Taking It Personally...A Conversation About Market-Driven Quality,* to all employees. It is an obvious attempt to explain IBM's goals for enhancement of its customer relationship philosophy through the practice of several aftermarketing strategies (most notably, total quality management). The booklet provides ample reasons for change: the Baldrige criteria, the needs of the market, eliminating defects and reducing cycle time. It identifies its purpose as follows:

> Profound changes are taking place within IBM and the business community world-wide. Competition continues to increase. Customers are expecting—demanding—the best. And rightfully so.
>
> Each of us has to make more than simply an intellectual and emotional commit-ment to total customer satisfaction; we have to do whatever it takes to delight our cus-tomers and help them succeed.

The booklet contains a straightforward yet persuasive discussion of IBM's goal of attaining total quality management. It describes the goals and even out-lines some tools for use in work groups (quality circles are not proposed). The obvious goal is to rally the support of the workforce for IBM and for each other, achieving a positive team environment.

A positive, supportive organizational culture is absolutely necessary for after-marketing to be successfully practiced. After all, satisfying internal and external customers is demanding work. To emphasize the strenuousness of successful customer relationships, author Arlie Hochschild created a new form of work, which he calls "emotional labor."[10]

Emotional labor is not readily fostered by a highly formal, highly structured system. Rather, emotional labor is most easily rendered under conditions of employee empowerment. Employee empowerment means trusting employees enough to allow them to exercise their judgment in business matters, rather than confining them to a rigid set of rules.

Employee Empowerment

Employee empowerment has become a major rallying cry among customer ser-vice specialists. Just as aftermarketing promises greater respect for customers, so too must today's organizations promise greater respect (and therefore greater operational latitude) for their employees, especially those employees involved in customer contact.

Empowerment is complemented by, and at the same time fosters, a goal of involving employees in the management and conduct of the business. Either in formal quality circles (renamed quality teams since their flash-in-pan life in the early 1980s), or through informal improvement projects or work group activities, employees should be allowed to feel a sense of participation in the business. (Federal Express utilizes such teams to good advantage, using employees' insights to increase its productivity.)[11] Just as partnering with customers helps create customer satisfaction, so too will management's partnering with its employees help create a more satisfied workforce.

There are companies in which customer service reps are now asked to write product instructions, because through their interaction with customers they have a better understanding of how customers interact with products and services, and are also familiar with customers' language.[12]

Empowerment gives employees the freedom to shape procedures to the needs of particular customers. Because customers are so different from one another, no one set of rules is going to satisfy every customer. If the employee is forced to deal with every customer with the same set of rules, the employee will easily become frustrated and will pass this frustration along to customers.

Employee Teamwork

To accomplish quality production of goods or services and to establish customer relationships, American corporations need to begin thinking about employee teamwork. In times past, areas worked in virtual isolation from one another. Employees were not invited into another area and did not desire participation with another area. Marketing considered its job done when it passed consumers' reactions to a new product design over to engineering or manufacturing. To achieve quality work in today's market, functional areas within the organization must start working together on a project from the start, and remain as a team through its completion.

Proper Training Programs

Very often companies spend a great deal of training time indoctrinating new salespeople in the benefits of their products or services, but they fail to similarly induct other employees who will ultimately come into contact with customers (such as customer service representatives or even the collections department).

Some companies are accepting the value of training all new employees on how to interact with customers; this skill is becoming one of the most important aspects of corporate training programs.[13] Any employee who may ultimately interact with a customer should be taught the following:

- About the products or services the organization makes and sells.
- The types of customers the organization has.
- How customers use the organization's products.
- Proper comportment: cordiality, how to gracefully direct a customer's conversation to avoid a focus on price, and so forth.

But beyond knowing how to interact, employees must understand what their employer produces and sells. This means that the company sales message should be taught to *everyone,* sales through service, so that the entire workforce understands the corporate objectives. Part of the training message can be to motivate workers not just to serve customers, but to help retain customers. In this way every employee who may ever interact with a customer will be prepared and will have the companywide instructions.

Nowhere is this philosophy more evident than in the Disney amusement parks. So dedicated is the Disney organization to properly training all of its park employees that it reportedly spends four days training the seemingly least important employees in the park—the street sweeper. Disney realizes that its "popcorn guys" (so called because they sweep up the popcorn that visitors leave behind) get asked more questions than most other employees in the parks. So these employees play a pivotal role in satisfying a certain number of park visitors. In their four days of training the popcorn guys learn about the Disney culture (they are "hosts," visitors are "guests," at work they are "on stage," and they are expected to "perform" in a happy, friendly manner).

Hiring the Right People

Establishing a supportive corporate culture and a good training program are both important to adopting aftermarketing strategies. But a third requirement is hiring people with the basic traits that instinctively promote good customer interactions.

Two Harvard researchers have declared that the age of the "industrialization of service" (such as McDonald's reliance on cheap, semiskilled, easily replaceable employees) is over. Over the next 5 to 10 years, properly educated and trained service employees will become harder and harder to find and to hire. Studying a number of corporations, including Marriott, they conclude that "finding the right people not only improves service quality, but is also less costly than constantly replacing cheaper help."[14]

For example, Marriott attributes a 10 percent decrease in employee turnover with a 1 to 3 percent decrease in lost customers and a $50 million to $100 million increase in revenues! *Selectivity in hiring is the new watchword.* Nordstrom and the Mayo Clinic are accustomed to interviewing 10 or more candidates for every job opening to find that one particular individual with an interest in the job and the potential to deliver quality service.

With employers' selectivity increasing, personnel research has developed screening techniques to help identify job candidates who have such traits. Customer service employees hired through validated selection methods have been shown to interact more perceptively, politely, and competently.[15]

There is more purpose in hiring the right employees than in simply reducing personnel costs. In the marketplace of the 1990s customer-focused employees will be increasingly scarce. Hiring and retaining such employees may well be a key to survival for many organizations.[16] There is mounting evidence that satisfied employees (who remain longer at a company) create better satisfied customers. Exhibit 9–8 shows the concomitant cycle of good customer service. This cycle is doubly good news: higher employee retention (when good employees are becoming increasingly difficult to find), and higher customer retention, thereby increasing customer lifetime value.

EXHIBIT 9–8
The Cycle of Good Service

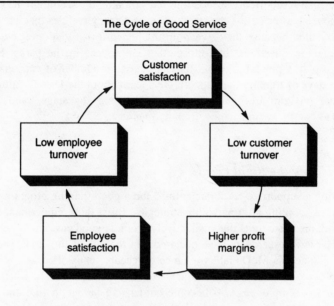

The Cycle of Good Service

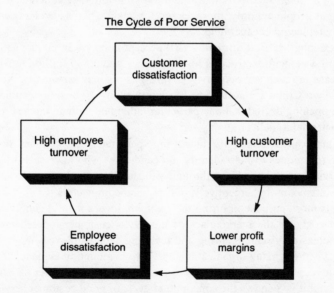

The Cycle of Poor Service

Rewarding Good Performance

Everyone in the company should accept customer relationships as his primary role. How to successfully instill this orientation is another question. If salespeople receive commissions for selling, shouldn't service people also receive commissions for retaining and satisfying customers?

Eastman Kodak's International Biotechnologies unit has tried a company-wide program to motivate care for customers. A point system was devised in which employees were given a point for each telephone call they took, and three points each time they made a follow-up call. Employees showing significant improvement from one month to the next could cash in their points for prizes such as paid time off.

Some firms have developed complex yet customer-focused incentive programs. Renex, a Woodbridge, Virginia–based computer connectivity company, treats its technical people more like salespeople. Customers help to evaluate technicians' performance, and they receive bonuses based on the satisfaction of customers they have helped. Technicians are rated both objectively (how readily they solve a problem) and subjectively (from customers and co-workers). Customers' and management's ratings comprise 80 percent of the evaluation; the remaining 20 percent comes from co-workers.

MBNA, the national credit card issuer, believes that customer retention as a priority should receive financial incentives. MBNA management observes service departments' performances for responsiveness and accuracy, the keys to customer retention. When all the departments achieve 97 percent of the performance standards, an allotment of the company's profits goes into a bonus pool. Bonuses at year's end can amount to 20 percent of an employee's take-home salary![17]

Not all managers and consultants recommend incentives. Some believe the gift-giving strategy sends the wrong message. They suggest that employees who receive rewards for providing customer service may soon come to think of it as above and beyond the call of duty. Philip Crosby, a noted quality consultant, says, "I never saw an incentive program that didn't turn out to be negative. As long as a company has prizes to give, workers play along. But when prizes run out, motivation can too. Incentive programs tend to trivialize the business work ethic."[18]

Bonus programs can also confuse employees if the bonus criteria are a change from past objectives. Most often this produces confusion between the goals of service *productivity* and service *quality*. GTE's California unit inadvertently communicated the wrong message to its employees through a new incentive program. Based on their perceptions of the past, the customer service reps incorrectly attempted to speed transactions rather than deliver customer satisfaction. Through subsequent spending of almost one-quarter of a million dollars in employee reeducation, employees have now accepted the customer-first priority, but they remain confused by GTE's continued interest in speed.

AFTERMARKETING WORKING
Customer Service at Delta Airlines

For 16 consecutive years, Delta has had the fewest complaints logged with the FAA of all the nation's major air carriers. According to Fred Elsberry, general manager of Consumer Affairs for Delta, "A lot of our policies that deal with customer service today, go back to our beginning. They go all the way back to our founder, C. E. Woolman. In fact, it's difficult to separate our customer service policies from the family spirit behind the company in its early years."

"Good employee relations translate into good customer service. It's the nucleus of Delta's customer service philosophy. Day in and day out we work very hard to try to keep our people happy," explains Elsberry.

The main challenge facing Delta is keeping the "family spirit" alive when its once small "family" now numbers over 60,000! To meet the challenge, the company believes in continuing the tradition. Here's how it does that:

• *Hiring.* The company's reputation draws many more applicants than jobs available; applicants with demonstrable people skills are sought.
• *Promotion.* Most senior officers have worked their way up from within.
• *Good job security.* Almost all Delta's employees are full-time and cared for during adverse economic times.
• *Regular personnel meetings.* Every 12 to 18 months Delta holds employee meetings in its 177-city network with senior management.
• *Frequent one-on-one contact* with senior management.
• *Recognition and incentive awards.* Two types of awards are given: on-the-job, customer service awards and community service awards, rewarding the Delta "family" members.
• *Training* that reflects the "Delta way".
• *Emphasis on helping each employee learn to solve problems.* Employees are encouraged to handle those problems they can, but to know when to seek help.
• *Consistency in approach.* The Delta Way—personal style and pride in one's job.

Source: "Delta Air Lines: Where Customer Service Is a Tradition," *Customer Service Management Bulletin*, #513, 7/10/91. Copyrighted material reprinted with permission of *Customer Service Management Bulletin* and Bureau of Business Practice, 24 Rope Ferry Road, Waterford, CT 06386.

Most consultants agree that asking for quality service from employees is not enough. Management must be prepared to acknowledge the behavior it is striving to accomplish. It should practice either recognition or rewarding or both. Acknowledging an employee's effective offering of service need not happen with money. Incentives, even a simple recognition such as a thank you, a plaque, or a trophy, are all effective.

Many companies are offering award programs for good service. Such awards range in form from gold rings to an Employee of the Month plaque. But only a few companies have recognized the importance of customer service through their salary structure. Hewlett-Packard is one such company. Support engineers, employees who help customers with technical problems over the telephone, are paid at the same scale as the engineers who design Hewlett-Packard's products!

Telephone consultations are followed up to see how satisfied the customer is. If they liked the service they received, the engineer is eligible for a quarterly raise or promotion. If the customer is unhappy, the support engineer is coached to do a better job in the future.

At some companies the job itself may be looked upon as sufficient reward. Sony Corporation in the United States considers establishing a quality interaction with a customer *the* job requirement for its customer relations specialists (an entry-level position at the company).

KEY POINTS OF THE CHAPTER

Customer Visits

A marketer can send a team to visit chosen customers to evaluate their use of and satisfactions with the marketer's products or services. The notion is that an on-site visit may better help marketers to understand the use-situation of their products and services.

House of Quality

This system helps the marketer act on customers' desires as expressed in a customer satisfaction survey. The system relates engineering characteristics of a product with customers' evaluations, helping the marketer act on customers' impressions to improve the product or service.

Management Assessment Survey

This survey is similar to a customer satisfaction survey, but is conducted among the organization's management. The results of the survey are compared to results of the customer satisfaction survey. The goal is to help managers better understand and accept customers' evaluations.

Management Monitoring

This is the occasional practice of eavesdropping on workers directly, indirectly, or electronically. The practice runs the risk of angering employees if not conducted properly. The value of such a study is identifying employees who are representing the marketer well and those who require some retraining.

Mystery Shopping

This involves the hiring of external interviewers to pose as shoppers of a business or service. The shoppers use an observation form to score the operation and the frontline people on a set of evaluative criteria. The results show management how the organization's frontline people respond to customers.

NOTES

1. J. M. Juran, noted quality advocate: J. M. Juran, *Juran on Planning for Quality* (New York: The Free Press, 1988), p. 246.
2. A well-designed mystery shopper program: L. Parker, " `Mystery Shopping' for Clues to Improve Service," *Bottomline,* October 1988, pp. 49-50.
3. One car dealership: J. Bohn, "Mystery Shoppers Rate Salespeople," *Automotive News,* July 30, 1984, p. 4.
4. The rate of successful reviews has doubled: L. Brokaw, "The Mystery-Shopper Questionnaire," *Inc.,* June 1991, pp. 94-97.
5. Customer visits are also important: E. F. McQuarrie, "The Customer Visit: Qualitative Research for Business-to-Business Marketers," *Marketing Research,* March 1991, pp. 15-28.
6. One method that has found considerable favor: J. R. Hauser and D. Clausing, "The House of Quality," *Harvard Business Review,* May-June 1988, pp. 63-73.
7. My role was to talk primarily to marketers: D. Schmalansee, "Marketers Must Lead Quality Improvement or Risk Becoming Irrelevant," *Marketing Services Newsletter,* Vol. 7, Issue 1, (Spring 1991), pp. 1-2.
8. According to Professor Michael LeBoeuf: K. Bertrand, "Sales and Service: One Big Happy Family?", *Business Marketing,* December 1988, pp. 36-38, 40.
9. When a company lacks unremitting pressure: W. H. Davidow and B. Uttal, *Total Customer Service: The Ultimate Weapon* (New York: Harper & Row, 1989), p. 95.
10. A positive, supportive organization: A. Hochschild, *The Managed Heart: Commercialization of Human Feeling* (Berkeley, CA: University of California Press, 1983).
11. Federal Express uses such groups: F. Rose, "Now Quality Means Service Too," *Fortune,* April 22, 1991, p. 107.
12. There are companies in which customer service reps: "Keeping Them Happy," *CSI Report,* Customer Service Institute, December 1989, no. 5, pp. 1-2.
13. At Polysar Ltd. in Leominister, Mass.: K. Bertrand, "Sales and Service: One Big Happy Family?", *Business Marketing,* December 1988, pp. 36-38, 40.
14. Two Harvard researchers have declared: L. Schlesinger and J. L. Heskett, "The Service Driven Service Organization," *Harvard Business Review,* September-October 1991, pp. 71-81.
15. Personnel research has developed screening techniques: G. E. Paajanen, "For Better Customer Service, Select the Right Employees," *Chain Store Age Executive,* September 1990, p. 96.
16. Hiring and retaining such employees: P. Sellers, "What Customers Really Want," *Fortune,* June 4, 1990, pp. 58-63.
17. MBNA, a national credit card issuer: P. Sellers, "What Customers Really Want."
18. Philip Crosby, noted quality consultant: J. E. Rigdon, "More Firms Try to Reward Good Service, But Incentives May Backfire in Long Run," *Wall Street Journal,* December 5, 1990, pp. B-1, 6.

Chapter Ten

Quality and Aftermarketing
The Key Components of Relationship Marketing

It has been said that marketing has, over the years, shifted in its orientation from *tricking* customers to *blaming* customers to *satisfying* customers. Its future success depends upon its skill to integrate customers systematically into the conduct of business. Whether this is an accurate characterization or not, marketing's posture to date has caused an escalating confidence gap between marketers and consumers. Today, consumers cynically anticipate marketers making a profit by exploiting them rather than by satisfying their wants and needs.

Even the most well-intentioned companies can lose sight of their most important objective—satisfying customers. They can single-mindedly get caught up in the process of creating new products, or of aggressively competing with other companies; both perspectives are fatal. Both perspectives allow marketers to overlook their most important consideration: *satisfying and thereby retaining current customers.*

Ironically, marketers' attentions have only recently focused on understanding the expectations that customers bring when they consider buying products and services offered by marketers. Marketing researchers have generally busied themselves studying aggregate phenomena such as customer segments or product attributes. They have tended to ignore information at the level of specific customers, overlooking their opportunity to answer such questions as "What expectations did customer X have, and were these satisfied?"

Throughout this discussion of aftermarketing, quality in products and services has been treated as a given. But in the real world it is often not quite so plentiful. Quality represents an investment; it is a commitment undertaken only by those managers who have a strong personal conviction.

Aftermarketing strategies cannot succeed in the absence of quality. And, interestingly, quality in the absence of a strong aftermarketing program may be far less successful than anticipated.

It therefore seems reasonable to conclude this book on relationship marketing with a chapter reviewing the key components of the necessary partnership between quality and aftermarketing.

QUALITY: AT THE "BOTTOM LINE"

Ultimately, aftermarketing means strengthening the loyalty of customers by meeting and managing their expectations. Consumers have expectations for the *basic quality* of the product or service they have purchased as well as expectations for the degree of servicing they desire (and deserve) to receive. Quality and servicing ought to accompany every product and service offered in the marketplace. In addition, although everyone's customers will differ somewhat in their specific definition of these elements, the marketing community is beginning to learn about *quality* and *servicing* in general terms.

The Definition of Quality

In Chapter 1 a brief definition of quality was offered; it is time to review and refine this definition. A more extensive definition will still, however, present problems. Quality is not easily defined. For example, in his definitive book *Managing Quality,* David Garvin offers five different definitions to fully represent the range of existing opinions.[1] With some minor modification made to allow equal applicability to services as well as products, they comprise the following:

- The *transcendent definition* treats quality as an ephemeral state of achievement and excellence:

    Quality is a condition of excellence implying fine quality as distinct from poor quality. . . . Quality is achieving or reaching for the highest standard as against being satisfied with the sloppy or fraudulent. (B. Tuchman, "The Decline of Quality," *The New York Times Magazine,* November 2, 1980, p. 38.)

- An *offering-based definition* considers quality to be measurable; high quality is achieved by having more of an element or attribute:

    Quality refers to the amounts of the unpriced attributes contained in each unit [or experience] of the priced offering. (K. B. Leffler, "Ambiguous Changes in Product Quality," *American Economic Review,* December 1982, p. 956.)

- A *user-based definition* relies on the premise that quality is only in the eye of the user. Users' appraisals of their satisfaction are the only appropriate benchmarks for quality:

    In the final analysis of the marketplace, the quality of a product depends on how well it fits patterns of consumer preferences. (A. Kuehn and R. Day, "Strategy of Product Quality," *Harvard Business Review,* November–December 1962, p. 101.)

- A *production-based definition* is almost diametrically opposed to the user-based definition. Production definitions deal with conformance to [production] requirements:

    Quality is the degree to which a specific product [or service] conforms to a design or specification. (H. Gilmore, "Product Conformance Cost," *Quality Progress,* June 1974, p. 16.)

EXHIBIT 10–1
Characteristics of Quality in Automobiles (Ranked by Consumers in Order of Importance)

1970	1975	1980	1985	1990
Styling	Fuel economy	Reliability	Value for the money	Safety
Value for the money	Styling	Fuel economy	Ease of handling	Reliability
Ease of handling	Prior experience with make	Value for the money	Fuel economy	Trouble-free maintenance
Fuel economy	Size and weight	Riding comfort	Reliability	Ease of handling
Riding comfort	Ease of handling	Prior experience with make	Safety	Fuel economy

Adapted from Takeuchi and Quelch, "Quality Is More Than Making a Good Product," *Harvard Business Review,* July–August 1983.

- A *value-based definition* ties customer needs and production requirements together; as an offering meets customers' needs at a lower price, it is declared to have greater value:

    Quality is the degree of excellence at an acceptable price and the control of variability at an acceptable cost. [R. Broh, *Managing Quality for Higher Profits* (New York: McGraw-Hill, 1982).]

Agreeing on a definition of quality is an important step toward identifying how to fully satisfy customers. Although there may always be some differences of opinion on the issue, the discussion itself keeps management and employees focused on what is really important.

Some marketers believe that they understand how their customers define quality, and some may actually understand. However, what very few marketers recognize is that customers' definitions may change over time. Take for example the changes in cues consumers have used to define quality in automobiles (see Exhibit 10–1).

Whereas styling was the most important quality indicant in 1970, safety and reliability had assumed this position by 1985. Not only will rankings change, but the consumers' understanding of many of the characteristics also will change, usually becoming more demanding over time. The American luxury car market is a market in which aggressive competition, especially from the Japanese, has dramatically redefined consumers' threshold expectations in each quality characteristic. This has been to the consumers' benefit, but manufacturers who have failed to recognize the changes and the increasing thresholds of *minimum acceptability* in quality characteristics have lost substantial business and market share.

One way marketers can keep up with consumers' dynamic definitions of quality is to conduct a periodic quality audit. A quality audit will continuously monitor customers' appraisal of quality, specifically how they determine quality, and what they consider to be the key attributes of quality in the particular product or service industry. Actually, the CSP (described in Chapter 6) can easily provide this information without necessitating a separate research project. But it is important to remember to include questions regarding the determination of quality when fielding a customer satisfaction study.

Correlates of Quality

Quality has an altruistic appeal, but most businesses require bottom-line proof that investing in quality will produce positive changes in market share and profitability. The relationship between marketplace behavior and quality has been studied in many different ways, from laboratory-type experiments to the examination of longitudinal data from the marketplace. The results are not always in agreement and do not always show positive correlations between quality and market share and profitability. Some researchers explain the conflicting results with the ambiguity of the term *quality*, suggesting that if a uniform definition were used, results would necessarily be more consistent.

Quality and price. Economically, quality and price ought to be positively correlated; as quality increases, so should price. In general this appears to be a reasonable observation because higher quality usually means that additional material, labor, or capital was employed in the production of the "higher-quality" good or service. This is especially true in situations in which consumers have an abundance of information with which to compare products or brands. In categories or situations in which information is limited or in which consumers feel unable to accurately compare products, price will become much more important, unless the marketer reinforces price information with other "evidence," as discussed in Chapter 4. An exception to the positive correlation appears to occur when marketers, recognizing the relationship between price and *perceived quality*, raise price without a requisite increase in quality.

Quality and market share. If high quality is defined according to the product definition, it will be manifested by superior performance or a large number of features. Such a quality product will sell for a higher price and therefore in smaller numbers. If, however, quality is defined according to a user definition, fitness for use, superior aesthetics, and improved conformance, it need not sell for a higher price. All of the studies investigating market share have generally used the PIMS database (of the Strategic Planning Institute), and therefore have used a uniform definition (similar to the second case). The PIMS studies have reportedly found a positive correlation between quality and market share.[2]

Quality and cost. There are two very different points of view regarding the impact of quality on production costs. One view, the production-based view, sees quality and cost as positively related, reasoning that, as performance, features, and durability of the product increase, so will the material and production costs.

An opposite view, related to operations management and typified by the commitment of Japanese manufacturers to continuous improvement, states that quality and cost are negatively correlated. This view holds that errors in production are quality costs that will ultimately have to be paid. For example, according to estimates by General Electric, error costs rise substantially each time a defective product moves one step closer to the ultimate consumer. An error that would only cost $.003 to correct on the production line may end up costing $300—100,000 times as much—if left undiscovered until the product reaches the final customer.

Quality and advertising. Garvin qualifies his description of the possible linkage between quality and advertising by dichotomizing products and services into "search" and "experience" varieties. Search goods and services can be investigated for their inherent quality prior to purchase (for example, the sound of a stereo system can be listened to prior to purchase). The quality of experience goods cannot be predetermined, but must be learned through experience.

It has been suggested that, among experience goods, higher-quality products will be accompanied by higher levels of advertising. It is reasoned that producers of high-quality goods (which sell for higher prices) will be able to afford more advertising to persuade nonpurchasers to try their products. This is justified by the higher customer value represented by potential purchasers of the more expensive, higher-quality products. This hypothesis has been extended to also include the concept of risk aversion. Higher quality products provide justification for making improved claims, thus alleviating consumers' perceptions of risk in purchasing the product. Empirical data investigating this linkage is apparently weak and contradictory.

Quality and profitability. Quality can be conceptually linked to profitability through one of two scenarios: *market gains* (gains in share and the ability to charge a higher price) or *cost savings* (through increased productivity, lower "scrap" costs and lower warranty and repair costs). In the area of profitability, investigations using the PIMS database are more consistent. In general, a positive relationship exists between quality and profitability.

The Progression of Quality

It is said that American management has passed through three stages in its flirtation with quality, moving the consideration of quality from the production line into the corporate boardroom. In the late 1970s, when Japanese marketers began

AFTERMARKETING WORKING
Benchmarking Service Quality

Donald Porter, director of customer service quality assurance, describes British Airways' first customer survey in *Service America!* The study aimed to answer two questions: First, what factors did people really consider most important in their flying experiences; and second, how did British Airways stack up against the other airlines on those factors?

"After some extensive interviewing and data analysis, we discovered some very interesting facts. Of all the statements made by the air travelers we interviewed, four factors stood out from all the rest as being critically important. What took us aback was the fact that two of the four factors came more or less as a surprise to us—we hadn't really considered them consciously before."

According to BA's findings, says Porter, travelers seemed to be responding to four key factors as they moved through the chain of experience.

1. *Care and concern.* "This was fairly clear. We weren't surprised to find this a key factor, although I think we'd have to confess that we couldn't claim a very high level of performance on it."

2. *Spontaneity.* "This made us stop and scratch our heads a bit. Customers were saying, "We want to know that your frontline people are authorized to think. When a problem comes up that doesn't fit the procedure book, can the service person use some discretion on the customer's behalf?"

3. *Problem solving.* "This was pretty clear. Employees are expected to know the business of the company and execute it efficiently."

4. *Recovery.* "This factor threw us. It had never really occurred to us. 'Recovery' was the term we coined to describe a very frequently repeated concern: If something goes wrong, as it often does, will anybody make a special effort to set it right? Will someone go out of his or her way to make amends to the customer?"

"We were struck with a rather chilling thought; if two of these four primary evaluation factors were things we had never consciously considered, what were the chances that our people in the service areas were paying attention to them?"

The customer survey came up with some other interesting findings. When the interviewers asked air travelers to rate British Airways in comparison with other airlines they had personally dealt with, they found some interesting statistics. About 20 percent of the respondents considered British Airways superior to other airlines. About 15 percent considered British Airways inferior to others. The remaining travelers expressed no strong opinion one way or the other.

Initial reaction of company management to these figures was guardedly optimistic. One executive offered this interpretation: "It seems like 85 percent of the people think we're OK." But another wisely observed, "Perhaps it means 65 percent don't see any important difference between us and the other airlines! That doesn't strike me as very good news."

Source: K. Albrecht and R. Zemke, *Service America!* (Homewood, IL: Dow Jones-Irwin, 1985).

winning American customers over to their products based on their quality (rather than their inexpensive prices), U.S. marketers entered into an *inspection phase.* In this era sampling techniques were employed in factories to study how production quality might be controlled. In 1980 NBC aired a now-famous TV program, "If Japan Can...Why Can't We?" giving recognition to the ideas of the American quality control expert, W. Edwards Deming. At this point U.S. marketers appear to have begun to take the issue seriously, and they graduated into a *quality control phase.*

As marketers' attitudes toward quality continue to mature, they evolve into the third phase, *total quality management.* At this stage, quality becomes a strategic objective of the entire corporate organization. Quality is no longer confined to a quality control department but becomes the concern of *every employee.*[3]

Today, few people will argue *against* quality. The more insidious tact, however, may be to engage in lengthy discussions of just *how much* quality to offer. Motorola corporate ads in 1991 described the company's commitment to quality in the following statements:

> When you aim for perfection, you discover it's a moving target. Every advance in quality raises new expectations. The company that is satisfied with its progress will soon find its customers are not.

Even within the most dedicated companies there still may exist a gulf between what management wishes to accomplish and what the workforce perceives. A survey by the American Society for Quality Control (ASQC) found some interesting discrepancies between what management said it was doing and what the workforce perceived that it was doing, as shown in Exhibit 10–2.

Components of Product Quality

Garvin has proposed a list of eight components of quality as an analytical framework with which to better understand quality.[4] He has apparently not validated the list by subjecting it to consumers, but it is nevertheless frequently referenced as indicative of the components of quality.

- *Performance.* This refers to the primary operating characteristics of the product. Performance blends the production definition of quality with the user definition. Although entities can be ranked on their performance relative to a certain capacity, individual customers will often evaluate performance on different criteria.

- *Features.* Features are described by Garvin as the "bells and whistles" of products. Such secondary characteristics supplement the product's basic functioning. Performance criteria and features may often be difficult to separate and may exchange elements customer to customer. The key has to do with the centrality or degree of importance of the characteristic to the customer.

EXHIBIT 10–2
Discrepancies Between Management's Statements and Actions

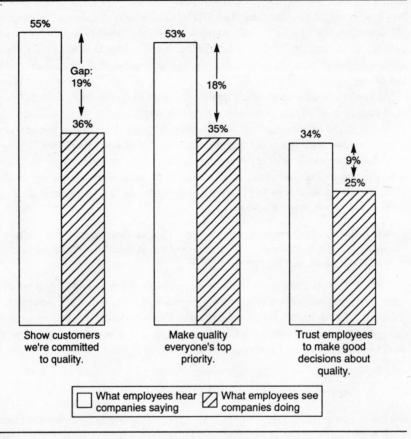

Source: J. Ryan, "Quality: A Job with Many Vacancies," *Quality Progress*, November 1990, p. 24.

- *Reliability.* Reliability deals with the likelihood of the product failing or malfunctioning within a specified period of time. Because time is involved, this characteristic is more important for durables than for products consumed instantaneously.
- *Conformance.* This has to do with how closely a product's design and operation match preestablished specifications or users' expectations or both.
- *Durability.* Durability is literally the amount of use one gets from a product before it physically deteriorates or becomes obsolete, requiring repair or replacement.

EXHIBIT 10–3
Volunteered Components of Product Quality

Volunteered Component	Equivalent to Garvin's	1985	1991	Change
Brand name	Reputation	31%	21%	−10
Word of mouth	Reputation	11	20	+ 9
Past experience	No equivalent	15	16	+ 1
Performance	Performance	16	13	− 3
Durability	Durability	9	12	+ 3
Workmanship	Conformance	26	11	−15
Price	No equivalent	16	11	− 5
Manufacturer's reputation	Reputation	6	11	+ 5
Design and style	Aesthetics	9	6	− 3
Advertising	Reputation	7	6	− 1
Warranty	Serviceability	–	5	+ 5
Dependability	Dependability	–	1	+ 1
Features	Features	–	1	+ 1
Number of items mentioned		1.5	1.7	

Adapted from: ASQC, *An International Survey of Consumers' Perceptions of Product and Service Quality*, Milwaukee, WI, 1991.

- *Serviceability.* Serviceability denotes the speed, courtesy, competence, and ease of repair of a product. Customers are concerned not only about the reliability of products but about how quickly they can be repaired once they fail.

- *Aesthetics.* Highly subjective, aesthetics concern the elements of personal judgment surrounding the consumption of a product. Although it is highly individualistic, there appears to be consensus among customers in some product categories concerning the specific attributes to use to judge the aesthetics of products in those categories.

- *Reputation.* In the absence of complete information and when discrete attributes are difficult to judge, consumers often resort to indirect measures of product comparison. Images, advertising, and company reputation support convenient comparisons.*

Consumers may bring somewhat different priorities to bear on the definition of quality. In an annual survey of Americans, the ASQC has been asking consumers

*D. Garvin, *Managing Quality*, (New York: The Free Press, 1988, pp. 49–60).

EXHIBIT 10–4
The Elements of Quality Service

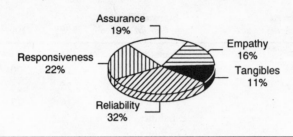

to describe their criteria of quality since the mid-1980s.[5] Garvin's items all appear in the consumers' volunteered listing, but with drastically different weights. Consumers' priorities are heavily skewed to the reputational aspects of the *confirmation of quality* (rather than Garvin's more intellectual approach to the *constitution of quality*). Things are changing, however. Exhibit 10–3 shows a more diverse definition of quality in 1991 than was evidenced in previous years and a lessening of reliance on brand name and workmanship.

Components of Service Quality

Zeithaml, Parasuraman, and Berry, three marketing professors, have been engaged in an investigation of quality in services, first underwritten by the Marketing Sciences Institute in 1983. In the first four phases of this project the authors have identified what they believe to be the five most important aspects of service quality.[6] They have created a scale (SERVQUAL) to rate companies and organizations on these five aspects, and they have conducted 16 focus groups with customers of four different service industries to investigate the universality of the SERVQUAL quality dimensions.

The five aspects of quality in services are identified, and their relative importance is shown in Exhibit 10–4. *Reliability,* the most important aspect, is approximately three times as important as *tangibles,* the least important of the five. The definitions of quality service proposed by Zeithaml and her colleagues are described in Exhibit 10–5.

The ASQC has also investigated the elements of quality services based on consumers' volunteered explanations. Exhibit 10–6 shows the most recent results from this investigation. There is even less agreement between the qualitatively derived SERVQUAL quality components and consumers' volunteered dimensions of service quality than is evident between Garvin's dimensions of product qualities and consumers' volunteered descriptions.

EXHIBIT 10–5
Definitions of Quality Service Elements

Element	Definition	Examples
Reliability	The ability to perform the promised service dependably and accurately.	Is the credit card statement free of errors? Is the washing machine repaired right the first time.
Responsiveness	Willingness to help customers and provide prompt service.	Does the company answer letters or phone calls? Is the stockbroker willing to answer my questions?
Assurance		
Competence	Possession of the required skills and knowledge to perform the service.	Does the repair person appear to know what he is doing?
Courtesy	Politeness, respect, consideration, and friendliness of contact personnel.	Does the bank teller have a pleasant demeanor?
Credibility	Trustworthiness, believability, honesty of the service provider.	Does the bank have a good reputation?
Security	Freedom from danger, risk, or doubt.	Is the credit card protected from unauthorized use?
Empathy		
Access	Approachability and ease of contact.	Does the company have a 24-hour toll-free telephone number?
Communication	Keeping the customers informed in language they can understand and listening to them.	Can the customer service representative clearly explain the billing procedures?
Understanding the customer	Making the effort to know customers and their needs.	Do communications from the company acknowledge the customer's unique needs?
Tangibles	Appearance of physical facilities, equipment, personnel, and communication materials.	Are the bank's facilities attractive? Do the tools used by the repair person look modern?

Source: V. Zeithaml, A. Parasuramen, and L. Berry, *Delivering Quality Service* (New York: The Free Press, 1990), pp. 21–22.

American consumers' awareness of service quality and their ability to articulate its components does not yet seem well exercised. Unlike their awareness of product quality, in which consumers' vocabulary (and hence expectations) has

EXHIBIT 10–6
Volunteered Components of Service Quality

Volunteered Component	Equivalent to Zeithaml's	1985	1991	Change
Courteous/Polite	Courtesy	21%	20%	– 1
Word of mouth	Credibility	12	15	+ 3
Friendliness	Courtesy	8	14	+ 6
Past experience	No equivalent	13	11	– 2
Satisfy customer requests	Responsiveness	18	11	– 7
Promptness	Responsiveness	12	10	– 2
Good service	Reliability	4	8	+ 4
Price	No equivalent	11	8	– 3
Helpful personnel	Competence	9	8	– 1
Attitude of personnel	Courtesy	10	7	– 3
Reputation	No equivalent	7	7	nc
Dependability	Reliability	3	6	+ 3
Advertising	No equivalent	6	3	– 3
Number of items mentioned		1.4	1.4	

Source: ASQC, *An International Survey of Consumer's Perceptions of Product and Service Quality,* Milwaukee, WI, 1991.

increased in the six years, 1985 to 1991, in service quality consumers have expressed approximately the same number of items each year, and there have been no substantive shifts in saliency of particular items. One could conclude from this survey evidence that consumers are still relatively naïve as far as quality in service products. Marketers have the opportunity to educate them and to control their expectations at the same time.

The SERVQUAL procedure is a tested method for asking customers to rate the quality of the service received from one or more companies in a service industry. The questionnaire consists of 22 questions which are usually administered in a two-step process. First, the questions are used to understand expectations, then they are used to rate the actual performance of two or more service providers. A SERVQUAL score is calculated as a measure of the disparity or gap between expectations and performance of each service provider.

In a series of focused group discussions, Zeithaml, Parasuraman, and Berry collected a series of interesting anecdotal examples of each of their servicing elements. Exhibit 10–7 reproduces some of these anecdotes.

EXHIBIT 10–7
Service Customers Want the Basics

Type of Service	Type of Customer	Principal Expectations
Automobile repair	Consumer	Be competent. "Fix it right the first time." Explain things. "Explain why I need the suggested repairs—provide an itemized list." Be respectful. "Don't treat me as a dumb female."
Automobile insurance	Consumer	Keep me informed. "I shouldn't have to learn about insurance law changes from the newspaper." Be on my side. "I don't want them to treat me like a criminal just because I have a claim." Play fair. "Don't drop me when something goes wrong." Protect me from catastrophe. "Make sure my estate is covered in the event of a major accident." Provide prompt service. "I want fast settlement of my claims."
Hotel	Consumer	Provide a clean room. "Don't have a deep pile carpet that can't be completely cleaned…You can literally see germs down there." Provide a secure room. "Good bolts and a peephole on the door." Treat me like a guest. "It is almost like they're looking you over to decide whether or not they're going to let you have a room." Keep your promise. "They said the room would be ready, but it wasn't at the promised time."
Equipment repair	Business customers	Share my sense of urgency. "Speed of response is vital. One time I had to buy a second piece of equipment because of the huge downtime in the first place." Be competent. "Sometimes I quote stuff from your instruction manuals to your own people, and they don't even know what it means." Be prepared. "Have all the parts ready."

SERVICING: AT THE BOTTOM LINE

In this chapter (as in this book), servicing is differentiated from services. *Servicing is aftermarketing care for the customer and should accompany any market offering,* both products and services. Servicing is the care, concern, and attention focused on customers of either products or services. A prompt replacement policy for defective goods is an example of servicing. The extra attention and advice given by an investment counselor, exceeding the financial service originally contracted for, is also an example of servicing.

Generally, servicing is post-purchase attention and assistance that is unexpected by customers but helps them derive greater satisfaction from a product or service.

The Components of Servicing

The appropriate offering of servicing can set apart a customer interaction from the routine. Good servicing is really the start of aftermarketing. Servicing consists of four components:

- *Spontaneity.* Servicing, to be properly distinguished from service, must be unexpected. The support that is offered must occur spontaneously without the customer requesting it. It is rendered in the spirit of doing something special to make an interaction with the organization useful, meaningful, and memorable.

- *Sincerity.* Servicing must be perceived by the customer as rendered with sincerity; otherwise it can be interpreted as only another marketing ploy or gimmick to increase sales.

- *Significance.* The customer ought to feel important because the organization recognizes him and seeks him out to express its appreciation.

- *Consistency.* Actions that classify as servicing ought to be performed with consistency over the entire customer base, and routinely in similar situations.

And so it is the combination of quality (in the products or services sold) and the practice of aftermarketing which guarantees the establishment of long-term relationships with customers.

REWARDING AN AFTERMARKETING PERSPECTIVE

In 1987 the U.S. Congress, sensing the country's decline in production of high-quality products and services, established a national award to commend those companies who truly satisfy their customers with superior products or services and with superior follow-up servicing (aftermarketing). No doubt patterned after Japan's prestigious Deming Award for quality, the Malcolm Baldrige National Quality Award (named after the late Secretary of Commerce) was created. Three application categories exist: manufacturing (SIC codes 01–39); service companies (SIC 40–89); and small businesses. As many as two awards may be made in each category per year. The award is privately funded and is administered by the National Institute of Standards and Technology.

The program has been established to recognize superior achievement in customer satisfaction, and to serve as an educational tool as well. It is the intent of the application and review process to provide significant educational feedback to applicants as well as to showcase exemplary companies for others to study and emulate.

The application process requires the submission of a detailed written application followed by an extensive on-site visit (conducted among those applicants selected from screening the written applications). Many believe the application process is too demanding and actually becomes counterproductive. It is certain that extensive resources will be required to satisfactorily complete the application. For example, according to Xerox's own estimates, its application was a year-long process consuming 20 full-time people and 5 part-timers plus teams of 4 to 12 people in each of Xerox's 75 U.S. branches (a cost approaching $5 million). Considering the fact that Xerox won, and developed their Total Satisfaction Guaranteed program as a result of the application, the cost may be more than justified.

Many companies are applying simply to experience the process of self-examination and benefit from the Baldrige examiners' critique of their operations.

> We didn't think we'd win, says Sharon Shiflet, Director of Quality and Training at Citicorp Credit Card Services. Winning wasn't the point of applying anyway. It's a great self-assessment tool. We use Baldrige criteria now in evaluating where we are. We didn't hire writers or highly-paid consultants to help us with the application. We formed a cross-functional team to complete the application. Spending all that money on winning the award doesn't give us any payback. What we really wanted was an assessment tool.[7]

Others have said that even a simple review of the application criteria, without any intention of preparing a formal application, is a very worthwhile practice. Some companies (a division of IBM and Lockheed Corporation, among others) have adopted the Baldrige criteria as an internal scorecard with which to track performance and improvement. But others question the rather sterile process of using the application procedure for only self-examination with no intention of actually applying.

> The nice thing about it [applying] is that once you have applied, long before you get the feedback report, that intense self-examination shows you many things. I don't think you can do that without formally applying, without going through that discipline, says Marty Landy at Preston Trucking in Preston, MD. The application process, Landy adds, forces entrants to look outside their own industry for ideas to improve their service. There are other people you can compare yourself to who are better than anybody in your own industry. So we benchmark against American Express for billing, Federal Express for on-time delivery, etc.

EXHIBIT 10-8
Baldrige Applications/Winners

Category	1988 Applications/ Winners		1989 Applications/ Winners		1990 Applications/ Winners		1991 Applications/ Winners	
Manufacturing	45	1	23	2	45	2	38	2
Service	9	0	6	0	18	1	21	0
Small business	12	2	11	0	34	1	47	1
Totals	66	3	40	2	97	4	106	3

Category	1992 Applications/ Winners		1993 Applications/ Winners		1994 Applications/ Winners	
Manufacturing	31	2	32	1	23	0
Service	15	2	13	0	18	2
Small business	44	1	31	1	30	1
Totals	90	5	76	2	71	3

Overall, the number of applicants has increased from 66 in 1988, peaking in 1991 at 106, with 71 applicants in 1994. At the same time the total number of application requests has skyrocketed, from 65,000 in 1989 to over 150,000 in 1993.[8] Still, out of the 42 possible awards which could have been made from 1988 to 1994, the committee has seen fit to confer only 22 Baldrige Awards (see Exhibit 10–8). Scores for applying companies have been reportedly low, almost 50 percent falling in the 401 to 600 point range out of a possible 1,000 and very few scoring above 750 points!

The award specifies seven major categories of performance review. Exhibit 10–9 shows the weighted importance allocated to each of these seven categories. Of the seven, customer satisfaction and focus and business results are assigned the most points. Each of the seven categories has been further divided across specific actions, or behaviors. These further subdivisions are shown in Exhibit 10–9.

A Critique of the Baldrige Program

It is curious that while the most important component of the Baldrige criteria is customer satisfaction, not one customer is ever interviewed in the application review process! The Baldrige examiners appear to focus on the *process* instituted to deliver customer satisfaction, but they fail to examine the *results* of the customer satisfaction process! In this sense, the award examination procedure may be considered as myopic as any other *manufacturing process control*.

EXHIBIT 10–9
The Relative Importance of the Balridge Criteria

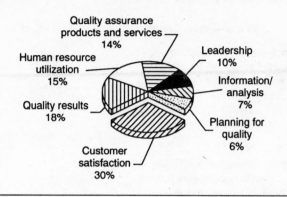

The award has also been accused of distracting applicants from the conduct of their business, being expensive to apply for, not being correlated with marketplace success, and possibly biased to companies who have funded the award. While none of these accusations can be proven, there is probably some element of truth to each of them.

Nevertheless, most fans and critics alike seem to feel that the creation of the award is timely. Companies are acknowledged to be discovering the value of quality, and the award is seen as providing an extra impetus. Dr. Curt Reimann, director of the Baldrige program at the National Institute of Standards and Technology, says, "Although many companies are admittedly intensifying their efforts for quality programs, it's hard for me to believe that the award is the only reason. I think companies want to improve quality anyway; and if they didn't they'd never succeed. A quality program is not something they can just slap together. They have to plan, and I don't know if they would find it worthwhile to do all that work just to win the award."[9]

ESTABLISHING AN AFTERMARKETING PROGRAM

By now the reader ought to visualize the sort of continuous activity that aftermarketing will require to accomplish its goal of customer retention. Aftermarketing must be a conscious, organizationwide mode of conducting business. It cannot reside in one area, department, or function. It includes a philosophy, a prescription for how business ought to be conducted; it is not simply another campaign or sales program.

AFTERMARKETING WORKING
The Baldrige Awards Criteria

1995 Examination Categories/Items and Point Values

Customer Focus and Satisfaction		*250*
Customer Satisfaction Results	100	
Customer Satisfaction Comparison	60	
Customer and Market Knowledge	30	
Customer Relationship Management	30	
Customer Satisfaction Deteminations	30	
Business Results		*250*
Company Operational and Financial Results	130	
Product and Service Quality Results	75	
Supplier Performance Results	45	
Process Management		*140*
Design and Introduction of Products and Services	40	
Process Management: Product and Service Production and Delivery	40	
Process Management: Support Services	30	
Management of Supplier Results	30	
Human Resource Development and Management		*140*
Employee Education, Training and Development	50	
High Performance Work Systems	45	
Employee Well-Being and Satisfaction	25	
Human Resource Planning and Evaluation	20	
Leadership		*90*
Senior Executive Leadership	45	
Leadership System and Organization	25	
Public Responsibility and Corporate Citizenship	20	
Information and Analysis		*75*
Analysis and Use of Company-Level Data	40	
Management of Information and Data	20	
Competitive Comparisons and Benchmaking	15	
Strategic Planning		*55*
Strategy Development	35	
Strategy Deployment	20	
TOTAL POINTS		1,000

Source: Malcolm Baldrige National Quality Award, National Institute of Standards and Technology, Gaithersburg, MD 20899, (301) 975-2036

This book has described seven aftermarketing activities to help a company achieve relationship marketing. They are listed here in the order in which they might be implemented as an overview of a complete aftermarketing program.

- Identifying the customer base.
- Acknowledging customers.
- Mapping customer interactions.
- Providing customer access.
- Measuring customer satisfaction.
- Maintaining contact.
- Reclaiming lost customers.

Identifying the Customer Base

With the availability and capacity of today's micro- and minicomputers, even small organizations can maintain complex customer profiles (customer information files) and access information from the CIF as they interact with each customer.

- *For service organizations,* a customer, subscriber, client, or membership list will probably already exist. If customers must apply for the service, much more will already be known about each customer than her name and address. The goal is to make such customer application information available for marketing purposes.

- *Manufacturers of durables* may already have owner registration cards returned from owners which can be used as the start for a good CIF.

- *Other marketers (consumer packaged goods, small-scale services)* will have to begin the task of identifying their customers before they can establish a computerized CIF. The size of the customer base will, of course, affect the costs and ease of identifying customers. Marketers with large customer bases should think about running a special promotion. (The Pepsi Big Chill Sweepstakes and the Miller Lite T-shirt Giveaway each succeeded in registering millions of customers' names.)

The name-collecting step need not cost a fortune. There are plenty of good, inexpensive ways to encourage customers to register their names and addresses. Notice that coupons are increasingly providing space for the redeemer's name and address.

Once customer names are known, the architecture of the CIF has to be specified. Establishing the structure of the CIF is a decision that warrants some consideration.

Experts can assist in designing the database to be most efficient for the marketer's specific uses.

When the customer base is fairly large, it is wise to start on a smaller segment of customers, gaining experience and information and demonstrating to management the value of the CIF before computerizing the entire customer base (which could delay aftermarketing activities for 1 to 3 years).

Acknowledging Customers

Once customers' identities are stored in a Customer Information File, the next step is to acknowledge customers for the business they have given the company and its products or services. This includes expressing appreciation for their patronage and expressing a desire to communicate with them (either by company-initiated messages or through their incoming calls and letters). A contact program can be designed to match the size of the customer base, the degree of personalization desired, and the established budget.

Newsletters or magazines are a popular way of maintaining the company's outward-bound communications. The key thing to remember here is to provide real customer benefit in whatever material is sent out. If the material is purely sales brochures, the marketer is not acknowledging and thanking customers for their current business; he is prospecting, asking for more or new business. This will be painfully clear to customers and is *not* aftermarketing.

Maintaining Contact with Customers

Not only should the marketer initiate outbound communication, he should also establish a mechanism for customers to easily contact him. In opposition to such a posture, some marketers express worries about opening the flood gates to disgruntled, bothersome, and just plain curious customers by making themselves readily available. However, there is a growing amount of information that suggests that 800 telephone numbers (and other access vehicles) provide many more benefits than the costs involved. In fact, TARP has demonstrated to several marketers that 800 facilities can actually be thought of as profit centers!

Successful operations such as the GE Answer Center and Ford's commitment to customer service exemplify the value of a strong commitment to customer access. But such facilities are not inexpensive. Whether a telephone center is run internally or subcontracted externally, call handling runs about $12 per call.

Mapping Customer Contact Points

Identifying all of the points at which the organization has or could have contact with customers provides vital information for properly managing present interactions. It also offers ideas for how to increase contact points and how to better exploit those that currently exist.

Customer contact points may be easily accomplished using a relatively new technique called customer blueprinting. The object is to pictorially list all contact points, identifying who is interacting with the customer and what are the primary objectives of the interaction. An estimate can be made (or an actual measurement taken) of the satisfactoriness of the current contact. The employees who are interacting, as well as their role and training, should also be identified. Once all customer contacts have been evaluated, plans may be specified to focus more attention (usually implying better contact people and better training) on those contacts identified as critical in providing the customer a satisfactory experience.

Measuring Customer Satisfaction

A most important component of the aftermarketing process is the measurement of customer satisfaction. This activity offers two benefits: the marketer collects valuable information allowing her to supply the marketplace with truly valued products and services, and the marketer can demonstrate her care and appreciation of customers by asking them for input into future production and management decisions. So customer satisfaction programs have both an *informational benefit* and *a marketing benefit.*

Such surveys ought to be conducted on a periodic basis and may involve the entire customer base (to maximize marketing benefits) or only a sample of customers (to minimize costs). The survey should always be presented to customers clearly indicating the benefits to them by completing it. Also, all responding customers should be acknowledged and thanked for their participation.

Elements that will generally be assessed include the following:

- The delivery system for the product or service.
- The actual performance of the product or service (that is, how does it live up to expectations?).
- Employees' conduct, performance, and abilities.
- The general image of the organization.
- The perceived price-to-value relationship of the product or service.
- Competitors' strengths and weaknesses.
- Customers' demographics and lifestyles (optional).

Incorporating the results of a CSP into production and managerial practices takes some experience. It is sometimes difficult to relate customer ratings with production or staffing decisions.

Maintaining Contact

The true test of an aftermarketing program (and the management commitment behind it) is whether or not the program is maintained. Once customers' identities are known and they have been contacted in some way, it is highly desirable to maintain a formal interaction with them (in addition to their business transactions with the organization). Newsletters, magazines, and special customer events are all mechanisms that can be used to help maintain contact.

Under no circumstances should a program of this nature be considered a quick-fix, one-shot effort. It is a major commitment that requires the dedication of upper-level management, the budgeting of substantial funds, and the involvement of all of the organization's workforce. Once the Customer Information File is in place, it must be used to be kept up to date. Contact with customers must be maintained, and should occur periodically.

While returns on this investment will not be immediate, they will be forthcoming and they will be more enduring than returns from any shorter-range tactical efforts.

SOME FINAL THOUGHTS

Many outsiders criticize marketing and marketers. They say marketing is guilty of advertising unneeded products, stimulating unwholesome demand, and making products and services appear bigger and better than they really are. Some of these criticisms are probably true. Many more were probably true in the past. But today marketing has become a more responsible citizen of the business world. Today's marketing professionals recognize that they and their companies will not prosper by quick sales void of customer service. They are beginning to understand that it is long-term relationships that will help companies through the "valleys of recession" and the exigencies of customers' reduced budgets.

Aftermarketing strategies that achieve relationship marketing make winners out of both the marketer and the customer. Like customer-oriented marketing before it, aftermarketing is based on satisfying the customer. But beyond customer satisfaction, aftermarketing recognizes the value to both marketer and customer of a continued relationship and a shared responsibility between the two parties. Aftermarketing tells marketers to view any customer problem as a test of the relationship. If the marketer stands by the customer rather than holding out for his own selfish (or egotistical) concerns, then the relationship will grow and prosper.

Stew Leonard, the dairy-store marketer par excellence, captured the philosophy of aftermarketing best, in retelling the story of how he came to realize that the customer should always be right:

> About a week after opening our small dairy store in 1969, I was standing at the entrance when a customer came up to me and angrily said, "This eggnog is sour!" I took the half-gallon carton, opened it, and tasted it. It tasted all right to me, so I said, "You're wrong, it's perfect." Then to prove the customer really was wrong, I added, "We sold over 300 half-gallons of eggnog this week, and you're the only one who's complained." The customer was boiling mad. She demanded her money back. As she turned and left the store, I heard her say, "I'll never shop here again!"

That night, at home, I couldn't get the incident out of my head. As I carefully analyzed it, I realized that I was in the wrong. First, I didn't listen. Second, I contradicted
the customer, and third, I humiliated her and practically called her a liar. I realized I
had watched $5,000 a year walk out my door. Here I was just starting in business, and
I was already losing a valuable customer. From that day on, I vowed I'd do everything
possible to retain the trust of my customers.[10]

Several mail-order clothing firms (L.L. Bean, Lands' End, Eddie Bauer) have
unconditional, no questions asked, in perpetuity satisfaction guarantees. Buy a
jacket from any one of these firms and notice a frayed cuff one year later, and
chances are they will replace the item or offer a full refund! Franklin International, printers of the Day Planner diaries, routinely replaces day planners free of
charge for owners who have lost or had theirs stolen.

All of these marketers are communicating something very important to customers: "We want your business. We appreciate your business. We're here to
support you and the purchases you have made from us." This turns the seller-
buyer single transaction into a lifelong relationship. And relationships keep customers coming back.

KEY POINTS OF THE CHAPTER

Aftermarketing.   This involves providing continuing satisfaction and
reinforcement to those groups of individuals or organizations who are past or
current customers. American marketing must readjust its perspective to embrace
current customers, rather than always looking for new customers. Current customers are the life-blood of the organization and must be respected for their
importance.

Components of product quality.   Quality in products has been characterized by Garvin as consisting of eight components:

Performance.	Durability.
Features.	Serviceability.
Reliability.	Aesthetics.
Conformance.	Reputation.

Components of service quality.   As a result of the SERVQUAL
project, quality in services has been defined by five components:

Reliability.	Empathy.
Responsiveness.	Tangibles.
Assurance/competence.	

Quality.   While quality can simply be defined as meeting or exceeding customers' expectations in a product or service, more extensive definitions have been offered. They include:

The transcendent view—a condition of excellence.

The product view—the amount of attributes contained in the product.

The user view—how well the product fits consumer preferences.

The production view—the degree to which a product conforms to design specifications.

The value view—the degree of excellence at an acceptable price.

Servicing.   Servicing, as distinct from a service, has been described as an important element of the after-sale relationship with customers. Servicing includes:

Spontaneity—outreach offered unexpectedly.

Sincerity—offered as appreciation, not to stimulate cross-selling.

Significance—honors the customer.

Consistency—performed throughout the customer base.

Appendix Ten
HOW TO DETERMINE IF YOUR BUSINESS OR ORGANIZATION IS CONQUEST OR RETENTION ORIENTED

Answer this brief quiz to see how your firm scores on **Aftermarketing.** The questions may also serve as useful discussion topics to stimulate fellow executives' ideas on how to implement retention strategies.

1. **How are your marketing funds currently allocated between:**
   a) attracting new customers to win them over to your brand or company (conquest marketing)
   b) focusing on current customers to keep them from leaving your brand or company (aftermarketing)

   attracting new customers   ____%
   retaining current customers   ____%
           must equal   **100%**

   – *If retention spending is equal to or more than conquest spending score 4 points.*
   – *If retention spending equals half of conquest spending score 2 points.*
   – *If retention spending equals less than half of conquest spending score 1 point.*   ____

2. **Do your current formal marketing strategies mention "customer retention" as a goal?**
   [ ] yes *(1 point)*
   [ ] no *(0 points)*   ___

3. **Does your company have a database of your current customers?**
   [ ] yes *(1 point) If the database resides in the marketing department or the marketing department has free access add 2 more points*
      – *If the database has a complete name/address/phone/unique ID score 1 more point.*
      – *If the database tracks customer purchases and interactions score 3 more points.*
      – *If the database identifies actual end-users and decision-makers score 2 more points.*
   [ ] no *(0 points)*   ___

4. **Does your company make itself available to customers with an 800 telephone number?**
   [ ] yes *(1 point) If the calls are answered directly by operational people, add 3 points; if by clerks with management reports sent on a regular basis add 2 points.*
   [ ] no *(0 points)*   ___

5. **Does your firm regularly (at least once a year) initiate some form of contact with your customers?**
   [ ] yes *(1 point) If more than one contact per year add 1 point.*
   [ ] no *(0 points)*   ___

6. **Do you offer any "frequency" or customer appreciation buying programs which reward more frequent purchasers with something in return?**
   [ ] yes *(1 point)*
   [ ] no *(0 points)*   ___

7. **Are customer complaints regularly examined and analyzed?**
   [ ] yes *(1 point) If each complaint is personally acknowledged, add 2 points. If each complaint is reviewed for a functional response or process change, add 2 more points.*
   If marketing area operates this function or is involved in the analysis and implementation of correction activities add 2 more points.
   [ ] no *(0 points)*   ___

8. **Are customer purchase records audited to spot changes (or discontinuance) of purchasing?**
   [ ] yes *(1 point)*
   [ ] no *(0 points)*   ___

9. **Is there a system in place to automatically win back/"revive" lost or discontinuing customers?**
   [ ] yes *(2 points)*
   [ ] no *(0 points)*   ___

10. Are exiting or discontinuing customers interviewed?

[ ] yes *(1 point) If their identity is maintained in the main customer database or an account file, add 1 point. If their record is addressable by reason for leaving, add 2 points*

[ ] no *(0 points)* _____

11. Does your CEO play a participatory role in any customer audit or survey programs?

[ ] yes *(1 point) If on a regular basis, add 2 points; if only to review summary reports add 1 point.*

[ ] no *(0 points)* _____

12. Which of the following describe your operating staff's feelings about customer complaints:

[ ] they've tried to completely eliminate them *(subtract 3 point)*

[ ] they try to minimize them *(subtract 1 point)*

[ ] they service them as well as competitors *(add 1 point)*

[ ] they're trying to *increase* the opportunity to hear more complaints *(add 3 points)* _____

13. Considering your information priorities, would you say you are more concerned about capturing information regarding:

[ ] competitors *(0 points)*

[ ] customers *(1 point)* _____

14. Do you have a formal customer satisfaction measurement and analysis program?

[ ] yes *(2 points)*

[ ] no *(0 points)* _____

    – If participants are selected on a truly random fashion add 1 point.

    – If the survey is regularly scheduled every year add 1 point.

    – If the survey is regularly scheduled two or more times a year or more frequently add 2 points

Now, add your total points. Scores between:

    45 and 31   : Congratulations, you're customer retention focused!

    30 and 19   : You're on your way; you're customer retention aware.

    less than 19 : Lots of work to become customer retention focused.

TOTAL _____

NOTES

1. David Garvin offers five definitions: D. Garvin, *Managing Quality: The Strategic and Competitive Edge* (New York: The Free Press, 1988).
2. The PIMS studies have reportedly found a positive correlation: D. A. Garvin, *Managing Quality,* (New York: The Free Press, 1988), pp. 76–78.
3. It is said American management: F. Rose, "Now Quality Means Service Too," *Fortune,* April 22, 1991, pp. 99–108.
4. Garvin has proposed a list of seven components of quality: D. A. Garvin, *Managing Quality* (New York: The Free Press, 1988), pp. 49–60.
5. In an annual survey of Americans: The American Society for Quality Control, *An International Survey of Consumers' Perceptions of Product and Service Quality,* Milwaukee, WI, 1991.
6. Zeithaml, Parasuraman and Berry, three marketing professors, have engaged in an investigation of the quality of services: V. A. Zeithaml, A. Parasuraman, and L. Berry, *Delivering Quality Service: Balancing Customer Perceptions and Expectations* (New York: The Free Press, 1990), p. 28.
7. "We didn't think we'd win": W. Blanding, "A Closer Look at the Baldrige Award," *CSI Report No. 7,* Silver Spring, MD, Customer Service Institute, 1991.
8. Overall the number of applicants: R. Eisman, "Why It Pays To Lose the Baldrige Competition," *Incentive,* April 1991, pp. 33–43, 98.
9. "Although many companies are admittedly intensifying their efforts for quality": R. Eisman, "Why It Pays To Lose the Baldrige Competition," *Incentive,* April 1991, pp. 33–43, 98.
10. About a week after opening our small dairy store: S. Leonard, "Love Your Customer!," Advertising Supplement to *Newsweek,* July 27, 1988.

Appendix

Bibliography

BOOKS

Albrecht, K. *Service Within.* Homewood, IL: Business One-Irwin, 1990.

Albrecht, K. *The Only Thing That Matters.* New York: Harper Collins Publishers, 1992.

Albrecht, K. and L. J. Bradford. *The Service Advantage.* Homewood, IL: Dow Jones-Irwin, 1989.

Albrecht, K. and R. Zemke. *Service America!.* New York: Dow Jones-Irwin, 1985.

Arter, D. *Quality Audits for Improved Performance.* Milwaukee, WI: ASQC Quality Press, 1989.

Bandley, M. J. and E. Kearney. *Everyone Is a Customer.* Marina Del Rey, CA: Sterling Press, 1986.

Barsky, J. D. *World-Class Customer Satisfaction.* Burr Ridge, IL: Irwin Professional Publishing, 1995.

Bell, C. R. *Customers As Partners: Building Relationships That Last.* Austin, TX: Berrett-Koehler Publishers, Inc., 1994.

Berry, L. L., D. R. Bennett and W. Carter. *Service Quality.* Homewood, IL: Jones-Irwin, 1994.

Bickert, J. *Adventures in Relevance Marketing.* Denver: National Demographics & Lifestyles Inc., 1990.

Bowen, D. E., R. B. Chase and T. E. Cummings. *Service Management Effectiveness.* San Francisco, CA: Josey-Bass Publishers, 1990.

Bradley, G. *Managing Customer Value.* New York: The Free Press, 1994.

Bureau of Business Practice. *Excellence Achieved; Customer Service Blueprints For Action From 50 Leading Companies.* Waterford, CT: Bureau of Business Practice, 1990.

Buzzell, R. D. and B. T. Gale. *The Pims Principles.* New York: The Free Press, 1987.

CACI. *1990 Census: Today's Technology for Tomorrow's Business.* Washington, DC: CACI, Marketing Systems Inc., 1990.

Cannie, J. K. and D. Caplin. *Keeping Customers for Life.* New York: American Management Association, 1991.

Cannie, J. K. *Turning Lost Customers Into Gold ... and the Art of Achieving Zero Defections.* New York: American Management Association, 1994.

Carlzon, J. *Moments of Truth.* New York: Harper & Row, 1987.

Carr, C. *Front-Line Customer Service.* New York: John Wiley & Sons, 1990.

Christopher, M., A. Payne, and D. Ballantyne. *Relationship Marketing: Bringing quality customer service, and marketing together.* Oxford, England: Butterworth Heinemann Ltd. 1991.

Congram, C. A. and M. L. Friedman. *The AMA Handbook of Marketing For The Service Industries.* New York: AMACOM, 1991.

Consumer Complaint Handling in America: An Update Study. Washington, DC: Technical Assistance Research Programs Institute, 1986.

Cottle, D. W. *Client-Centered Service: How to Keep Them Coming Back for More.* New York: John Wiley & Sons, 1990.

Crosby, P. B. *Let's Talk Quality: 96 Questions You Always Wanted to Ask Phil Crosby.* New York: Plume Books, 1989.

Crosby, P. B. *Quality is Free: The Art of Making Quality Certain.* New York: New American Libary, 1980.

Cross, R. and J. Smith. *Customer Bonding: Pathways to Lasting Customer Loyalty.* Lincolnwood, IL: NTC Publishing, 1994.

Czepiel, J., M. R. Solomon, and C. Suprenant. *The Service Encounter.* Lexington, MA: Lexington Books, 1985.

Davidow, W. H. and B. Uttal, *Total Customer Service: The Ultimate Weapon.* New York: Harper & Row, 1989.

Day, G. S. *Market-Driven Strategy: Processes for Creating Value.* New York: The Free Press, 1990.

Deming, W. E. *Out of the Crisis.* Cambridge, MA: Massachusetts Institute of Technology, 1986.

Desatnick, R. L. *Keep the Customer!: Making Customer Service Your Competitive Edge.* Boston: Houghton Mifflin, 1987.

Desatnick, R. L. *Managing to Keep the Customer: How to Achieve and Maintain Superior Customer Service Throughout the Organization.* San Francisco: Jossey-Bass, 1987.

Disend, J. E. *How to Provide Excellent Service in Any Organization: A Blueprint for Making All the Theories Work.* Radnor, PA: Chilton Book Co., 1991.

Dobyns, L. and C. Crawford-Mason. *Quality or Else: The Revolution in World Business.* Boston: Houghton-Mifflin, 1991.

Donnelly, J. H. Jr. *Close to the Customer: 25 Management Tips from the Other Side of the Counter.* Burr Ridge, IL: Irwin Professional Publishing, 1992.

Dutka, A. *AMA Handbook for Customer Satisfaction.* Lincolnwood, IL: NTC Business Books, 1994.

Eastman Kodak Company. *Keeping the Customer Satisfied: A Guide to Field Service.* Milwaukee, WI: American Society for Quality Control, 1989.

Eureka, W. E. and N. E. Ryan. *The Customer-Driven Company.* Dearborn, MI: ASI Press, 1988.

Excellence Achieved: Customer Service Blueprints For Action From 50 Leading Companies. Waterford, CT: Bureau of Business Practice, 1990.

Feigenbaum, A. *Total Quality Control,* 3rd edition revised. New York: McGraw-Hill, Inc. 1991.

Fine, S. and R. Dreyfack. *Customers: How to Get Them, How to Serve Them, How to Keep Them.* Chicago: Dartnell Corporation, 1983.

Francese, P. and R. Piirto. *Capturing Customers: How To Target The Hottest Markets of the '90s.* Ithaca, NY: American Demographics Press, 1990.

Gale, B. T. *Managing Customer Value.* New York: The Free Press, 1994.

Galvin, R. W. *The Idea of Ideas.* Chicago, IL: Motorola University Press, 1991.

Garvin, D. A. *Managing Quality: The Strategic and Competitive Edge.* New York: The Free Press, 1988.

Gerson, R. F. *Beyond Customer Service.* Los Altos, CA: Crisp Publications, Inc., 1992.

Graham, J. and S. Bennett. *Magnet Marketing.* New York: John Wiley & Sons, Inc., 1991.

Grenier, R. *Customer Satisfaction Through Total Quality Assurance.* New York: Hitchcock, 1988.

Guide to Understanding and Using Demographics. Metromail, The Information Corporation.

Hanan, M. and P. Karp. *Competing on Value.* New York: AMACOM, 1991.

Hanan, M. and P. Karp. *Customer Satisfaction: How to Maximize, Measure and Market Your Company's "Ultimate Product."* New York: AMACOM, 1988.

Harvard Business Review. *Seeking and Keeping Your Customers.* Boston: Harvard Business Press, 1991.

Heskett, J. L., W. E. Sasser, Jr., and C. W. L. Hart. *Service Breakthroughs: Changing the Rules of the Game.* New York: The Free Press, 1990.

Hilton, C. *Be My Guest.* New York: Prentice Hall, 1957.

Hinton, T. D. *The Spirit of Service: How to Create a Customer-Focused Service Culture.* Dubuque, IA: Kendall/Hunt Publishing Company, 1991.

Honeycombe, G. *Selfridges.* London, England: The Rainbeid Publishing Group Ltd., 1984.

Hughes, A. M. *The Complete Database Marketer: Tapping Your Customer Base to Maximize Sales and Increase Profits.* Chicago, IL: Probus Publishing, 1991.

Hughes, A. M. *Strategic Database Marketing.* Chicago, IL: Probus Publishing Co., 1994.

Jackson, B. B. *Winning and Keeping Industrial Customers: The Dynamics of Customer Relationships.* Lexington, MA: Lexington Books, 1985.

Jackson, R. and P. Wang. *Strategic Database Marketing.* Lincolnwood, IL: NTC Publishing, 1994.

Jacques, H. and M. J. Panak. *Putting the World's Best Programs to Work.* Burr Ridge, IL: Irwin Professional Publishing, 1994.

Juran J. M. *Juran on Planning for Quality.* New York: The Free Press, 1988.

Katz, B. *How to Turn Customer Service into Customer Sales.* Lincolnwood, IL: NTC Business Books, 1988.

Klug, J. *Customer Communications: The New Marketing Discipline.* Customer Communication Group, 1993.

LaLonde, B. J., and M. C. Cooper, *Partnerships in Providing Customer Service: A Third-Party Perspective.* Oak Brook, IL: Council of Logistics Management, 1989.

LaLonde, B. J., M. C. Cooper, and T. G. Noordewier. *Customer Service: A Management Perspective.* Oak Brook, IL: Council of Logistics Management, 1988.

Lash, L. M. *The Complete Guide to Customer Service.* New York: John Wiley & Sons, 1989.

Lazer, W., P. LaBarbera, J. M. MacLachlan, and A. E. Smitth. *Marketing 2000 and Beyond.* Chicago: American Marketing Association, 1990.

LeBoeuf, M. *How To Win Customers and Keep Them For Life.* New York: Berkley Books, 1987.

Lele, M. M. with J. Sheth. *The Customer is Key.* New York: John Wiley & Sons, 1987.

Levitt, T. *The Marketing Imagination.* New York: The Free Press, 1983.

Liswood, L. A., *Serving Them Right: Innovative and Powerful Customer Retention Strategies.* New York: Harper Business, 1990.

Lovelock, C. H. *Managing Services: Marketing, Operations, and Human Resources.* Englewood Cliffs, NJ: Prentice Hall, 1988.

Martin, W. and M. G. Crisp. *Managing Quality Customer Service.* Los Altos, CA: Crisp Publications, 1989.

McAlindon, H. *Customer Care: Innovative Thoughts on Customer Service.* Lombard, IL: Great Quotations, Inc. 1989.

McKenna, R. *The Regis Touch, Million-Dollar Advice from America's Top Marketing Consultant.* Reading, MA: Addison-Wesley Publishing Co., 1985.

McKenna, R. *Relationship Marketing: Successful Strategies for the Age of the Customer.* Reading, MA: Addison-Wesley Publishing Co., 1992.

Naumann, E. *Creating The Path To Sustainable Customer Competitive Advantage Value.* Cincinnati, OH: Thomson Executive Press, 1995.

Nykiel, R. A. *You Can't Lose If the Customer Wins: Ten Steps to Service Success.* Stamford CT: Longmeadow Press, 1990.

Nykiel, R. A. *Keeping Customers In Good Times and Bad.* Stamford. CT: Longmeadow Press, 1992.

Peppers, D. and M. Rogers. *The One to One Future: Building Relationships One Customer at a Time.* New York: Bantam Doubleday Dell Publishing Group, 1993.

Peters, T. *Thriving on Chaos: Handbook for a Management Revolution.* New York: Alfred A. Knopf, 1987.

Peters, T. J. and N. Austin. *A Passion for Excellence.* New York: Random House, 1985.

Peters, T. J. and R. H. Waterman,. Jr. *In Search of Excellence: Lessons From America's Best-Run Companies.* New York: Warner Communications Company, 1982.

Quinn, F. *Crowning the Customer,* Dublin, Ireland: The O'Brien Press, 1990.

Rapp, S. and T. L. Collins. *MaxiMarketing: The New Direction in Advertising Promotion and Marketing Strategy.* New York: McGraw-Hill, 1987.

Rapp, S. and T. L. Collins. *The Great Marketing Turnaround: The Age of the Individual—and How to Profit from It.* Englewood Cliffs, NJ: Prentice Hall, 1990.

Ries, A. and J. Trout. *Bottom-Up Marketing.* New York: McGraw Hill, 1989.

Rosenbluth, H. F. and D. McFerrin Peters. *The Customer Comes Second: And Other Secrets of Exceptional Service.* New York: William Morrow and Co., Inc. 1992.

Schnaars, S. P. *Marketing Strategy: A Customer-Driven Approach.* New York: The Free Press, 1991.

Seeking and Keeping Your Customers. Boston, MA: Harvard Business School Publishing Division, 1991.

Sewell, C. and P. B. Brown. *Customers For Life: How to Turn That One-Time Buyer into a Lifetime Customer.* New York: Doubleday, 1990.

Shepard, D. *The New Direct Marketing.* Homewood, IL: Dow Jones-Irwin, 1990.

Smilor, R. W. ed. *Customer-Driven Marketing: Lessons from Entrepreneurial Technology Companies.* Lexington, MA: Lexington Books, 1989.

Stanley, T. J. *Marketing to the Affluent.* Homewood, IL: Dow Jones-Irwin, 1988.

Steps to Improving Service Quality and Customer Satisfaction. Washington, DC: American Bankers Association, 1990.

Stone, B. *Successful Direct Marketing Methods.* Chicago: Crain Books, 1979.

Sviokla, J. J. and B. P. Shapiro. ed. *Keeping Customers.* Boston, MA: Harvard Business School Publishing Corp., 1993.

Tannehill, R. *Achieving Service Excellence: Guidelines for Supervisors.* Amherst, NY: Robert Tannehill Associates, 1990.

Tjosvold, D. *Teamwork for Customers.* San Francisco, CA: Jossey-Bass Publishers, 1993.

Tucker, R. B. *Managing the Future: 10 Driving Forces of Change for the '90's.* New York: The Putnam Berkley Group, 1991.

Walker, D. *Customer First: A Strategy for Quality Service.* Gower, England: Gower Publishers Company, 1990.

Walther, G R. *Upside-Down Marketing: Turning Your Ex-Customers Into Your Best Customers.* New York: McGraw-Hill, Inc., 1994.

Whiteley, R. C. *The Customer Driven Company Moving From Talk to Action.* Reading, MA: Addison-Wesley Publishing, Co., 1991.

Woods, R. *What's in It for Me? A Marketer's Guide to Establishing an Equal Partnership with Consumers.* Ontario, Canada: WIFM Marketing, 1990.

Zeithaml, V. A., A. Parasuraman, and L. L. Berry. *Delivering Quality Service.* New York: The Free Press, 1990.

Zemke, R. *The Service Edge: 101 Companies That Profit From Customer Care.* New York: NAL Books, 1988.

Zemke, R. and C. Bell, eds. *Service Wisdom.* Minneapolis: Lakewood Publications, 1988.

Zemke, R., and D. Schaaf. *The Service Edge: 101 Companies That Profit from Customer Care.* New York: Plume Books, 1989.

NEWSLETTERS

The Customer Communicator, Customer Service Institute, 1010 Wayne Avenue, Silver Spring, MD 20910. (301) 585-0730

Customer Profit Report, Customer Service Institute, 1010 Wayne Avenue, Silver Spring, MD 20910. (301) 585-0730.

Customer Service Bulletin, Arthur D. Little, Acorn Park, Cambridge, MA 02140. (617) 864-5770.

Customer Service Management Bulletin, Bureau of Business Practice, Rope Ferry Road, Waterford, CT 06386. (203) 442-4365.

Customer Service Newsletter, Customer Service Institute, 1010 Wayne Avenue, Silver Spring, MD 20910. (301) 585-0730.

Executive Report on Customer Satisfaction, Alexander Research & Communications, 215 Park Avenue South—Suite 1301, New York, NY 10003, (212) 228-0246

Positive Impact, Resort Impressions, Ltd., P.O. Box 4018, Evergreen, CO. (303) 670-1001.

The Service Edge, Lakewood Publications, 50 South Ninth Street, Minneapolis, MN 55402. (800) 328-4329.

Index

Y

Yankelovich Clancy Shulman Monitor, 7
Your Company, 192
Yugo America, 22

Z

Zeithaml, Valerie A., 274, 275n, 276, 277n,
  291n

Zemke, Ron, 99, 112n, 255, 270
Zero defections, 215
Zero defects, 218, 235
Zone of visibility/invisibility, 103
Zunin, L., 98, 112n
Zunin, N., 98, 112n

Other books of interest to you from Irwin Professional Publishing...

HIGH PERFORMANCE SALES ORGANIZATIONS
Best Practices from Global Sales Leaders
Kevin J. Corcoran, Laura K. Petersen, Daniel B. Baitch, and Mark T. Harr

High Performance Sales Organizations provides insights into the principles and practices used by some of the world's leading sales organizations. In particular, the book highlights the findings of a recent study of sales leaders in three world markets: North America, Europe, and Japan.
ISBN: 0-7863-0352-2

THE ULTIMATE GUIDE TO SPORT EVENT MANAGEMENT AND MARKETING
Stedman Graham, Joe Jeff Goldblatt, CSEP, and Lisa A. Delpy, Ph.D.

The Ultimate Guide to Sport Event Management and Marketing is the first book to go behind the scenes, from the back office to the front office, from the locker room to the television control room to explain how special events in sports can be effective, successful, and profitable.
ISBN: 0-7863-0244-5

THE NEW DIRECT MARKETING
How to Implement a Profit-Driven Database Marketing Strategy, Second Edition
David Shepard Associates

The New Direct Marketing shows how to cost-effectively acquire the data you need to identify and profile your best customers and prospects.
ISBN: 1-55623-809-6

Also available in fine bookstores and libraries everywhere.